8th Linguistic Annotation Workshop 2014

Held at COLING 2014

Dublin, Ireland
23 - 24 August 2014

ISBN: 978-1-63439-219-8

Printed from e-media with permission by:

Curran Associates, Inc.
57 Morehouse Lane
Red Hook, NY 12571

Some format issues inherent in the e-media version may also appear in this print version.

Printed by Curran Associates, Inc. (2014)

For permission requests, please contact the Association for Computational Linguistics at the address below.

Association for Computational Linguistics
209 N. Eighth Street
Stroudsburg, Pennsylvania 18360

Phone: 1-570-476-8006
Fax: 1-570-476-0860

acl@aclweb.org

Additional copies of this publication are available from:

Curran Associates, Inc.
57 Morehouse Lane
Red Hook, NY 12571 USA
Phone: 845-758-0400
Fax: 845-758-2634
Email: curran@proceedings.com
Web: www.proceedings.com

Preface

The Linguistic Annotation Workshop (The LAW) is organized annually by the Association for Computational Linguistics Special Interest Group for Annotation (ACL SIGANN). It provides a forum to facilitate the exchange and propagation of research results concerned with the annotation, manipulation, and exploitation of corpora; work towards harmonization and interoperability from the perspective of the increasingly large number of tools and frameworks for annotated language resources; and work towards a consensus on all issues crucial to the advancement of the field of corpus annotation.

The series is now in its eighth year, with these proceedings including papers that were presented at LAW VIII, held in conjunction with the COLING conference in Dublin, Ireland, on August 23-24 2014. As in previous years, more than 40 submissions have originally been received in response to the call for papers. After careful review, the program committee accepted 11 long papers and three short papers for oral presentation, together with eight additional papers to be presented as posters. The topics of the long papers revolve quite nicely around major linguistic levels of description: part of speech, syntax, semantics, and discourse; and thus we arranged them in theses groups in the program. The short papers report on interesting experiments or new tools.

Our thanks go to SIGANN, our organizing committee, for its continuing organization of the LAW workshops, and to the COLING 2014 workshop chairs for their support: Jennifer Foster, Dan Gildea and Tim Baldwin. Also, we thank the COLING 2014 publication chairs for their help with these proceedings.

Most of all, we would like to thank all the authors for submitting their papers to the workshop, and our program committee members for their dedication and their thoughtful reviews.

Lori Levin and Manfred Stede, program co-chairs

Workshop Chairs

Lori Levin (Carnegie Mellon University)
Manfred Stede (University of Potsdam)

Organizing Committee

Stefanie Dipper (Ruhr University Bochum)
Chu-Ren Huang (The Hong Kong Polytechnic University)
Nancy Ide (Vassar College)
Adam Meyers (New York University)
Antonio Pareja-Lora (SIC & ILSA, UCM / ATLAS, UNED)
Massimo Poesio (University of Trento)
Sameer Pradhan (Harvard University)
Katrin Tomanek (University of Jena)
Fei Xia (University of Washington)
Nianwen Xue (Brandeis University)

Program Committee

Collin Baker (UC Berkeley)
Archna Bhatia (Carnegie Mellon University)
Nicoletta Calzolari (ILC/CNR)
Christian Chiarcos (University of Frankfurt)
Stefanie Dipper (Ruhr University Bochum)
Tomaž Erjavec (Josef Stefan Institute)
Dan Flickinger (Stanford University)
Udo Hahn (University of Jena)
Chu-Ren Huang (The Hong Kong Polytechnic University)
Nancy Ide (Vassar College)
Aravind Joshi (University of Pennsylvania)
Valia Kordoni (Humboldt University Berlin)
Adam Meyers (New York University)
Antonio Pareja-Lora (SIC & ILSA, UCM / ATLAS, UNED)
Massimo Poesio (University of Trento)
Sameer Pradhan (Harvard University)
James Pustejovsky (Brandeis University)
Katrin Tomanek (University of Jena)
Yulia Tsvetkov (Carnegie Mellon University)
Andreas Witt (IDS Mannheim)
Marie-Paule Péry-Woodley (Université de Toulouse 2)
Fei Xia (University of Washington)
Nianwen Xue (Brandeis University)
Heike Zinsmeister (University of Hamburg)

Table of Contents

Workshop Program

Saturday, August 23

8.50-9:00 Opening remarks

Parts of Speech

9:00–9:30 *STTS 2.0? Improving the Tagset for the Part-of-Speech-Tagging of German Spoken Data*
Swantje Westpfahl

9:30–10:00 *Use of Coreference in Automatic Searching for Multiword Discourse Markers in the Prague Dependency Treebank*
Magdalena Rysova and Jiří Mírovský

10:00–10:30 *POS Error Detection in Automatically Annotated Corpora*
Ines Rehbein

10:30-11:00 Break

Syntax

11:00–11:30 *Aligning Chinese-English Parallel Parse Trees: Is it Feasible?*
Dun Deng and Nianwen Xue

11:30–12:00 *Sentence Diagrams: their Evaluation and Combination*
Jirka Hana, Barbora Hladka and Ivana Luksova

12:00-12:30 Poster Boasters

12:30-14:00 Lunch

Short Papers

14:00–14:20 *Finding Your "Inner-Annotator": An Experiment in Annotator Independence for Rating Discourse Coherence Quality in Essays*
Jill Burstein, Swapna Somasundaran and Martin Chodorow

14:20–14:40 *Optimizing Annotation Efforts to Build Reliable Annotated Corpora for Training Statistical Models*
Cyril Grouin, Thomas Lavergne and Aurelie Neveol

14:40–15:00 *A Web-based Geo-resolution Annotation and Evaluation Tool*
Beatrice Alex, Kate Byrne, Claire Grover and Richard Tobin

15:00-15:30 Break

Saturday, August 23 (continued)

(15:30-17:00) Poster session

Annotating Uncertainty in Hungarian Webtext
Veronika Vincze, Katalin Ilona Simkó and Viktor Varga

A Corpus Study for Identifying Evidence on Microblogs
Paul Reisert, Junta Mizuno, Miwa Kanno, Naoaki Okazaki and Kentaro Inui

Semi-Semantic Part of Speech Annotation and Evaluation
Qaiser Abbas

Multiple Views as Aid to Linguistic Annotation Error Analysis
Marilena Di Bari, Serge Sharoff and Martin Thomas

Annotating a Large Representative Corpus of Clinical Notes for Parts of Speech
Narayan Choudhary, Parth Pathak, Pinal Patel and Vishal Panchal

Part-of-speech Tagset and Corpus Development for Igbo, an African Language
Ikechukwu Onyenwe, Chinedu Uchechukwu and Mark Hepple

Annotating Descriptively Incomplete Language phenomena
Fabian Barteld, Sarah Ihden, Ingrid Schröder and Heike Zinsmeister

Annotating Discourse Connectives in Spoken Turkish
Isin Demirsahin and Deniz Zeyrek

Sunday, August 24

Discourse

9:00–9:30 *Exploiting the Human Computational Effort Dedicated to Message Reply Formatting for Training Discursive Email Segmenters*
Nicolas Hernandez and Soufian Salim

9:30–10:00 *Annotating Multiparty Discourse: Challenges for Agreement Metrics*
Nina Wacholder, Smaranda Muresan, Debanjan Ghosh and Mark Aakhus

10:00–10:30 *Towards Automatic Annotation of Clinical Decision-Making Style*
Limor Hochberg, Cecilia Ovesdotter Alm, Esa M. Rantanen, Qi Yu, Caroline M. DeLong and Anne Haake

10:30-11:00 Break

Semantics

11:00–11:30 *Interactive Annotation for Event Modality in Modern Standard and Egyptian Arabic Tweets*
Rania Al-Sabbagh, Roxana Girju and Jana Diesner

11:30–12:00 *Situation Entity Annotation*
Annemarie Friedrich and Alexis Palmer

12:00–12:30 *Focus Annotation in Reading Comprehension Data*
Ramon Ziai and Detmar Meurers

12:30-14:00 Lunch

14:00-15:00 Presentation of NSF Community Infrastructure proposal

15:00-15:30 Break

15:30-16:30 Discussion of NSF Community Infrastructure proposal

16:30-17:30 LAW Business Meeting and Discussion of Shared Task

STTS 2.0? Improving the Tagset for the Part-of-Speech-Tagging of German Spoken Data

Swantje Westpfahl
Institut für Deutsche Sprache, Mannheim
westpfahl@ids-mannheim.de

Abstract

Part-of-speech tagging (POS-tagging) of spoken data requires different means of annotation than POS-tagging of written and edited texts. In order to capture the features of German spoken language, a distinct tagset is needed to respond to the kinds of elements which only occur in speech. In order to create such a coherent tagset the most prominent phenomena of spoken language need to be analyzed, especially with respect to how they differ from written language. First evaluations have shown that the most prominent cause (over 50%) of errors in the existing automatized POS-tagging of transcripts of spoken German with the Stuttgart Tübingen Tagset (STTS) and the treetagger was the inaccurate interpretation of speech particles. One reason for this is that this class of words is virtually absent from the current STTS. This paper proposes a recategorization of the STTS in the field of speech particles based on distributional factors rather than semantics. The ultimate aim is to create a comprehensive reference corpus of spoken German data for the global research community. It is imperative that all phenomena are reliably recorded in future part-of-speech tag labels.

1 Introduction

In the Institute for German Language (Institut für Deutsche Sprache, IDS Mannheim) a large reference corpus of German spoken data is currently being built. It already contains more than 100 hours of transcribed audio material, i.e. about one million tokens. The aim of my dissertation is to annotate the corpus with Part-of-Speech-tags (POS-tags) and thus to tackle the theoretical problems which originate from the differences between spoken and written language. On the one hand, as the corpus is growing fast, ways must be found to automate this, i.e. without manual correction. On the other hand there are no tools to accomplish such a task at present. First tests running the treetagger (Schmid 1995) with the Stuttgart Tübingen Tagset (STTS) (Schiller et al. 1999), which on written data show an accuracy of 97.53% (Schmid 1995) have shown that the accuracy of these tools on spoken data is far below acceptable, i.e. they only show an accuracy of 81.16% (Westpfahl and Schmidt 2013). There are two main reasons for this. First of all, the structure of German spoken language is quite different from the structure of German written language due to many elliptic structures, disruptions, repetitions etc. Furthermore, punctuation is not annotated in the corpus; hence the algorithms have no "proper sentences" to work with.

As was shown in the studies of Westpfahl and Schmidt (2013) and Rehbein and Schalowski (2013), the mistakes in annotating POS-tags on German spoken language are due to a lack of suitable categories in the tagset; namely categories which reflect the manifold speech particles, vernacular use of pronouns, verbs and items which are impossible to categorize grammatically. As can be seen in Table 1, a first analysis of tagging errors showed that more than 50% of the mistakes are due to mis-tagged discourse markers, interjections and speech particles. Hence, to reach the goal of an automatized POS-tagging, the tagset must firstly be adapted to those phenomena. It is the aim of this paper to provide a theoretical foundation on how to comply with the need to re-categorize the existing tag set for speech particles; creation of new tags and merging of existing tags are both proposed as seems relevant for the particular data. Problems which are due to verbs, pronouns and non-words cannot be discussed here.

Table 1: Errors in POS annotation > 5% (Westpfahl and Schmidt 2013)

Errors in POS annotation	**> 5%**
Particles and interjections	51,59%
Pronouns	13,43%
Verbs	9,14%
XY non words	8,18%

LAW VIII - The 8th Linguistic Annotation Workshop, pages 1–10,
Dublin, Ireland, August 23-24 2014.

2 Related work

Various spoken language corpora which are annotated with POS tags already exist. English language corpora are for example the BNC (Burnard 2007), the Switchboard corpus (Godfrey et al. 1992), Vienna-Oxford International Corpus of English (VOICE) (VOICE 2013) and the Christine Corpus (Sampson 2000). While both the Switchboard corpus and the BNC use POS tag-sets developed for written data, VOICE and the Christine corpus adapted theirs specifically for spoken language. VOICE added 26 POS tags to the Penn treebank POS tagset which include tags for, among others, discourse markers or response particles and also non-verbal elements like laughter and breathing. The Christine corpus uses a very fine grained tagset with more than 400 tags annotating morpho-syntactic as well as rich pragmatic information.

A POS tagset which has been especially designed for a corpus of spoken language is the tagset of the Spoken Dutch Corpus (Oosterdijk 2000). However, although the tagset consists of more than 300 tags, all discourse related items are tagged as interjections.

For the German language there is the Tübingen Treebank of Spoken German (TüBa-D/S), which uses the STTS with no alterations whatsoever (Telljohann et al. 2012).

In order to find a solution on how to tag non-standard texts with the STTS, an interest group was set up in 2012. Within this interest group a work group formed which especially focused their attention on the adaption of the STTS for spoken language and computer mediated language (CMC), namely for the corpora Kietz-Deutsch Corpus, the Dortmund chat corpus and our corpus (DGD2/FOLK). As a first result, three papers were published with some suggestions on which phenomena should be represented in an adapted tagset (Rehbein and Schalowski 2013; Bartz et al. 2013; Westpfahl and Schmidt 2013). The present paper is meant to give an overview of a theoretical foundation on how to comply with the need to recategorize the tagset with respect to speech particles, as so far only a "purely data-driven" approach has been discussed (Rehbein and Schalowski 2013).

3 Speech particles in the original STTS

The Stuttgart Tübingen Tagset (STTS) was conceptually developed for a corpus of newspaper articles and only those classes of words which were frequently used were represented in the tagset. Therefore, modal particles, speech particles or discourse markers were not at the center of attention of Schiller et al. (1999) as their use in written texts is commonly understood to be 'bad style'. To understand the changes I have made in the tagset I shall first present the categories used for particles and discourse markers in the original tagset:

Table 2 categories for speech particles in the original STTS

Tags	Description	Example	Literal English translation
PTKVZ	verbal particles	[er gab] auf	[he gave] up
PTKZU	particle used with infinitives	zu [gehen]	to [walk]
PTKA	particle used with adjectives or adverbs	am [schönsten], zu [schnell]	most [beautiful], too [fast]
PTKNEG	negation particle	nicht	not
PTKANT	response particles	ja, nein, danke, bitte	yes, no, thanks, please
ITJ	interjections	mhm, ach, tja	uhum, oh, well

As one can see, the STTS is structured hierarchically; for particles, the basis tag would be "PTK" for "Partikel" and there are five subcategory tags. Furthermore, the tagset provided one category for interjections: ITJ, defining them after Bußmann (1990) as words which serve to express emotions, swearing and curses and for getting in contact with others. Formally they are invariable and syntactically independent from the sentence as well as having, strictly speaking, no lexical meaning (Schiller et al. 1999, S. 73).

Concerning modal particles, intensity particles or focus particles etc., the guidelines published with the tagset do not assign them their own category. It is implicitly clear from the cited examples that modal particles or intensity particles are to be tagged as adverbs "ADV". (Schiller et al. 1999)

On running the STTS with the treetagger on three transcripts of German spoken data (11029 tokens), one finds that 35.76% of all corrected items were incorrectly tagged as adverbs and yet again 85.87% of those items tagged as adverbs were actually particles or interjections (Westpfahl and Schmidt 2013). Thus, the first step in restructuring the tagset would be finding categories differentiating adverbs from particles as well as interjections and discourse markers.

4 Features of spoken German - Speech particles in German grammar references

In order to explain the categorization employed in our proposed STTS 2.0 one has to take a deeper look at how transcripts of spoken German differ from 'normal' written language. First of all, in our corpus, no punctuation is annotated and there also is no annotation on where a speaker's turn starts or ends. Secondly, it is typical of spoken language that not all utterances form "proper" sentences but are quite often disrupted, e.g. marked by extensions or anacolutha, apokoinu-constructions, repairs etc. All this would be represented as such in the transcripts.

Furthermore, there are also differences in the choice of words, i.e. some closed categories contain other or more tokens in spoken language and some speech phenomena simply do not occur in written language except for, maybe, in quoting direct speech. Some of those phenomena are even hard to describe as syntactic categories, e.g. hesitation markers or backchannel signals. Nevertheless, exactly those phenomena are particularly interesting in working with a corpus of spoken language.

The approach used for finding categories was to first take a look at the canon of German grammars and then check whether the classifications made there could be applied for the corpus data.

The most consulted grammars for the German language are (Duden 2006), (Zifonun 1997), (Engel 2004), (Helbig 2011), (Hoffmann 2013), (Weinrich 2005) and the online grammar grammis 2.0 (Institut für deutsche Sprache 2013). The most consulted articles dealing with speech particles are (Burkhardt 1982), (Hentschel and Weydt 2002), (Schwitalla 2012) and (Diewald 2006).

Looking at this literature it becomes obvious that research on this topic has, so far, not lead to a unified classification of speech particles, but rather to a plethora of classifications and concepts differing at times quite radically in definition and nomenclature. Even the terminology and definitions used for the supercategory 'particles' vary quite drastically. For some, particles are all word classes which do not inflect, hence conjunctions and prepositions would be counted as particles as well (Engel 2004). Others differentiate between 'particles sensu lato' (particles in the wider sense) and 'particles in the strict sense' or synsemantica (Hentschel and Weydt 2002; Duden 2006; Burkhardt 1982). Yet again others differentiate between those which distributionally contribute to the compositional structure of the sentence and those which can form sentence-independent units (Diewald 2006; Weinrich 2005; Hoffmann 2013; Zifonun 1997; Institut für deutsche Sprache 2013). For those 'sentence-independent' units, e.g. interjections and response particles, yet again a variety of terms is used: interactive units ("Interaktive Einheiten") (Hoffmann 2013; Zifonun 1997; Institut für deutsche Sprache 2013), discourse particles (Diewald 2006), speaker signals and particles of the dialogue ("Sprechersignale und Dialogpartikeln") (Weinrich 2005) or 'words of speech' ("Gesprächswörter") (Burkhardt 1982).

As for statistical POS tagging the most important feature is distribution, the differentiation between sentence-independent particles and sentence-internal particles seems to be a reasonable basis for classification. Hence we propose these two major categories for the tagset. However, there are also particles which are neither sentence-independent nor sentence-internal but are either in the pre-front field or in the end field of a sentence, namely discourse particles ("Diskurspartikeln"). Quite surprisingly, these phenomena are hardly mentioned in any standard grammar reference at all. The DUDEN (2006), Weinrich (2005), Burkhardt (1982) and Diewald (2006) subsume e.g. reinsurance signals ("Rückversicherungssignale") and starting signals ("Startsignale") under the term structuring particles ("Gliederungspartikeln"), however, no distinction is made on whether they can stand independently from the sentence or not (Duden 2006). The other grammars simply do not mention them at all. Nevertheless, a differentiation can be made between sentence-independent, sentence-internal and sentence-external particles. By 'external', I mean that they are not part of the core sentence yet 'need' the sentence. So how can these categories be subclassified now and which phenomena fall into these classes?

4.1 Non-grammatical or sentence-independent elements

Regarding those particles which are sentence-independent, e.g. "ähm" or "hmm", it is crucial to bear in mind that these phenomena cannot be classified according to their distribution or any syntactic features. Hence, the only criterion by which to differentiate them is with respect to their pragmatic function. Taking a look at the grammar reference canon, one finds that DUDEN (2006) differentiates between interjections and onomatopoeia and subclassifies the former ones into simple and complex interjections, i.e. between those which have homonyms in other word classes and those which do not. The GDS (Zifonun 1997), Hoffmann's grammar (2013) and grammis 2.0 (Breindl and Donalies 2012) differentiate between interjections and response particles (“Responsive”) and Engel’s grammar (2004) adds initiating particles (“Initiativpartikeln”) and reaction particles (“Reaktive Partikeln”) to those. In contrast to that, Harald Weinrich’s grammar (2005) only defines interjections, but subclassifies those into situational, expressive and imitative interjections. Just looking at the terminology used for their classifications, one can get a hint of how contradictory the various definitions of interjections are. Whether response particles, onomatopoeia, inflectives or filled pauses are all interjections or separate classes of their own always depends on how broad or strict a definition for the interjection would be.

4.2 Sentence-external elements

Sentence-external particles, namely discourse markers (“Diskursmarker”) and tag questions (“Rückversicherungspartikeln”), are not classes which are explicitly named as such in any grammar reference yet are controversially debated in the research field of conversation analysis. Only the DUDEN uses the term “Diskursmarker” but not in describing it as word class of its own, but only to differentiate subjunctions from the use of the same lexeme (e.g. *weil* or *obwohl*) with main clauses. Nevertheless, in the grammars we do find classes which could be subsumed under these concepts even though they are classified as, for example, structuring particles (“Gliederungspartikeln”) (Hentschel and Weydt 2002; Burkhardt 1982), dialogue particles (“Dialogpartikeln”) (Weinrich 2005) or “Sequenzpartikeln” (sequencing particles) (Hentschel and Weydt 2002). However, in all of these classes no differentiation is made between those which are really distributionally bound to the pre-front field or the end field and those which are sentence-independent. In the literature on discourse markers there is no agreement on what is to be subsumed under that term either. Traugott (1997) and Auer and Günthner (2005) define them as every utterance which has a peripheral syntactical position and a ‘metapragmatic function’. What seems clear is that these phenomena came into existence through grammaticalization or degrammaticalization (Gohl and Günthner 1999; Brinton 1996; Günthner 2005; Leuschner 2005; Auer and Günthner 2005), hence most of them are homophones of adverbs, conjunctions, subjunctions etc. Imo (2012) yet again clearly differentiates between discourse markers and tag questions as, according to him, they have a different function, namely only to demand attention or sequencing turns whilst discourse markers would project the continuation of a speaker’s turn (Imo 2012).

4.3 Sentence-internal elements

Analyzing those particle categories, the only ones which seem to be quite indisputable are verbal particles and the ones which are defined by their form, i.e. the particle “zu” used with the infinitive (PTKZU), “am” preceding an adjective (PTKA) and the negation particle “nicht” (PTKNEG), although the online grammar grammis 2.0 defines it to be a subclass of the focus particle (Breindl and Donalies 2011).

Table 3 Comparison of criteria for modal particles and Abtönungspartikeln in the literature

grammar / criteria	DUDEN	HSK		GDS		Diewald		Schwitalla		Grammis	Hoffmann		Weinrich		Engel		Burkhardt	
	MP+AP	MP	AP	MP	AP	MP	AP	MP	AP	MP+AP	MP	AP	MP	AP	MP	AP	MP	AP
express speaker attitude	+		+		+	+		+		+	+	+	+		+			+
changing the illocution			(+)	+		+		+		+						+		+
changing the proposition		+		+		+					+		+					
answer for yes/no questions		+		+			n/a		n/a		+		-	n/a	+	-	n/a	
has constituency value		-			-	-				-		(-)	-					
may be negated		-			-					-						-		
can appear in front field	-		-		-	-		-		-		-	-		+	-		
always unstressed	+		+		+			+		+								

AP Abtönungspartikeln
MP modal particles
\+ criterion is explicitly mentioned
(+) criterion is implicitly mentioned
– criterion is explicitly denied
(–) criterion is implicitly denied

By contrast, table 3 shows that there is much disagreement on how to define or differentiate "Abtönungspartikeln" (I'm not able to find a translation; literally translated it would be something like 'shading' or 'coloration' particles, A/N) from modal particles ("Modalpartikeln"), such as German *mal, halt, doch*, or *ja*. Furthermore, there are differences on whether to make a distinction between these two terms, whether to treat them as synonyms (Duden 2006; Breindl and Donalies 2011a) or having only one class of items at all (Schwitalla 2012; Diewald 2006; Weinrich 2005; Burkhardt 1982).
Looking at the table one can find that the core definitions of those types of particles are very similar to each other. Criteria used to describe both types of particles in nearly all definitions are:

- the expression of attitudes, expectations, assumptions, and appraisal of the speaker and the addressee
- the inability to appear in the front field
- they never form constituents of a sentence and thus cannot be moved at all
- apart from a few exceptions, they cannot be stressed.

Also quite problematic is the differentiation of what is termed focus particles ("Fokuspartikeln"), scalar particles ("Gradpartikeln") and intensifying particles ("Intensitätspartikeln") such as German nur,sogar, sehr etc. as can be seen in table 4.

Table 4 Comparison of criteria for focus particles, scalar particles and intensifying particles in the literature

grammar / properties	DUDEN			grammis 2.0			GDS			HSK			Engel		
	FP	SP	IP[1]	FP	SP	IP	FP[2]	SP	IP	FP	SP[3]	IP	FP	SP	IP
modify NPs	+	–		(+)	(+)	–	+		–	n/a	n/a		n/a	+	n/a
may modify AdjPs, VPs, and words of number	+	+		(+)	(+)	+	+		+	n/a	n/a		n/a	+	n/a
scaling function	+	+		+	+	n/a	+		n/a	+	n/a		n/a	+	n/a
focus item they precede	+	n/a		+	+	n/a	+		n/a	+	n/a		n/a	+	n/a
intensifying or weakening function	n/a	+		n/a	n/a	+	+		+	n/a	+		n/a	+	n/a
grading function	(+)[4]	+		+	+	n/a	+		n/a	n/a	+		n/a	+	n/a
may be stressed	n/a	+		n/a	n/a	n/a	n/a		n/a	n/a	n/a		n/a	n/a	n/a
may appear in the front field	n/a	(–)[5]		–	–	–	(–)[6]		n/a	n/a	n/a		n/a	–	n/a
no effect on proposition of the sentence if omitted	(–)	+		n/a	n/a	+	+		n/a	–	n/a		n/a	n/a	n/a

FP focus particles
SP scalar particles
IP intensifying particles
+/(+)/–/(–) see table 3

It becomes obvious that the definitions of this group of particles are quite similar to each other except for the focus particles not being omittable without changing the proposition of the sentence and intensifying particles not being able to precede noun phrases. However, looking at spoken language, the last definition can be easily contradicted – e.g. considering the statement: "Das ist aber *sehr* fünfzehntes Jahrhundert" (This is *very* fifteenth century). Looking at the data of our corpus, quite a lot of examples come up where one could not easily decide whether the particles used would be only used for intensifying, bringing something into focus or for their scaling function, e.g.: "weil ich bin jetzt *echt* müde" (FOLK_E_00002_SE_01_T_01_DF_01, 00:30:46.94 - 00:30:53.93) (because I'm really tired now) or "*voll* die sau" (FOLK_E_00021_SE_01_T_16_DF_01, 02:07:20.34 - 02:07:26.09) (truly/utterly a pig).

A third group of phenomena which are quite inconsistently classified are connective particles ("Konnektivpartikeln"), maneuvering particles ("Rangierpartikeln") and conjunctive adverbs ("Konjunktionaladverbien") such as German *allerdings, deshalb* etc. On grammis 2.0 for example it is stated that the term connective particles is simply a synonym of maneuvering particles and conjunctive adverbs (Breindl and Donalies 2010). These terms are also used in the DUDEN (2006) and in (Engel

1 DUDEN claims that intensifying particles are synonyms to scalar particles.
2 The GDS claims that focus particles are synonyms to scalar particles.
3 The HSK claims that intensifying particles are synonyms to scalar particles.
4 DUDEN vaguely claims that only 'some' items of the class have a grading function.
5 DUDEN vaguely claims that 'most' of them can stand in the pre-front field.
6 GDS claims that they cannot stand in the pre-front field except for the words "noch" and "schon".

2004), however, they define them as something different than what is defined as connective particles in Zifonun (1997), Hoffmann (2013), Breindl and Donalies (2010). The problem here is based on the linguistic level on which they are defined. Some grammars define them according to their semantics and classify them as to their conjunctive function albeit not being conjunctions. Others define them according to their distribution in which case they rather have to be classified as adverbs rather than particles.

5 The STTS 2.0 – new categories for speech particles

5.1 Preliminary considerations

Restructuring the tagset is a task which requires some thoughts in advance. First of all, as the tagset is structured in a hierarchical way, new categories must fit into that hierarchical system. Secondly, as the aim of the restructuring is not just a theoretical one but aims at practical use for the research community, it needs to be comprehensible. However, the aim is not to follow a single grammar or theory but rather to build an unambiguous system of categories which are mutually exclusive and allow for an exhaustive categorization when applied to data of transcribed spoken language. The general principles followed were to construct the tagset as detailed as possible, to allow the research community to find as many phenomena typical for spoken language as possible, yet as coarse as necessary in order to maintain consistency and to create mutually exclusive categories. In contrast to, say, the VOICE corpus, in which several possible word class categories can be assigned to a token if it is ambiguous (VOICE 2013), in an automatized tagging relying only on statistical values, ambiguity – especially with respect to pragmatic information – cannot be taken into account as the tagging will not be manually corrected. Consistent with the original guidelines of the STTS each item shall receive only one tag (Schiller et al. 1999). As a result, multiword expressions will not be tagged as one item either, even when the pragmatic information in such cases might be lost. However, the new structures built should be coherent concerning the linguistic levels on which the annotation is based. It has been discussed whether e.g. pragmatic and syntactic information should be specifically annotated on different annotation levels (see e.g. Rehbein 2013). One of the main reasons to annotate only one level of POS tags in our corpus is that, looking at spoken data, the syntactic function of an item is often deeply intertwined with its pragmatic function. Nevertheless, this paper suggests a reclassification which on a theoretical level aims at a clear representation of the distinction between the linguistic levels which shall be assigned through POS tags.

In addition, as the transcripts are based on spoken language and follow the cGAT conventions, one has to take into account that there are many utterances transcribed which cannot even be seen as 'words', like sighing, laughing or breathing. Hence, the categories created for typical spoken language phenomena will still adhere to the concept of a "word" and only those items shall receive a POS tag.

Being aware that the classical concept of the sentence cannot be applied to these transcripts of spoken data, the concept of the verbal bracket (Verbklammer) is still fundamental for the new categorization in order to describe the items in the utterances syntactically and also to determine whether they apply to a syntactical concept at all.

5.2 Extensions to the STTS

An overview on the structure of the categorization is given in table 5. Firstly, items like e.g. hesitation markers, interjections, onomatopoeia, inflectives or backchannel signals cannot be looked at on a syntactic linguistic level as they are not part of the syntax of a sentence. They shall be tagged as non-grammatical elements and thus receive the supercategory tag NG. As one category for all non-grammatical items would hardly be satisfactory to depict these various typical spoken language phenomena, one needs to consider a different linguistic level in order to further categorize them; namely their pragmatic function.

To ensure that the subcategories are mutually exclusive, a closer look into the corpus data was necessary to check whether one (and only one) pragmatic function could be assigned to items that are considered non-grammatical. Wherever this was not the case and one item could have several pragmatic functions, the items would have to be categorized into a 'broader' class of items. Finally, items like onomatopoeia, inflectives and hesitation markers only have this one pragmatic function and thus get their own POS tag categories NGONO (Onomatopoetika), NGAKW (Aktionswörter) and NGHES

(Hesitationspartikeln). However, response particles, backchannel signals and interjections do quite often take each other's functions, e.g. in the following example it is not clear whether "ach" is used as a response particle, a backchannel signal or an interjection.

LB °h isch ne GUte frage, ((schmatzt)) °hh des hat einfach mit der diagNOse zu tun.
(that's a good question ((smacking lips)) it's just about the diagnosis)
(0.22)
LB gucke ma uns NAchher mal an dann.
(we'll have a closer look at that later)
ML ACH so;
(ah)
LB ja?
(yes) (FOLK_E_00008_SE_01_T_01_DF_01, 00:15:21.66 - 00:15:28.84)

Hence, although on a theoretical level there might be differences between those classes, in analyzing spoken language these differentiations cannot be made in every case. Thus, there will only be one POS tag for those items in the STTS 2.0 which have the function of signaling response, backchanneling or interjections – the NGIRR for "Interjektionen, Rezeptionssignale und Responsive". Obviously, what formerly has been tagged as answering particle PTKANT (Antwortpartikel) will subsequently be tagged as NGIRR. This restructuring needs to be done as the response particles "yes", "no", "maybe" etc. are not – like the other particles which are tagged with the supercategory PTK – syntactically integrated in the sentence, i.e. located in the middle field of a sentence.

Secondly, there is the group of speech particles which are not part of the core sentence construction, yet pragmatically cannot stand on their own. These 'sentence external' (SE) elements can be subclassified into two classes. Discourse markers stand in the pre-front field and need a sentence to follow, i.e. they open up a projection which needs to be filled by the following. Tag questions stand in the end field and are used to raise the hearer's attention. Hence, two new POS tags are introduced to tag those items: SEDM (discourse particles) and SEQU (tag questions).

Table 5 schematic overview on the reclassification of speech particles

subject	POS tagging	distributional features	proposed tags	examples
Items in the corpus	**no tags assigned** No stable phonetical form, annotated according to cGAT conventions (e.g. sighing, laughing, breathing etc.).			((stöhnt)), ((lacht)), °hhh (sighs) (laughs) (breathing)
	tags assigned	**sentence-independent → non grammatical elements (NG)**	**NGIRR** interjections, response signals and backchannel behavior	ach, ja, hmhm (oh, yes, uhum)
			NGHES hesitation signals	äh, ähm (uhh, uhm)
			NGAKW action words (inflectives)	lol, grins, seufz (lol, grin, sighing)
			NGONO onomatopoeia	muh, miau, kikeriki (moo, meow, cock-a-doodle-doo)
		dependent on grammatical constructions yet not part of them → sentence-external elements (SE)	**SEDM** discourse particles	also [ich glaube …] (well [I think])
			SEQU tag questions	[ist gut] ne? ([it's good] isn't it?)
		sentence-internal → particles (PTK) (other than PTKZU, PTKA, PTKNEG, PTKVZ)	**PTKIFG** intensifying, focus, and scalar particles	sehr [schön], nur [sie], viel [mehr] (very [nice], only [her], much [more])
			PTKMA modal particles und Abtnungs-partikeln	halt, mal, ja, schon (just, once)[7]
			PTKLEX particles which are part of a multi-word expression	[noch] eine/r, immer [noch] (another, still)

Finally, there are those speech particles which are syntactically integrated in the core sentence, i.e. are situated in the middle field. Those which are already represented in categories in the tagset and which are categorized based on their syntactic features will remain. The PTKANT tag will be removed from this category. Additionally, those sentence-internal particles which formerly have been tagged as

[7] There are hardly any Abtönungspartikeln in the English language, thus no literal translations are possible.

adverbs, i.e. modal, focus, scalar or intensifying particles shall be categorized as particles. Although the naming and the concepts for those particles are highly debated in the literature, syntactically, one can clearly differentiate them from adverbs as adverbs can stand in the front field on their own whilst speech particles cannot (Breindl and Donalies 2011). Moreover, as Hirschmann (2013) pointed out, one can divide all these speech particle concepts into two groups: those which can be moved to the front field together with their mother phrase and those which cannot be moved at all. The latter ones are either modal particles or Abtönungspartikeln, the former ones intensifying particles, focus particles and scalar particles (Breindl and Donalies 2011b). As evidently not even the grammars can give clear guidelines for the distinction of these classes, a categorization can only be based on distributional features. Consequently, there shall be two new POS tag categories PTKIFG (Intensitäts-, Fokus- und Gradpartikeln) and PTKMA (Modal- und Abtönungspartikeln). However, annotating data one comes across a set of sentence-internal particles which have not been accounted for so far. Hirschmann (2013) presented an analysis of items which are part of multi-word lexemes. They are bound to other lexemes not by modifying them as an intensifyer, focus, or scalar particle, but they have to be considered parts of multi-word constructions. This can be proven by the fact that the elements in question lose the meaning which they possess without the element they are joint with. From an orthographic point of view, however, those particles, together with the other item, build a phrasal constituent. For example, "immer" and "noch" in: "Baba ist *immer noch* brummelig" (Baba is still grumpy) (FOLK_E_00016, 13), together semantically form one lexeme which can also be seen in the translation where both together are translated as "still". Crucially, the word "immer" is neither an adverb with the usual meaning "always" here, nor is it an intensifier with the meaning "increasingly" as in "immer besser" (increasingly well/better). In this one idiosyncratic case ("immer noch"), "immer" can onlybe interpreted together with "noch" which can only be moved as a multi-word lexeme in the sentence. The adverb "noch" can still be interpreted as the head of the whole expression. In this respect, lexicalized particles are similar to the group of PTKIFG, with the difference that they neither have an intensifying, scaling or focusing function. It seems like they are a very interesting group of particles, as one can analyze the gradual grammaticalization cline in such items. Finding that it is a very restricted group of possible items they shall receive their own tag PTKLEX for "particle in a multi-word lexeme".

6 Conclusion and outlook

This paper presented a proposal as to how new tag categories for an improved version of the STTS (STTS 2.0) in the field of speech particles could look like.

To see whether these new categories work for part of speech annotation, guidelines have been written and the work on annotating a gold standard of about 100,000 tokens has begun. In order to evaluate and validate the proposed tagset and the guidelines, Cohen's kappa will be used to assess the inter-annotator agreement. In addition, post-processing has been implemented that already helps to improve the accuracy of the output, e.g. by assigning POS-tags to those items which do not have any homonyms in other word classes, i.e. through a list of items which shall receive this tag. A first analysis shows that this proved to be extremely useful for the categories NGIRR, NGONO, NGHES, NGAKW and SEQU.

However, in order to fully automatize part of speech tagging of transcripts of spoken language, a re-training of the tagger will be necessary. Moreover – although the errors due to mis-tagged speech particles were the most prominent cause for the low precision rate – additional sources of errors will have to be analyzed to be able to create a coherent tagset for spoken language annotation. The analysis of the colloquial use of pronouns, verbs, foreign language material or in the STTS so called 'non-words' might call for a further recategorization of the Stuttgart Tübingen tagset.

References

Auer, Peter; Günthner, Susanne (2005): Die Entstehung von Diskursmarkern im Deutschen - ein Fall von Grammatikalisierung? In: Torsten Leuschner (Hg.): Grammatikalisierung im Deutschen. Berlin: De Gruyter (Linguistik - Impulse & Tendenzen), S. 335–362.

Bartz, Thomas; Beißwenger, Michael; Storrer, Angelika (2013): Optimierung des Stuttgart-Tübingen-Tagset für die linguistische Annotation von Korpora zur internetbasierten Kommunikation: Phänomene, Herausforderungen, Erweiterungsvorschläge. In Journal for Language Technology and Computational Linguistics (28(1)), pp. 155–198.

Breindl, Eva; Donalies, Elke (2011): Abtönungspartikel. grammis 2.0. das grammatische informationssystem des instituts für deutsche sprache (ids). Institut für deutsche Sprache. Online verfügbar unter http://hypermedia.ids-mannheim.de/call/public/sysgram.ansicht?v_typ=d&v_id=392, zuletzt aktualisiert am 05.05.2011, zuletzt geprüft am 11.09.2013.

Breindl, Eva; Donalies, Elke (2011): Fokuspartikel. grammis 2.0. das grammatische informationssystem des instituts für deutsche sprache (ids). Institut für deutsche Sprache. Available online at http://hypermedia.ids-mannheim.de/call/public/sysgram.ansicht?v_typ=d&v_id=408, updated on 5/5/2011, checked on 8/20/2013.

Breindl, Eva; Donalies, Elke (2012): Intensitätspartikel. grammis 2.0. das grammatische informationssystem des instituts für deutsche sprache (ids). Institut für deutsche Sprache. Available online at http://hypermedia.ids-mannheim.de/call/public/sysgram.ansicht?v_typ=d&v_id=391, updated on 1/12/2012, checked on 8/20/2013.

Breindl, Eva; Donalies, Elke (2012): Interaktive Einheiten. grammis 2.0. das grammatische informationssystem des instituts für deutsche sprache (ids). Institut für deutsche Sprache. Online verfügbar unter http://hypermedia.ids-mannheim.de/call/public/sysgram.ansicht?v_typ=d&v_id=370, zuletzt aktualisiert am 12.01.2012, zuletzt geprüft am 13.01.2014.

Breindl, Eva; Donalies, Elke (2011): Konnektivpartikel. grammis 2.0. das grammatische informationssystem des instituts für deutsche sprache (ids). Institut für deutsche Sprache. Online verfügbar unter http://hypermedia.ids-mannheim.de/call/public/sysgram.ansicht?v_id=410, zuletzt aktualisiert am 05.05.2011, zuletzt geprüft am 08.10.2013.

Brinton, Laurel J. (1996): Pragmatic Markers in English: Grammaticalization and Discourse Functions. Berlin, Germany: Mouton de Gruyter (Topics in English Linguistics (TopicsEL): 19).

Burkhardt, Armin (1982): Gesprächswörter. Ihre lexikologische Bestimmung und lexikographische Beschreibung. In: Wolfgang Mentrup (Hg.): Konzepte zur Lexikographie. Studien zur Bedeutungserklärung in einsprachigen Wörterbüchern. Tübingen: Niemeyer (Reihe Germanistische Linguistik), S. 138–171.

Burnard, Lou (Ed.) (2007): Reference Guide for the British National Corpus. Available online at http://www.natcorp.ox.ac.uk/docs/URG/, checked on 5/1/2014.

Diewald, Gabriele (2006): Discourse particles and modal particles as grammatical elements. In: Kerstin Fischer (Hg.): Approaches to discourse particles. 1. Aufl. Amsterdam, Heidelberg: Elsevier (Studies in pragmatics), S. 403–425.

Duden. Die Grammatik: unentbehrlich für richtiges Deutsch (2006). Mannheim: Dudenverlag (Duden in zwölf Bänden, 4).

Engel, Ulrich (2004): Deutsche Grammatik. Neubearbeitung. Heidelberg: Groos.

Godfrey, J. J.; Holliman, E. C.; McDaniel, J. (1992): Switchboard: Telephone speech corpus for research and development. In Proceedings of the IEEE International Conference on Acoustics, Speech and Signal Processing, pp. 517–520.

Gohl, Christine; Günthner, Susanne (1999): Grammatikalisierung von weil als Diskursmarker in der gesprochenen Sprache. In: Zeitschrift für Sprachwissenschaft 18 (1). DOI: 10.1515/zfsw.1999.18.1.39.

Günthner, Susanne (2005): Grammatikalisierungs-/Pragmatikalisierungserscheinungen im alltäglichen Sprachgebrauch. Vom Diskurs zum Standard? In: Eichinger, Ludwig M. und Kallmeyer, Werner (Hg.): Standardvariation. Wie viel Variation verträgt die deutsche Sprache? Berlin, New York: De Gruyter, S. 41–62.

Helbig, Gerhard (2011): Deutsche Grammatik. Ein Handbuch für den Ausländerunterricht. Unter Mitarbeit von Joachim Buscha. [Neubearb.]. Berlin, München, Wien, Zürich: Langenscheidt.

Hentschel, Elke; Weydt, Harald (2002): Die Wortart "Partikel". In: David A. Cruse (Hg.): Lexikologie. Lexicology, Bd. 2. 2 Bände. Berlin [u.a.]: De Gruyter (Handbücher zur Sprach- und Kommunikationswissenschaft, 21), S. 646–653.

Hirschmann, H., Lestmann, N., Rehbein, I., and Westpfahl, S. (2013). Erweiterung der Wortartenkategorien des STTS im Bereich 'ADV' und 'PTK'. Presentation at STTS Workshop, Hildesheim, Germany.

Hoffmann, Ludger (2013): Deutsche Grammatik: Grundlagen für Lehrerausbildung, Schule, Deutsch als Zweitsprache und Deutsch als Fremdsprache. Berlin: E. Schmidt. Online verfügbar unter http://deposit.d-nb.de/cgi-bin/dokserv?id=4057806&prov=M&dok%5Fvar=1&dok%5Fext=htm.

IDS, Datenbank für Gesprochenes Deutsch (DGD2). Online verfügbar unter http://dgd.ids-mannheim.de:8080/dgd/pragdb.dgd_extern.welcome?v_session_id=, zuletzt geprüft am 04.07.2014.

Imo, Wolfgang (2012): Wortart Diskursmarker? In: Björn Rothstein (Hg.): Nicht-flektierende Wortarten. Berlin: De Gruyter (Linguistik, Impulse & Tendenzen, 47), S. 48–88.

Institut für deutsche Sprache (2013): grammis 2.0. das grammatische informationssystem des instituts für deutsche sprache (ids). Unter Mitarbeit von Marek Konopka, Jacqueline Kubczak, Roman Schneider, Bruno Strecker, Eva Breindl-Hiller, Elke Donalies et al. Online verfügbar unter http://hypermedia.ids-mannheim.de/index.html, zuletzt geprüft am 17.07.2013.

Leuschner, Torsten (Hg.) (2005): Grammatikalisierung im Deutschen. Berlin: De Gruyter (Linguistik - Impulse & Tendenzen).

Oosterdijk, Nelleke (2000): The spoken Dutch corpus. Overview and first evaluation. Proceedings of the Second International Conference on Language Resources and Evaluation (LREC).

Rehbein, Ines; Schalowski, Sören (2013): STTS goes Kiez – Experiments on Annotating and Tagging Urban Youth Language. In Journal for Language Technology and Computational Linguistics (28(1)), pp. 199–227, checked on 4/30/2014.

Sampson, Geoffrey (2000): CHRISTINE Corpus: Documentation. University of Sussex. Available online at http://www.grsampson.net/ChrisDoc.html, updated on 8/18/2000, checked on 5/1/2014.

Schiller, Anne; Teufel, Simone; Stöckert, Christine; Thielen, Christine (1999): Guidelines für das Tagging deutscher Textcorpora mit STTS. (Kleines und großes Tagset). Universität Stuttgart, Institut für maschinelle Sprachverarbeitung; Universität Tübingen, Seminar für Sprachwissenschaft. Online verfügbar unter http://www.sfs.uni-tuebingen.de/resources/stts-1999.pdf, zuletzt geprüft am 26.02.2014.

Telljohann, H.; Hinrichs, E.; Kübler, S.; Zinsmeister, Heike (2012): Stylebook for the Tübingen Treebank of Written German (TüBa-D/Z). University of T¨ubingenre.

Traugott, Elizabeth Closs (Hg.) (1997): The discourse connective "after all": A historical pragmatic account. 10th International Congress of Linguists. Paris, July.

VOICE (2013): Part-of-Speech Tagging and Lemmatization Manual. With assistance of Barbara Seidlhofer, Stefan Majewski, Ruth Osimk-Teasdale, Marie-Luise Pitzl, Michael Radeka, Nora Dorn. The Vienna-Oxford International Corpus of English. Available online at http://www.univie.ac.at/voice/documents/VOICE_tagging_manual.pdf, checked on 5/1/2014.

Weinrich, Harald (2005): Textgrammatik der deutschen Sprache. 3. Aufl. Hildesheim: Olms.

Westpfahl, Swantje; Schmidt, Thomas (2013): POS für(s) FOLK - Part of Speech Tagging des Forschungs- und Lehrkorpus Gesprochenes Deutsch. In: Journal for Language Technology and Computational Linguistics (28 (1)), S. 139–153, zuletzt geprüft am 16.04.2014.

Zifonun, Gisela (1997): Grammatik der deutschen Sprache: [Bd. 1-3]. Hg. v. Ludger Hoffmann und Bruno Strecker. Berlin [u.a.]: De Gruyter (Schriften des Instituts für Deutsche Sprache, 7).

Use of Coreference in Automatic Searching for Multiword Discourse Markers in the Prague Dependency Treebank

Magdaléna Rysová
Charles University in Prague
Faculty of Arts
[magdalena.rysova@post.cz]

Jiří Mírovský
Charles University in Prague
Faculty of Mathematics and Physics
[mirovsky@ufal.mff.cuni.cz]

Abstract

The paper introduces a possibility of new research offered by a multi-dimensional annotation of the Prague Dependency Treebank. It focuses on exploitation of the annotation of coreference for the annotation of discourse relations expressed by multiword expressions. It tries to find which aspect interlinks these linguistic areas and how we can use this interplay in automatic searching for Czech expressions like *despite this* (*navzdory tomu*), *because of this fact* (*díky této skutečnosti*) functioning as multiword discourse markers.

1 Introduction

The aim of the paper is to introduce possibilities of interplay between two linguistic phenomena – discourse[1] and coreference relations – annotated in the Prague Dependency Treebank (PDT). The paper demonstrates how the annotation of coreference relations (finished in 2011) may facilitate automatic searching for alternative lexicalizations of discourse connectives like *due to this fact* (*kvůli této skutečnosti*), *in addition to this* (*kromě toho*) in the corpus that offers annotation of several linguistic phenomena at once. In other words, the paper tries to show how we can build on existing annotation of coreference to improve another level of annotation – discourse.

1.1 Annotation of Discourse Relations in the Prague Dependency Treebank

The Prague Dependency Treebank is a corpus of almost 50 thousand sentences of Czech journalistic texts that offers linguistic data manually annotated on three layers – it interlinks morphological, syntactic and complex semantic (or tectogrammatic) annotation (Hajič et al., 2006, Bejček et al., 2012). For the semantic layer of PDT, there also exists annotation of coreference (Nedoluzhko et al., 2011), and discourse (as the only annotated corpus of Czech; see Poláková et al., 2012a).

Discourse relations are marked between two verbal arguments (i.e. two relevant parts of text) if they are signalled by a certain discourse marker – see an example from PDT:

(1) *The mattress was terrible, no quality at first sight.*
However, he did not care.
(In original: *[Matrace] byla na první pohled strašná, nekvalitní. On na to ale vůbec nedbal.*)

[1] In this paper, we understand discourse in narrow sense, i.e. as text relations between sentences (verbal arguments). Coreference is here used as an umbrella term for grammatical and textual coreference and bridging relations expressed in section 4. Although bridging relations differ from coreference in traditional sense, as they express an indirect relation based on association, we use the general term coreference in the text for better transparency.

LAW VIII - The 8th Linguistic Annotation Workshop, pages 11–19,
Dublin, Ireland, August 23-24 2014.

In this example, there are two verbal arguments: the first is *the mattress was terrible, no quality at first sight* (*[matrace] byla na první pohled strašná, nekvalitní*) and the second *he did not care* (*on na to ale vůbec nedbal*). Between these two arguments, there is a discourse relation of opposition signalled by the conjunction *however* (*ale*). Therefore, in this case, *however* (*ale*) has a function of discourse marker.

In the first phase of discourse annotation (see the Prague Discourse Treebank 1.0, Poláková et al., 2012a), only discourse relations (between verbal arguments) introduced by explicit connectives have been captured. Explicit connectives are understood as closed class expressions with connecting function at the level of discourse description (see Poláková et al., 2012b) belonging among certain parts of speech – especially conjunctions (*therefore, however, or – proto, ačkoli, nebo*), adverbs (*then, afterwards – potom, pak*) and particles (mainly rhematizers as *too, only – také, jen*).

However, during annotation, there occurred also other expressions exactly with the same connecting function that differed from connectives in both lexical and syntactic aspect. These expressions were called alternative lexicalizations of discourse connectives (shortly AltLexes) in the Penn Discourse Treebank[2] (see Prasad et al., 2010); their examples are *this is the reason why* (*to je důvod, proč*), *due to this fact* (*kvůli tomu*) etc. In some cases, explicit discourse connectives and their alternative lexicalizations are even interchangeable – see an example from PDT:

(2) *Almost every mined diamond has a quality of a jewel.*
<u>This is the reason why</u> such an expensive output from the sea is worth for the company.

(In original: *Téměř každý vytěžený diamant má kvalitu drahokamu.*
<u>To je důvod, proč</u> se tak nákladná těžba z moře firmě vyplácí.)

In this example, there is an AltLex *this is the reason why* (*to je důvod, proč*) signalling a discourse relation of reason and result. This AltLex is replaceable by the connective *therefore* and the meaning remains exactly the same.

The example demonstrates that a complete discourse annotation should contain also relations expressed by AltLexes. Therefore, a detailed research on AltLexes is useful and needed. In this respect, the present paper tries to demonstrate how the new instances of Czech AltLexes may be automatically found in the Prague Dependency Treebank on the basis of the already finished coreference annotation.

2 Alternative Lexicalizations of Discourse Connectives in PDT

Alternative lexicalizations of discourse connectives were firstly described in detail for English (see Prasad et al., 2010). English AltLexes were examined from the lexico-syntactic and semantic point of view. Similar analysis has been made also for Czech (see Rysová, 2012a) – the research was carried out on the basis of the annotated data from PDT.

In the first stage of discourse annotation in PDT (i.e. annotation of Czech data), the annotators (trained students of linguistics) were asked to fill a comment "AltLex" to such expressions that function in the text, according to their interpretation, as Czech AltLexes. The aim of the first stage (regarding the AltLexes) was to collect an adequate sample of material that allowed the preliminary analysis of Czech AltLexes (see Rysová, 2012a).

Altogether, PDT contains 49,431 sentences with the annotation of discourse. Within them, there were 306 expressions (or tokens) with the annotators' comment "AltLex". This number seems to be rather low. However, the annotators did not mark all instances of AltLexes – in the first stage, the aim was not a final and complete annotation (as Czech AltLexes are a new and uninvestigated topic) but a collection of material for further research. So for example, we found out that the Czech AltLex *because of* (*díky*) appears in PDT in 14 instances although firstly, it was marked in the annotators' comment just in one case.

[2] The terms AltLex's and explicit discourse connectives are used in the Prague Dependency Treebank and Penn Discourse Treebank not fully identically. For example, Penn Discourse Treebank captures prepositional phrases as connectives whereas Prague Dependency Treebank as AltLex's etc. However, both understand connectives as closed class expressions and AltLex's as open class expressions with connecting function at the level of discourse.

Therefore, it is obvious that the preliminary number 306 of Czech AltLexes will considerably grow and that in the following stage of annotation, it is necessary to search for Czech AltLexes more systematically.

3 A Specific Group of Czech AltLexes: Preposition + an Anaphoric Expression

On the basis of the 306 tokens gained from the first stage of annotation, there was created a preparatory list of Czech AltLexes (see Rysová, 2012b). It appeared that one significant group of them is formed by Czech prepositions followed by an anaphoric expression referring to the previous argument. These are expressions like *because of this* (*kvůli tomu*), *due to this fact* (*díky této skutečnosti*), *despite this situation* (*navzdory této situaci*) etc. – see an example from PDT:

(3) *President Fernando Collor probably hoarded millions to his own pocket.*
<u>*Because of this,*</u> *he is supposed to fail.*

(In original: *Prezident Fernando Collor si údajně nahrabal do vlastní kapsy milióny.*
<u>*Kvůli tomu*</u> *pravděpodobně padne.*)

In the example, there is a discourse relation of reason and result introduced by the AltLex *because of this* (*kvůli tomu*) that is replaceable by the connective *therefore* (*proto*) in this case.

In this group of AltLexes, it is the preposition that carries the core of lexical meaning as well as the property of being an AltLex (see Rysová, 2012b). It means that the preposition carries the information about the type of the discourse relation – e.g. the example (3) demonstrates that it is the expression *because of* (*kvůli*) that signals a relation of reason and result and therefore the preposition is also the fixed part of the AltLex. At the same time, the preposition obligatorily combines with an anaphoric reference that may vary – in the example (3), it is the pronoun *this* (*tomu*) but it is variable with other anaphoric expressions, so there are such variants of AltLexes like *because of this / this fact / this situation* (*díky tomu / této skutečnosti / této situaci*) etc.

Other examples of prepositions (meant in the Czech originals – see Kroupová, 1984) from this group of AltLexes are *in addition to* (*kromě*), *due to* (*kvůli*), *unlike* (*na rozdíl od*), *on the basis of* (*na základě*), *despite* (*navzdory*), *in spite of* (*přes*), *due to* (*vinou*), *considering* (*vzhledem k*).

As said above, these types of AltLexes must combine with some complementation due to their valency. Therefore, it is impossible to use, for example, **because of, I will do it* (**kvůli to udělám*), but only *because of this, I will do it* (*kvůli tomu to udělám*). So if there is some obligatory complementation, i.e. a general rule in all of these AltLexes, we may use this information for their automatic searching.

Moreover, all of these prepositions function as AltLexes only if they combine with some anaphoric expression referring to the previous argument. If they occur with a non-anaphoric expression, they are not AltLexes, like in this example:

(4) *I was ill a whole month.*
I could not sleep <u>*due to cough*</u> *at night.*

(In original: *Marodila jsem celý měsíc.*
V noci jsem nemohla spát <u>*kvůli kašli.*</u>)

It is obvious that the expression *due to cough* (*kvůli kašli*) from the second sentence does not refer to any part of the previous one and that it does not signal any discourse relation between the two sentences. On the contrary, there is the following example of the same preposition with anaphoric reference functioning as AltLex:

(5) *Italy saves.*
<u>*Because of this,*</u> *some journals will no longer come out.*

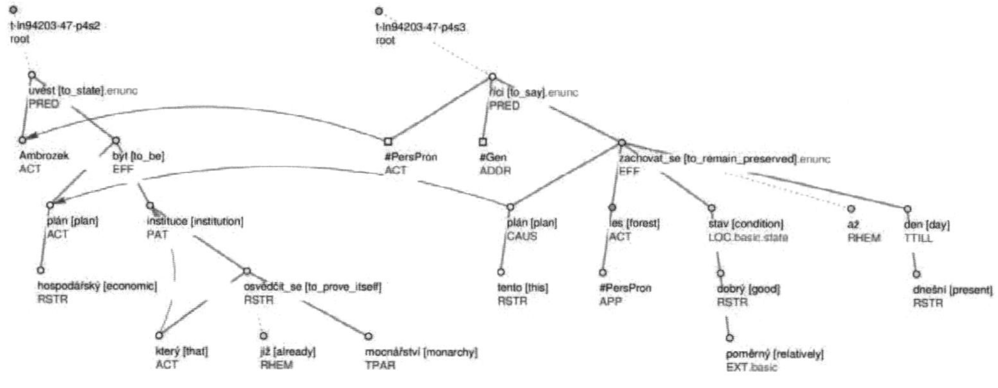

Figure 1. An example of a textual coreference with a noun as the antecedent.

(In original: *Itálie šetří.*
<u>*Kvůli tomu*</u> *tam přestanou vycházet některé deníky.*)

In this example, the whole expression *because of this* (*kvůli tomu*) introduces a discourse relation of reason and result between the two arguments. We may replace it, for example, by the connective *therefore* (*proto*).

It is obvious that combination of prepositions as *due to* (*kvůli*), *because of* (*díky*) with an anaphoric reference is, for them, a condition for being AltLex. This condition may be well used especially in corpora with annotated coreference as the Prague Dependency Treebank.

4 Annotation of Coreference in PDT and Its Use for Discourse

4.1 Types of Coreference

Annotation of coreference in PDT was finished in 2011 (cf. Nedoluzhko et al., 2011). The annotated relations are divided into four groups: a) grammatical coreference – mostly inter-sentential coreference derivable using Czech grammatical rules (the vertical arrow in Fig. 1); b) textual coreference – inter- and intra-sentential coreference of pronouns and nouns derivable only from the sentence meaning (the horizontal arrows in Fig. 1); c) bridging anaphora – inter- and intra-sentential relations such as part-whole, subset-set, function etc.; d) special types of reference (exophora – referring to elements outside the text, and segment – referring to an unspecified larger part of the preceeding context) (see Nedoluzhko, 2011).

4.2 AltLexes – Coreference Leading to the Verbal Argument

As said in the section 3, there is one group of Czech AltLexes functioning as discourse markers only in combination with some anaphoric expression. The second condition is that this anaphoric expression must refer to a (whole) verbal argument. PDT captures it in the tree structure with the highest verbal node representing the whole argument (discourse relations are realized by thick orange arrows leading between two verbal nodes symbolising the two arguments).[3] It means that when searching for tokens from this group of AltLexes, we may omit anaphoric expressions referring to non-verbal parts of text – see an example from PDT, depicted in Figure 1:

---

[3] It is important to understand that coreference and all discourse relations, although technically annotated between two nodes, in fact express a relation between the whole subtrees of the two nodes, as (on the tectogrammatical layer of PDT) a node represents the whole subtree it governs. (In case of discourse, more complex arguments can be specified in a dedicated attribute *range*.)

(6) *Ambrozek stated that the economic plan is an institution that proved itself already in the monarchy. Because of this plan, our forests remained preserved in a relatively good condition until the present days, he said.*

(In original: *Ambrozek uvedl, že hospodářský plán je instituce, která se osvědčila již za mocnářství. Díky tomuto plánu se naše lesy zachovaly v poměrně dobrém stavu až do dnešních dnů, řekl.*)

In the example, there is the preposition *because of* (*díky*) that combines with the anaphoric expression *this plan* (*tento plán*). However, *this plan* (*tento plán*) does not refer to the whole previous argument (sentence) but only to its nominal part *plan* (*plán*) – it means that there is annotated a coreference relation between these two nouns (see Figure 1 and the dark curved arrow between the two nodes *plan* in the two trees). Therefore, the expression *because of this plan* (*díky tomuto plánu*) is not an AltLex here.

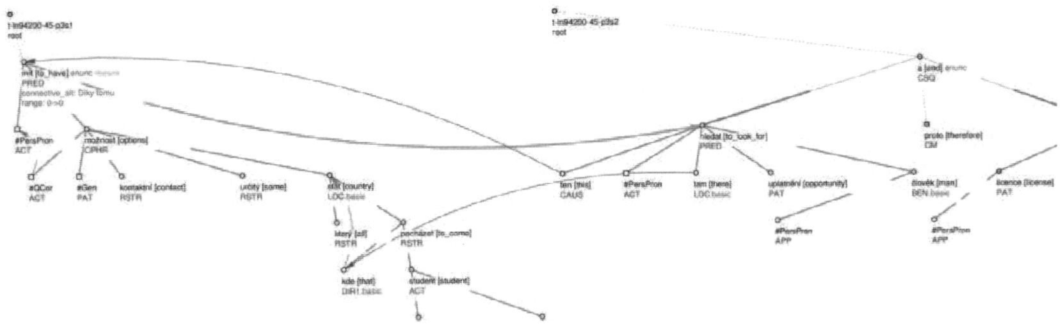

Figure 2. An example of a coreference to a verbal node. The trees have been cropped to fit the page.

On the other hand, there is another example, depicted in Figure 2:

(7) *We have some contact options in all countries that foreign students in the former Czechoslovakia came from.*
Because of this, we might be able to look there for opportunities for our people, and our license is therefore designed quite broadly.

(In original: *Máme určité kontaktní možnosti ve všech státech, odkud pocházeli zahraniční studenti v bývalém Československu.*
Díky tomu bychom tam mohli hledat uplatnění pro naše lidi, a naše licence je proto pojata dosti široce.)

Again, there is the preposition *because of* (*díky*) with an anaphoric expression *this* (*tomu*) that, in this case, fulfils also the second condition, as it refers to the whole previous argument (sentence) represented by the finite verb in the main clause *to have* (*mít*) – see Figure 2 with the annotated coreference relation going from *this* (*ten*) to a verb *to have* (*mít*). The discourse relation is represented by a thick orange arrow going from the verb *to have* (*mít*) to a verb *to look for* (*hledat*).

These examples demonstrate that tokens of this type of AltLexes in PDT may be automatically looked up on the basis of the two conditions: a) the preposition must combine with an anaphoric expression; b) this expression must be in a coreference or bridging relation (according to the finished annotation of coreference – see Nedoluzhko et al., 2011) with some verbal node (representing the whole argument).

4.3 Searching in the Data

The primary format of PDT is called Prague Markup Language (PML). It is an abstract XML-based format designed for annotation of treebanks. For editing and processing data in the PML format, a highly customizable tree editor TrEd[4] was developed (Pajas and Štěpánek, 2008). The search was performed in PML Tree Query (PML-TQ)[5], a powerful client-server based query engine for treebanks (Pajas and Štěpánek, 2010), with the client part implemented as an extension to the tree editor TrEd.

Using the query engine, we searched for places in the data with a given preposition and an anaphoric expression relating to a verbal node either as grammatical coreference, textual coreference, bridging anaphora, or coreference to segment. The antecedent of the relation could either be directly the verbal node or a coordination or apposition of verbal nodes, or it could be unspecified in case of coreference to segment.

Let us present a simplified example of such a query; this particular query searches for relevant places in the PDT data with a preposition *due to* (*vinou*) plus an anaphoric expression:

```
1 t-node $t :=
2 [ (1+x coref_gram.rf t-node
3        [ gram/sempos = "v" ] or
4    1+x coref_text/target-node.rf t-node
5        [ gram/sempos = "v" ] or
6    1+x bridging/target-node.rf t-node
7        [ gram/sempos = "v" ] or
8    1+x coref_gram.rf t-node
9        [ nodetype = "coap", t-node
10           [ gram/sempos = "v" ] ] or
11   1+x coref_text/target-node.rf t-node
12       [ nodetype = "coap", t-node
13           [ gram/sempos = "v" ] ] or
14   1+x bridging/target-node.rf t-node
15       [ nodetype = "coap", t-node
16           [ gram/sempos = "v" ] ] or
17   coref_special = "segm"),
18  a/lex.rf|a/aux.rf a-node
19      [ m/form ~ "^[Vv]inou$" ] ];
20
21 >> give $t.id
```

Line 1 declares a tectogrammatical node (and names it $t for later reference), lines 2–17 specify a disjunction of seven possible ways of an anaphoric reference (lines 2 and 3 define a grammatical coreference from the given node to a verbal node (semantic part-of-speech equals "v"), lines 4 and 5 define the same condition for textual coreference, lines 6 and 7 for bridging anaphora. Lines 8–16 express the same three relations, this time with an anaphoric verbal node being a part of a coordination or apposition (the relation is between the given node $t and the node representing the coordination or apposition (nodetype="coap")), and line 17 searches for a coreference to a not further specified segment). Lines 18 and 19 express that on the surface, the given node $t represents the preposition *due to* (*vinou*). Finally, an output filter on line 21 gives identifiers of positions in the data found by the query.

For each preposition from a given list (see Table 1 below), the query produced a list of positions in the data. These positions were gone through by human annotators and discourse relations with all required additional information were marked there.

4.4 Results, Evaluation and Discussion

Altogether, PDT contains 1,482 tokens of selected prepositions (we worked with the types of prepositions that were, in some instances, marked as AltLexes in the preliminary phase of annotation). Within them, we have automatically looked up 89 instances functioning as AltLexes.

The results demonstrate that using coreference annotation significantly helped reduce the final number of relevant instances (i.e. those being AltLexes) and that it substantially facilitated the annotation of discourse (instead of 1,482 instances, the human annotators had to go only through 89 of them, i.e. only through 6 % out of the total number in the whole PDT) – see Table 1 that introduces the total number of all instances of given prepositions (in any role) in PDT and their final reduced numbers in the role of Alt-

[4] http://ufal.mff.cuni.cz/tred/

[5] http://ufal.mff.cuni.cz/pmltq/

Lexes. So, for example, the preposition *in addition to* (*kromě*) appears altogether in 309 instances in PDT, within which there are 44 instances in the function of AltLex (automatically looked up). All automatically retrieved instances have then been manually checked and validated.

Preposition	Instances as AltLexes	Total
Because of (*díky*)	14	191
In addition to (*kromě*)	44	309
Due to (*kvůli*)	5	130
Unlike (*na rozdíl od*)	1	95
On the basis of (*na základě*)	7	167
Despite (*navzdory*)	2	30
In spite of (*přes*)	9	389
Due to (*vinou*)	1	14
Considering (*vzhledem k*)	6	157
Total	**89**	**1482**

Table 1. Occurrences of AltLexes in the data of PDT

4.4.1 Reliability of Coreference in the Annotation

We are aware of the fact that our method is dependent on the good annotation of coreference and that if there are some mistakes on the level of coreference, they will mirror also in discourse, logically. Therefore, we have chosen one preposition (*because of* / *díky*) and manually checked all its tokens in PDT to examine the validity of searching for AltLexes on the basis of coreference.

We found out that coreference in PDT is annotated reliably. Within 191 of all instances, there were 35 with annotated coreference relations (14 leading to a verbal node, 21 to a non-verbal node) and 156 without any annotated relation. Within these 156 instances[6], we found only 3 disputable cases where the coreference could be annotated. However, these examples are definitely not clear cases of coreference, but they are rather questionable – see one of the examples from PDT:

(8) *Their immortality is born from the blood until John begins to age incredibly fast.*
Because of his disease, also a young doctor Sarah is pulled inevitably to a fatal whirl of bloody passions and mystery of life and death...

(In original: *Z krve se rodí jejich nesmrtelnost až do doby, než John začne neuvěřitelně rychle stárnout. Díky jeho chorobě je do osudového víru krvavých vášní a tajemství života i smrti neodvratně vtažena také mladá lékařka Sarah...*)

It is disputable whether the expression *his disease* (*jeho chorobě*) is interpretable as coreferential to *John begins to age incredibly fast* (*John začne neuvěřitelně rychle stárnout*). We consider this example ambiguous and therefore the annotation of similar examples is dependent on the decision of the individual annotator. Moreover, it is disputable whether we can consider expressions like *because of his disease* (*díky jeho chorobě*) to be discourse markers. Also other data from PDT demonstrated that AltLexes of this type mostly contain rather general and abstract words like *these facts* / *this situation* / *this problem* (*tyto skutečnosti* / *tato situace* / *tento problém*).

4.4.2 Difference between the Preliminary and Final Annotation

The final number of AltLexes like *due to this* (*vinou toho*), *despite this* (*navzdory tomu*) found in PDT using the queries is 89. Some of them have been captured already in the preliminary annotation – it means

[6] The instances have been discussed by two trained linguists.

they were provided with the annotators' comment AltLex. There were altogether 306 of such comments in PDT, i.e. expressions that were interpreted as AltLexes (of all types, not only the prepositions) by first annotators. In the section 2, we demonstrated that this number is rather approximate, as not all instances of AltLexes have been captured. For illustration, see Table 2 for prepositions with preliminary numbers of tokens that had the comment AltLex after the first phase of annotation. The table shows that the preliminary annotation captured only 9 out of 89 final AltLex instances of prepositions. It means that the real number of this AltLex type grew almost ten times.

Preposition	**Annotated as AltLex in the preliminary annotation**	**Final number of AltLex instances**
Because of (*díky*)	1	14
In addition to (*kromě*)	0 (1)[7]	44
Due to (*kvůli*)	2	5
Unlike (*na rozdíl od*)	1	1
On the basis of (*na základě*)	1	7
Despite (*navzdory*)	0 (1)	2
In spite of (*přes*)	2	9
Due to (*vinou*)	1	1
Considering (*vzhledem k*)	1	6
Total	**9**	**89**

Table 2. Difference between the preliminary and final annotation in numbers

5 Conclusion

The paper demonstrates the possibilities of using the present annotation of the Prague Dependency Treebank for practical annotations of discourse relations. The aim of the paper was to introduce how we can use the annotation of coreference for searching for the so called alternative lexicalizations of discourse connectives like *considering this situation* (*vzhledem k této situaci*), *on the basis of this* (*na základě toho*). In this way, we significantly reduced the amount of manual annotation work, as we demonstrated in the evaluation part.

This method may be used not only for prepositions like *due to* (*díky*), but also for all other multiword discourse markers containing an anaphoric expression, for example verbs like *this means* (*to znamená*), *this leads to* (*to vede k*), *this is related to* (*s tím souvisí*) etc. for which the presence of an anaphoric expression leading to the previous verbal argument is also compulsory.

Acknowledgment

The authors gratefully acknowledge support from the Czech Science Foundation (project n. P406/12/0658), from the Ministry of Education, Youth and Sports (project LH14011) and support from the project "*Discourse Connectives in Czech*" (n. 36213) solved at the Faculty of Arts at the Charles University in Prague from the resources of the Charles University Grant Agency in 2013–2015. This work has been using language resources developed, stored and distributed by the LINDAT/CLARIN project of the Ministry of Education, Youth and Sports of the Czech Republic (project LM2010013).

[7] The note *0 (1)* means that this token was finally interpreted as not relevant, i.e. not as AltLex because the anaphoric expression did not refer to the verbal but nominal node in this case. Therefore, this token (although provided with the comment AltLex) was excluded from the final number.

References

Nicholas Asher. 1993. *Reference to Abstract Objects in Discourse.* Dordrecht: Kluwer Academic Publishers.

Eduard Bejček, Jarmila Panevová, Jan Popelka, Pavel Straňák, Magda Ševčíková, Jan Štěpánek, Zdeněk Žabokrtský. 2012. Prague Dependency Treebank 2.5 – a revisited version of PDT 2.0. In: *Proceedings of the 24th International Conference on Computational Linguistics (Coling 2012)*, Bombay, India, pp. 231–246.

Jan Hajič, Jarmila Panevová, Eva Hajičová, Petr Sgall, Petr Pajas, Jan Štěpánek, Jiří Havelka, Marie Mikulová, Zdeněk Žabokrtský, and Magda Ševčíková-Razímová. 2006. *Prague Dependency Treebank 2.0.* Software prototype, Linguistic Data Consortium, Philadelphia, PA, USA, ISBN 1-58563-370-4, http://www.ldc.upenn.edu, Jul 2006.

Libuše Kroupová. 1984. Klasifikace sekundárních předložek z hlediska jejich tvoření. In: *Naše řeč 67 (3)*, pp. 113–116.

Anna Nedoluzhko, Jiří Mírovský, Eva Hajičová, Jiří Pergler, Radek Ocelák. 2011. *Extended Textual Coreference and Bridging Relations in PDT 2.0.* Data/software, ÚFAL MFF UK, Prague, Czech Republic, https://ufal-point.mff.cuni.cz/xmlui/handle/11858/00-097C-0000-0005-BCCF-3, Dec 2011.

Anna Nedoluzhko. 2011. Rozšířená textová koreference a asociační anafora (Koncepce anotace českých dat v Pražském závislostním korpusu). Institute of Formal and Applied Linguistics, Prague, Czech Republic, ISBN 978-80-904571-2-6, 268 pp., Dec 2011.

Petr Pajas, Jan Štěpánek. 2008. Recent advances in a feature-rich framework for treebank annotation. In *Proceedings of the 22nd International Conference on Computational Linguistics (Coling 2008),* Manchester, pp. 673–680.

Lucie Poláková, Pavlína Jínová, Šárka Zikánová, Eva Hajičová, Jiří Mírovský, Anna Nedoluzhko, Magdaléna Rysová, Veronika Pavlíková, Jana Zdeňková, Jiří Pergler, Radek Ocelák. 2012a. *Prague Discourse Treebank 1.0.* Data/software, ÚFAL MFF UK, Prague, Czech Republic, http://ufal.mff.cuni.cz/discourse/, Nov 2012.

Lucie Poláková, Pavlína Jínová, Šárka Zikánová, Zuzana Bedřichová, Jiří Mírovský, Magdaléna Rysová, Jana Zdeňková, Veronika Pavlíková, Eva Hajičová. 2012b. *Manual for Annotation of Discourse Relations in the Prague Dependency Treebank.* Technical Report No. 47, ÚFAL, Charles University in Prague.

Rashmi Prasad, Aravind Joshi, Bonnie Weber. 2010. Realization of Discourse Relations by Other Means: Alternative Lexicalizations. In: *Proceedings of the 23rd International Conference on Computational Linguistics (Coling 2010)*, Tsinghua University Press, Beijing, China, pp. 1023–1031.

Rashmi Prasad, Nikhil Dinesh, Alan Lee, Eleni Miltsakaki, Livio Robaldo, Aravind Joshi and Bonnie Webber. 2008. The Penn Discourse Treebank 2.0. In: *Proceedings of the 6th International Conference on Language Resources and Evaluation (LREC 2008)*, Marrakech, Morocco, pp. 2961–2968.

Magdaléna Rysová. 2012a. Alternative Lexicalizations of Discourse Connectives in Czech. In: *Proceedings of the 8th International Conference on Language Resources and Evaluation (LREC 2012)*, European Language Resources Association, Istanbul, Turkey, ISBN 978-2-9517408-7-7, pp. 2800–2807.

Magdaléna Rysová. 2012b. *Alternativní vyjádření konektorů v češtině.* Master thesis, Faculty of Arts, Charles University in Prague, Czech Republic, 98 pp., Jun 2012.

Jan Štěpánek, Petr Pajas. 2010. Querying Diverse Treebanks in a Uniform Way. In: *Proceedings of the 7th International Conference on Language Resources and Evaluation (LREC 2010)*, European Language Resources Association, Valletta, Malta, ISBN 2-9517408-6-7, pp. 1828–1835.

POS error detection in automatically annotated corpora

Ines Rehbein
SFB 632 Information Structure
German Department
Potsdam University
irehbein@uni-potsdam.de

Abstract

Recent work on error detection has shown that the quality of manually annotated corpora can be substantially improved by applying consistency checks to the data and automatically identifying incorrectly labelled instances. These methods, however, can not be used for automatically annotated corpora where errors are systematic and cannot easily be identified by looking at the variance in the data. This paper targets the detection of POS errors in automatically annotated corpora, so-called *silver standards*, showing that by combining different measures sensitive to annotation quality we can identify a large part of the errors and obtain a substantial increase in accuracy.

1 Introduction

Today, linguistically annotated corpora are an indispensable resource for many areas of linguistic research. However, since the emergence of the first digitised corpora in the 60s, the field has changed considerably. What was considered "very large" in the last decades is now considered to be rather small. Through the emergence of Web 2.0 and the spread of user-generated content, more and more data is accessible for building corpora for specific purposes.

This presents us with new challenges for automatic preprocessing and annotation. While conventional corpora mostly include written text which complies to grammatical standards, the new generation of corpora contain texts from very different varieties, displaying features of spoken language, regional variety, ungrammatical content, typos and non-canonical spelling. A large portion of the vocabulary are unknown words (that is, not included in the training data). As a result, the accuracy of state-of-the-art NLP tools on this type of data is often rather low. In combination with the increasing corpus sizes, it seems that we have to lower our expectations with respect to the quality of the annotations. Time-consuming double annotation or a manual correction of the whole corpus is often not feasible. Thus, the use of so-called *silver standards* has been discussed (Hahn et al., 2010; Kang et al., 2012; Paulheim, 2013), along with their adequacy to replace carefully hand-crafted gold standard corpora.

Other approaches to address this problem come from the areas of domain adaptation and error detection. In the first field, the focus is on adapting NLP tools or algorithms to data from new domains, thus increasing the accuracy of the tools. In error detection, the goal is to automatically identify erroneous labels in the data and either hand those instances to a human annotator for manual correction, or to automatically correct those cases. Here, the focus is not on improving the tools but on increasing the quality of the corpus and, at the same time, reducing human effort. These approaches are not mutually exclusive but can be seen as complementary methods for building high-quality language resources at a reasonable expense.

We position our work at the interface of these fields. Our general objective is to build a high-quality linguistic resource for informal spoken youth language, annotated with parts of speech (POS) information. As we do not have the resources for proofing the whole corpus, we aim at building a silver standard where the quality of the annotations is high enough to be useful for linguistic research. For automatic

LAW VIII - The 8th Linguistic Annotation Workshop, pages 20–28,
Dublin, Ireland, August 23-24 2014.

preprocessing, we use tagging models adapted to our data. The main contribution of this paper is in developing and evaluating methods for POS error detection in automatically annotated corpora. We show that our approach not only works for our data but can also be applied to canonical text from the newspaper domain, where the POS accuracy of standard NLP tools is quite high.

The paper is structured as follows. Section 2 reviews related work on detecting annotation errors in corpora. Section 3 describes the underlying assumptions of our approach. In Section 4, we describe the experimental setup and data used in our experiments, and we present our results in Section 5. We conclude in Section 6.

2 Related Work

Most work on (semi-)automatic POS error detection has focussed on identifying errors in POS assigned by *human annotators* where variation in word-POS assignments in the corpus can be caused either by ambiguous word forms which, depending on the context, can belong to different word classes, or by incorrect judgments made by the annotators (Eskin, 2000; van Halteren, 2000; Květoň and Oliva, 2002; Dickinson and Meurers, 2003; Loftsson, 2009).

The *variation n-gram algorithm* (Dickinson and Meurers, 2003) allows users to identify potentially incorrect tagger predictions by looking at the variation in the assignment of POS tags to a particular word ngram. The algorithm produces a ranked list of varying tagger decisions which have to be processed by a human annotator. Potential tagger errors are positioned at the top of the list. Later work (Dickinson, 2006) extends this approach and explores the feasibility of automatically correcting these errors.

Eskin (2000) describes a method for error identification using *anomaly detection*, where anomalies are defined as elements coming from a distribution different from the one in the data at hand. Květoň and Oliva (2002) present an approach to error detection based on a semi-automatically compiled list of *impossible ngrams*. Instances of these ngrams in the data are assumed to be tagging errors and are selected for manual correction.

All these approaches are tailored towards identifying human annotation errors and cannot be applied to our setting where we have to detect systematic errors made by automatic POS taggers. Thus, we can not rely on *anomalies* or *impossible ngrams* in the data, as the errors made by the taggers are consistent and, furthermore, our corpus of non-canonical spoken language includes many structures which are considered *impossible* in Standard German.

Rocio et al. (2007) address the problem of finding systematic errors in POS tagger predictions. Their method is based on a modified multiword unit extraction algorithm which extracts cohesive sequences of tags from the corpus. These sequences are then sorted manually into linguistically sound ngrams and potential errors. This approach addresses the correction of large, automatically annotated corpora. It successfully identifies (a small number of) incorrectly tagged high-frequency sequences in the text which are often based on tokenisation errors. The more diverse errors due to lexical ambiguity, which we have to deal with in our data, are not captured by this approach.

Most promising is the approach of Loftsson (2009) who evaluates different methods for error detection, including an ensemble of five POS taggers, where error candidates are defined as those instances for which the predictions of the five taggers disagree. His method successfully identifies POS errors and thus increases the POS accuracy in the corpus. Using the tagger ensemble, Loftsson (2009) is able to identify error candidates with a precision of around 16%. He does not report recall, that is how many of the erroneously tagged instances in the corpus have been found. We apply the ensemble method to our data and use it as our baseline.

Relevant to us is also the work by Dligach and Palmer (2011), who show how the need for double annotation can be efficiently reduced by only presenting carefully selected instances to the annotators for a second vote. They compare two different selection methods. In the first approach, they select all instances where a machine learning classifier disagrees with the human judgement. In the second approach, they use the probability score of a maximum entropy classifier, selecting instances with the smallest *prediction margin* (the difference between the probabilities for the two most probable predictions). Dligach and Palmer (2011) test their approach in a Word Sense Disambiguation task. The main ideas of this work, however, can be easily applied to POS tagging.

3 Identifying Systematic POS Errors

Taggers make POS errors for a number of reasons. First of all, anomalies in the input can cause the tagger to assign an incorrect tag, e.g. for noisy input with spelling or tokenisation errors. Another source of errors are out-of-vocabulary words, that is word forms unknown to the tagger because they do not exist in the training data. A third reason for incorrect tagger judgments are word forms which are ambiguous between different parts of speech. Those cases can be further divided into cases where the information for identifying the correct label is there but the tagger does not make use of it, and into cases that are truly ambiguous, meaning that even a human annotator would not be able to disambiguate the correct POS tag. Tagger errors can also be caused by ill-defined annotation schemes or errors in the gold standard (see Manning (2011) for a detailed discussion on different types of POS errors).

To assess the difficulty of the task, it might be interesting to look at the agreement achieved by human annotators for POS tagging German. The inter-annotator agreement for POS annotation with the STTS on written text is quite high with around 0.97-0.98 Fleiss κ, and for annotating spoken text using an extended version of the STTS similar numbers can be obtainded (Rehbein and Schalowski, 2013).

In this work, we are not so much interested in finding tokenisation and spelling errors but in identifying automatic tagger errors due to lexical ambiguity. Our work is based on the following assumptions:

> **Assumption 1:** Instances of word forms which are labelled differently by different taggers are potential POS errors.

> **Assumption 2:** POS tags which have been assigned with a low probability by the tagger are potential POS errors.

In the remainder of the paper, we present the development of a system for error detection and its evaluation on a corpus of informal, spontaneous dialogues and on German newspaper text. We report precision and recall for our system. *Precision* is computed as the number of correctly identified error candidates, divided by the number of all (correctly and incorrectly identified) error candidates *(number of true positives / (number of true positives + false positives))*, and *recall* by dividing the number of identified errors by the total number of errors in the data *(true positives / (true positives + false negatives))*.

4 Experimental Setup

The data we use in our experiments comes from two sources, i) from a corpus of informal, spoken German youth language (The KiezDeutsch Korpus (KiDKo) Release 1.0) (Rehbein et al., 2014), and ii) from the TIGER corpus (Brants et al., 2002), a German newspaper corpus.

4.1 Kiezdeutsch – Informal youth language

KiDKo is a new language resource including informal, spontaneous dialogues from peer-to-peer communication of adolescents. The current version of the corpus includes the audio signals aligned with transcriptions, as well as a normalisation layer and POS annotations. Additional annotation layers (Chunking, Topological Fields) are in progress.

The transcription scheme has an orthographic basis but, in order to enable investigations of prosodic characteristics of the data, it also tries to closely capture the pronunciation, including pauses, and encodes disfluencies and primary accents. On the normalisation layer, non-canonical pronunciations and capitalisation are reduced to standard German spelling. The normalisation is done on the token level, and non-canonical word order as well as disfluencies are included in the normalised version of the data (Example 1).

(1)	[transcription]:	isch	hab	au	(–)	isch	hab	isch	hab	auch	äh	FLATrate
	[normalisation]:	Ich	habe	au #	PAUSE	Ich	habe ,	ich	habe	auch	äh	Flatrate .
		I	have	too #		I	have ,	I	have	too	uh	flatrate .

"I have ... I have, I have a flatrate, too." (MuH23MT)

	KiDKo			TIGER	
Baseline taggers	avg. (5-fold)	dev	test	dev	test
Brill	94.4	94.7	93.8	96.8	96.8
Treetagger	95.1	95.5	94.8	97.2	97.4
Stanford	95.3	95.6	94.7	97.4	97.5
Hunpos	95.6	95.8	94.8	97.4	97.5
CRF	**96.9**	**97.4**	**96.1**	**97.9**	**98.0**

Table 1: Baseline results for different taggers on KiDKo and TIGER (results on KiDKo are given for a 5-fold cross validation (5-fold) and for the development and test set)

We plan to release the POS tagged version of the corpus in summer 2014. Due to legal constraints, the audio files will have restricted access and can only be accessed locally while the transcribed and annotated version of the corpus will be available over the internet via ANNIS (Zeldes et al., 2009).[1]

4.2 The TIGER corpus

The second corpus we use in our experiments is the TIGER corpus (release 2.2), a German newspaper corpus with approximately 50,000 sentences (900,000 tokens). We chose TIGER to show that our approach is not tailored towards one particular text type but can be applied to corpora of different sizes and from different domains.

4.3 Baseline

In our experiments, we use a subpart of KiDKo with 103,026 tokens, split into a training set with 66,024 tokens, a development set with 16,530 tokens, and a test set with 20,472 tokens. The TIGER data was also split into a training set (709,740 tokens), a development set (88,437 tokens) and a test set (90,061 tokens).

To test our first assumption, we trained an ensemble of five taggers on the two corpora (see list below), and checked all instances where the taggers disagreed. We consider all cases as disagreements where at least one of the five taggers made a prediction different from the other taggers.

The five taggers we use reflect different approaches to POS tagging (including Transformation-based Learning, Markov Models, Maximum Entropy, Decision Trees, and Conditional Random Fields):

- the Brill tagger (Brill, 1992)
- the Hunpos tagger[2]
- the Stanford POS tagger (Toutanova and Manning, 2000)
- the Treetagger (Schmid, 1995)
- a CRF-based tagger, using the CRFSuite[3]

Table 1 shows the accuracies of the different taggers on KiDKo and on TIGER (because of the smaller size of KiDKo, we also report numbers from a 5-fold cross validation on the training data). The CRF-based tagger gives the best results on the spoken language data as well as on TIGER. For more details on the implementation and features of the CRF tagger, please refer to (Rehbein et al., 2014).

For the KiDKo development set, we have 1,228 cases where the taggers disagree, that is 1,228 error candidates, and 1,797 instances in the test set. Out of those, 267 (dev) and 558 (test) are true errors (Table 2). This means that the precision of this simple heuristic is between 21.7% and 33%, with a recall between 61.1 and 70.8%. For TIGER, precision and recall are higher. Applying this simple heuristic, we are able to identify around 70% of the errors in the data, with a precision of around 27%. We consider this as our baseline.

[1]ANNIS (ANNotation of Information Structure) is a corpus search and visualisation interface which allows the user to formulate complex search queries which can combine multiple layers of annotation.

[2]The Hunpos tagger is an open source reimplementation of the TnT tagger (`https://code.google.com/p/hunpos`)

[3]`http://www.chokkan.org/software/crfsuite/`

	tokens	candidates	true err.	out of	% prec	% rec.
			KiDKo			
dev	16,530	1,228	267	437	21.7	61.1
test	20,472	1,797	558	788	33.0	70.8
			TIGER			
dev	88,437	4,580	1,280	1,818	27.9	70.4
test	90,061	4,618	1,246	1,754	27.0	71.0

Table 2: Number of error candidates identified by the disagreements in the ensemble tagger predictions (baseline)

5 Finding measures for error detection

When defining measures for error detection, we have to balance precision against recall. Depending on our research goal and resources available for corpus creation, we might either want to obtain a high precision, meaning that we only have to look at a small number of instances which are most probably true POS errors, or we might want to build a high-quality corpus where nearly all errors have been found and corrected, at the cost of having to look at many instances which are mostly correct.

5.1 Increasing precision

First, we try to improve precision and thus to reduce the number of false positives we have to look at during the manual correction phase. We do this by training a CRF classifier to detect errors in the output of the ensemble taggers. The features we use are shown in Table 3 and include the word form, the tags predicted by the tagger ensemble, ngram combinations of the ensemble POS tags, word and POS context for different context windows for the POS predicted by the CRF tagger and the Treetagger, a combination of word form and POS context (for CRF, Treetagger, and combinations of both; for window sizes of 3 and 4 with varying start and end positions), and the class label (1: error, 0: correct).

We experimented with different feature combinations and settings. Our basic feature set gives us high precision on both data sets, with very low recall. Only around 4-6% of all errors are found. However, precision is between 55-65%, meaning that the majority of the selected candidates are true errors.

Our extended feature sets (I and II) aim at improving recall by alleviating the sparse data problem. The extended feature set I extracts new features where the tags from the fine-grained German tagset, the STTS (Schiller et al., 1999), are converted into the coarse-grained universal tagset of Petrov et al. (2012),

basic features	**example**
word form	der (the)
lowercased word form	der
ensemble tags	PDS ART PDS PDS ART
POS context (CRF)	ADV:PROAV:VAFIN:APPR, PROAV:VAFIN:APPR:PDS, ...
POS context (tree)	PROAV:VAFIN:APPR, VAFIN:APPR:ART, ...
word form with POS context (CRF)	PROAV:VAFIN:APPR:der, VAFIN:APPR:der:APPR, ...
word form with POS context (CRF:tree)	PROAV:VAFIN:APPR:der, ..., der:APPR:ART:NN, ...
extended features I: universal POS	
universal ensemble tags	P D P P D
universal POS ngrams	P:D, P:P, P:P, ..., P:P:P:D, P:D:P:P:D
universal POS context (CRF)	ADV:P:VF:ADP, P:VF:ADP:P, ...
word form with universal POS context (CRF)	P:VF:ADP:der, VF:ADP:der:ADP, ADP:der:ADP:D, ...
word form with universal POS context (CRF:tree)	VF:VF:ADP:ADP:der, ADP:ADP:der:ADP:ADP, ...
extended features II: brown clusters	
brown cluster for word form	110111011111
brown cluster with universal POS context (CRF)	ADV:P:110111111110:ADP, P:110111111110:ADP:P, ...
class label (1 or 0)	1

Table 3: Features used for error detection

	tokens	candidates	true err.	out of	% prec	% rec
			KiDKo			
			basic features			
dev	16,530	32	21	437	65.6	4.8
test	20,472	59	32	788	54.2	4.1
			extended features I (universal POS)			
dev	16,530	77	38	437	49.3	8.7
test	20,472	172	88	788	51.2	11.2
			extended features II (universal POS, Brown clusters)			
dev	16,530	88	50	437	56.8	11.4
test	20,472	205	104	788	50.7	13.2
			TIGER			
			basic features			
dev	88,437	163	101	1,818	62.0	5.6
test	90,061	202	111	1,754	54.9	6.3
			extended features I (universal POS)			
dev	88,437	564	348	1,818	61.7	19.1
test	90,061	588	347	1,754	59.0	19.8
			extended features II (universal POS, Brown clusters)			
dev	88,437	501	318	1,818	63.5	17.5
test	90,061	518	298	1,754	57.5	17.0

Table 4: Number of error candidates identified by the classifier, precision (prec) and recall (rec)

with minor modifications.[4] On KiDKo, the universal POS features increase recall from around 5% up to 8-14%. On TIGER, the results are more substantial. Here, our recall increases from 5-6% up to nearly 20%, while precision is still in the same range (Table 4).

Our basic features were designed to add more (local) context useful for disambiguating between the different tags. Especially the right context (assigned POS) includes information which often helps, e.g. when distinguishing between a substitutive demonstrative pronoun (PDS) and a determiner (ART), which is a frequent error especially in the spoken language data.

We try to achieve further improvements by adding new features where we replace the word forms with Brown word cluster paths (Brown et al., 1992).[5] The extended features are designed to address the unknown word problem by generalising overvi t word forms. On the smaller KiDKo data set, this again has a positive effect, increasing both precision and recall. On TIGER, however, the results are mixed, with a higher precision on the development set but a somewhat lower recall for both, development and test sets. This is not surprising, as semi-supervised techniques are expected to help most for settings where data sparseness is an issue.

Overall, our error detection classifier is able to identify errors in the corpus with a good precision, meaning that only a small number of instances have to be checked manually in order to achieve an error rate reduction in the range of 11-17%. This approach seems suitable when limited resources are available for manual correction, thus asking for a method with high precision and low time requirements.

5.2 Increasing recall

While our attempts to increase precision were quite successful, we had to put up with a severe loss in recall. However, we would like to keep precision reasonably high but also to increase recall. Our next approach takes into account the marginal probabilities of the predictions (0: correct/1: error) of the CRF-based error detection classifier. We not only check those instances which the classifier has labelled as

[4] For instance, instead of converting all verb tags to V, we keep a tag for finite verbs (VF).

[5] The word clusters have been trained on the Huge German Corpus (HGC) (Fitschen, 2004), using a cluster size of 1000, a frequency threshold of 40 and a maximum path length of 12.

	tokens	threshold	candidates	true err.	out of	% prec	% rec
			KiDKo				
		extended features II (universal POS, Brown clusters)					
dev	16,530	0.8	286	120	437	42.0	27.5
dev	16,530	0.85	350	138	437	39.4	31.6
test	20,472	0.8	472	190	788	40.2	24.1
test	20,472	0.85	561	227	788	40.5	28.8
			TIGER				
		extended features I (universal POS)					
dev	88,437	0.8	1,208	602	1,818	49.8	33.1
dev	88,437	0.85	1,431	658	1,818	46.0	36.2
test	90,061	0.8	1,276	605	1,754	47.4	34.5
test	90,061	0.85	1,554	670	1,754	43.1	38.2

Table 5: Number of error candidates identified by the classifier using a marginal probability threshold

incorrect, but also those which have been labelled as correct, but with a marginal probability below a particular threshold. Table 5 gives results for a threshold of 0.8 and 0.85, using the best-scoring feature sets from the last experiment.

Our new measure results in a substantial increase in recall. Setting the threshold to 0.85, we are now able to detect around 30% of the errors in KiDKo and 36 to 38% in TIGER, while precision is still reasonably high. Figure 1 shows the relation between precision and recall for different thresholds from 0.95 to 0.1. Setting the threshold to 0.8, for example, would result in an error prediction presicion of around 40-42% for KiDKo and of around 47-50% for TIGER. Recall for error identification using a threshold of 0.8 would be in the range of 24-27.5% for KiDKo and 33-34.5% for TIGER. If we wanted to increase recall up to 50% for KiDKo, we would have to use a marginal probability threshold of approximately 0.65, and precision would drop to around 14%. This knowledge allows us to make an informed decision during corpus compilation, either starting from the POS accuracy we want to achieve, or from the resources we have for manual correction, and to predict the POS accuracy of the final corpus.

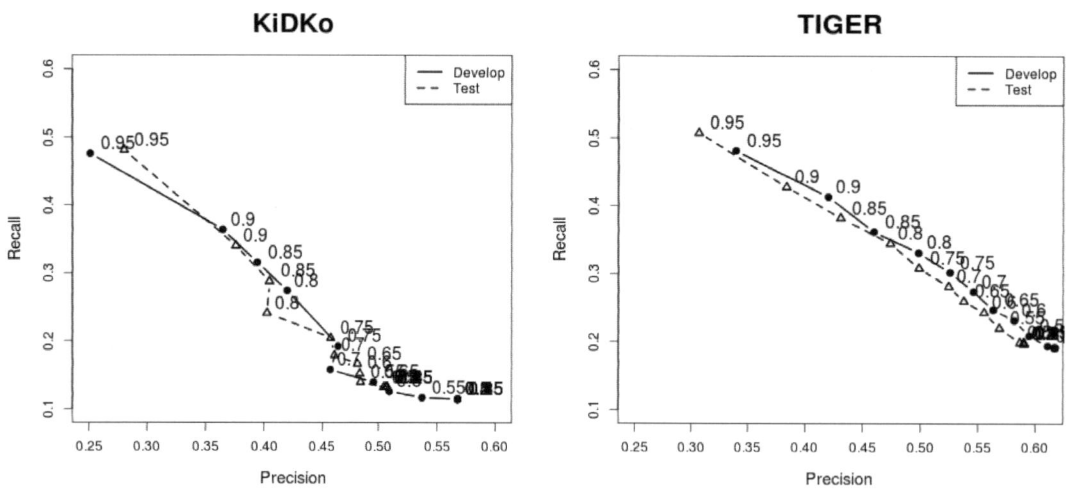

Figure 1: Trade-off between precision and recall for different marginal probability thresholds

6 Conclusions

In the paper, we presented and evaluated a system for automatic error detection in POS tagged corpora, with the goal of increasing the quality of so-called *silver standards* with minimal human effort. Our baseline, a simple heuristic based on disagreements in tagger predictions, allows us to identify between 60 and 70% of all errors in our two data sets, but with a low precision. We show how to refine this method, training a CRF-based classifier which is able to identify POS errors in tagger output with a much higher precision, thus reducing the need for manual correction.

Our method is able to find different types of POS errors, including the ones most frequently made by the tagger (adjectives, adverbs, proper names, foreign language material, finite verbs, verb particles, and more). Furthermore, it allows us to define the parameters which are most adequate for the task at hand, either aiming at high precision at the cost of recall, or increasing recall (and thus the annotation quality of the corpus) at the cost of greater manual work load. In addition, our method can easily be applied to different corpora and new languages.

References

Sabine Brants, Stefanie Dipper, Silvia Hansen, Wolfgang Lezius, and George Smith. 2002. The TIGER treebank. In *Proceedings of the First Workshop on Treebanks and Linguistic Theories*, pages 24–42.

Eric Brill. 1992. A simple rule-based part of speech tagger. In *3rd conference on Applied natural language processing (ANLC'92)*, Trento, Italy.

Peter F. Brown, Peter V. deSouza, Robert L. Mercer, Vincent J. Della Pietra, and Jenifer C. Lai. 1992. Class-based n-gram models of natural language. *Computational Linguistics*, 18(4):467–479.

Markus Dickinson and Detmar W. Meurers. 2003. Detecting errors in part-of-speech annotation. In *10th Conference of the European Chapter of the Association for Computational Linguistics (EACL-03)*.

Markus Dickinson. 2006. From detecting errors to automatically correcting them. In *Annual Meeting of The European Chapter of The Association of Computational Linguistics (EACL-06)*, Trento, Italy.

Dmitriy Dligach and Martha Palmer. 2011. Reducing the need for double annotation. In *Proceedings of the 5th Linguistic Annotation Workshop*, LAW V '11.

Eleazar Eskin. 2000. Automatic corpus correction with anomaly detection. In *1st Conference of the North American Chapter of the Association for Computational Linguistics (NAACL)*, Seattle, Washington.

Arne Fitschen. 2004. *Ein computerlinguistisches Lexikon als komplexes System.* Ph.D. thesis, Institut für Maschinelle Sprachverarbeitung der Universität Stuttgart.

U. Hahn, K. Tomanek, E. Beisswanger, and E. Faessler. 2010. A proposal for a configurable silver standard. In *The Fourth Linguistic Annotation Workshop*, LAW 2010, pages 235–242.

Ning Kang, Erik van Mulligen, and Jan Kors. 2012. Training text chunkers on a silver standard corpus: can silver replace gold? *BMC Bioinformatics*, 13(1):17.

Pavel Květoň and Karel Oliva. 2002. (Semi-)Automatic detection of errors in PoS-tagged corpora. In *19th International Conference on Computational Linguistics (COLING-02)*.

Hrafn Loftsson. 2009. Correcting a POS-tagged corpus using three complementary methods. In *Proceedings of the 12th Conference of the European Chapter of the ACL (EACL 2009)*, Athens, Greece, March.

Christopher D. Manning. 2011. Part-of-speech tagging from 97linguistics? In *Proceedings of the 12th International Conference on Computational Linguistics and Intelligent Text Processing - Volume Part I*, CICLing'11, pages 171–189.

Heiko Paulheim. 2013. Dbpedianyd - a silver standard benchmark dataset for semantic relatedness in dbpedia. In *CEUR Workshop*, CEUR Workshop Proceedings. CEUR-WS.org.

Slav Petrov, Dipanjan Das, and Ryan T. McDonald. 2012. A universal part-of-speech tagset. In *The Eighth International Conference on Language Resources and Evaluation (LREC-2012)*, pages 2089–2096.

Ines Rehbein and Sören Schalowski. 2013. STTS goes Kiez – Experiments on annotating and tagging urban youth language. *Journal for Language Technology and Computational Linguistics*.

Ines Rehbein, Sören Schalowski, and Heike Wiese. 2014. The KiezDeutsch Korpus (KiDKo) release 1.0. In *The 9th International Conference on Language Resources and Evaluation (LREC-14)*, Reykjavik, Iceland.

Vitor Rocio, Joaquim Silva, and Gabriel Lopes. 2007. Detection of strange and wrong automatic part-of-speech tagging. In *Proceedings of the Aritficial Intelligence 13th Portuguese Conference on Progress in Artificial Intelligence*, EPIA'07.

Anne Schiller, Simone Teufel, and Christine Thielen. 1999. Guidelines für das Tagging deutscher Textkorpora mit STTS. Technical report, Universität Stuttgart, Universität Tübingen.

Helmut Schmid. 1995. Improvements in part-of-speech tagging with an application to German. In *ACL SIGDAT-Workshop*.

Kristina Toutanova and Christopher D. Manning. 2000. Enriching the knowledge sources used in a maximum entropy part-of-speech tagger. In *Proceedings of the conference on Empirical methods in natural language processing and very large corpora*, EMNLP '00, Hong Kong.

Hans van Halteren. 2000. The detection of inconsistency in manually tagged text. In *Proceedings of the COLING-2000 Workshop on Linguistically Interpreted Corpora*, Centre Universitaire, Luxembourg, August.

Amir Zeldes, Julia Ritz, Anke Lüdeling, and Christian Chiarcos. 2009. Annis: A search tool for multi-layer annotated corpora. In *Corpus Linguistics 2009*.

Aligning Chinese-English Parallel Parse Trees: Is it Feasible?

Dun Deng and **Nianwen Xue**

Computer Science Department, Brandeis University
415 South Street, Waltham MA, USA
ddeng@brandeis.edu, xuen@brandeis.edu

Abstract

We investigate the feasibility of aligning Chinese and English parse trees by examining cases of incompatibility between Chinese-English parallel parse trees. This work is done in the context of an annotation project where we construct a parallel treebank by doing word and phrase alignments simultaneously. We discuss the most common incompatibility patterns identified within VPs and NPs and show that most cases of incompatibility are caused by divergent syntactic annotation standards rather than inherent cross-linguistic differences in language itself. This suggests that in principle it is feasible to align the parallel parse trees with some modification of existing syntactic annotation guidelines. We believe this has implications for the use of parallel parse trees as an important resource for Machine Translation models.

1 Introduction

Parallel treebanks have been proved to be a valuable resource in Machine Translation research (Gildea, 2003; Liu et al., 2009; Sun et al., 2010; Chiang, 2010; Xiao and Zhu, 2013), but one issue that hampers their utility is the incompatibility between the syntactic parse trees for a sentence pair (Chiang, 2010), as the trees are annotated based on independently developed monolingual syntactic annotation standards. For example, even though the Penn Chinese Treebank (Xue et al., 2005) and English TreeBank (Marcus et al., 1993) are often referred to collectively as the Penn series of treebanks and are both annotated with phrase structure trees in very similar annotation frameworks, different annotation decisions have led to divergent tree structures (Chiang, 2010). The purpose of this study is to investigate to what extent the divergences between Chinese-English parallel parse trees are caused by different annotation styles (and therefore can be avoided by revising the annotation guidelines), and to what extent they are caused by cross-linguistic differences inherent in language. The answer to this question would shed light on whether it is possible to align the parse trees in parallel treebanks, and on the feasibility of building Machine Translation systems based on these aligned parallel treebanks.

The question above cannot be answered without first having a concrete alignment specification and knowing what types of alignments are attempted. No incompatibility issue would arise for sentence-level alignment when sentences are aligned as a whole. By contrast, both word-level alignment (or the alignment of terminal nodes) and phrase-level alignment (or the alignment of non-terminal nodes) interact with syntactic structures, which could potentially cause incompatibility between the alignments and the tree structures. In the next section, we outline an alignment approach where we perform word alignments and phrase alignments simultaneously in a parallel Chinese-English treebank to prevent incompatibilities between word alignments and syntactic structures. The alignment approach alone, however, does not prevent incompatibilities between the two parse trees of a sentence pair, which are either due to inherent cross-linguistic divergences or differences in treebank annotation styles. In Section 3, we report three types of incompatibilities between the syntactic structures of a sentence pair that prevent proper

LAW VIII - The 8th Linguistic Annotation Workshop, pages 29–37,
Dublin, Ireland, August 23-24 2014.

phrase-level alignments. We analyze two of them and show how they make certain phrase alignments impossible. In Section 4, we discuss the third and also the most common type of incompatibility, which is caused by different annotation decisions as specified in the Penn Chinese and English Treebank syntactic bracketing guidelines (Xue and Xia, 2000; Bies et al., 1995). We propose modifications to the tree structures for the purpose of aligning the parse trees, which means that proper phrase alignment is possible if certain common patterns of incompatibility in syntactic parse trees are fixed. We conclude our paper in Section 5 and touch on the workshop theme. We argue that the quality and level of linguistic sophistication of an linguistic annotation project is tied to the purpose of the resource, and how it is going to be used.

2 Overview of the HACEPT Project

The purpose of the HACEPT (Hierarchically Aligned Chinese-English Parallel TreeBank) Project is to perform word-level and phrase-level alignments between parallel parse trees to develop a linguistic resource for Machine Translation models. We are currently in the process of aligning about 9,000 sentence pairs where syntactic parses already exist for sentences on both the Chinese and English side.

In our project, the annotator is presented with a pair of parallel Chinese-English sentences which have parse trees. The task of the annotator is to do both word and phrase alignments between the two parse trees. The reason for doing word alignments and phrase alignments simultaneously is to make sure word alignments and syntactic structures are harmonized to avoid both redundancies and incompatibilities. Let us use the concrete example in Figure 1 to illustrate the point.

A big challenge to word alignment comes from language-particular function words that do not have counterparts in the translation language. Take the sentences in Figure 1 for instance, the Chinese prenominal modification marker 的 has no English counterpart. Similarly, the English infinitive marker *to* has no Chinese counterpart. Word alignments done without taking syntactic structures into consideration generally glue a function word such as 的 and *to* here to a neighboring content word which has a counterpart and align the two words together to the counterpart of the content word (Li et al., 2009). Under this practice, the first 的 will be glued to 国家/country, and the two words 国家/country 的 as a whole will be aligned to *countries*. Similarly, *to* will be glued to *weigh in* and the whole string *to weigh in* will be aligned to 品评/weigh in. In our project, we take a different approach to word alignments: we leave all the words without a counterpart unaligned on the word level and mark them as "extra". For each unaligned word, we locate the appropriate phrase which contains the unaligned word and has a phrasal counterpart on the other side. By aligning the two phrases, the unaligned word is captured in its appropriate context. Under this new strategy, the Chinese 的 and the English *to* are both left unaligned on the word level. For 的, we align the NP 所有/all 国家/country 的 人民/people with the NP *people in all countries*, because the Chinese NP is the relevant context where 的 appears (的 is used in the NP to indicate that 所有/all 国家/country is the modifier of the noun 人民/people) and matches in meaning with the English NP. For *to*, we align the VP *use their own methods of expression to weigh in on this* with the VP 利用/use 自己/own 的 表达/expression 方式/method 品评/weigh in 此/this 事/thing, because *to* is used in the English VP to connect *use their own methods of expression* and *weigh in on this* and also because the English VP and the Chinese one matches in meaning.

Under our approach, word alignments and syntactic structures are harmonized, and both redundancies and incompatibilities between the two are avoided. For example, the phrase alignment between the two NPs 所有/all 国家/country 的 人民/people and *people in all countries* specifies the context for the occurrence of the function word 的. There is no need to glue 的 to the previous noun 国家/country on the word level. As a matter of fact, the host of 的 (namely the modifier signaled by it) is not the noun 国家/country but the NP 所有/all 国家/country. Similarly, the phrase alignment between *use their own methods of expression to weigh in on this* and 利用/use 自己/own 的 表达/expression 方式/method 品评/weigh in 此/this 事/thing captures the syntactic environment in which *to* appears. The phrase alignment also avoids an incompatibility issue caused by attaching *to* to *weigh in* and aligning the

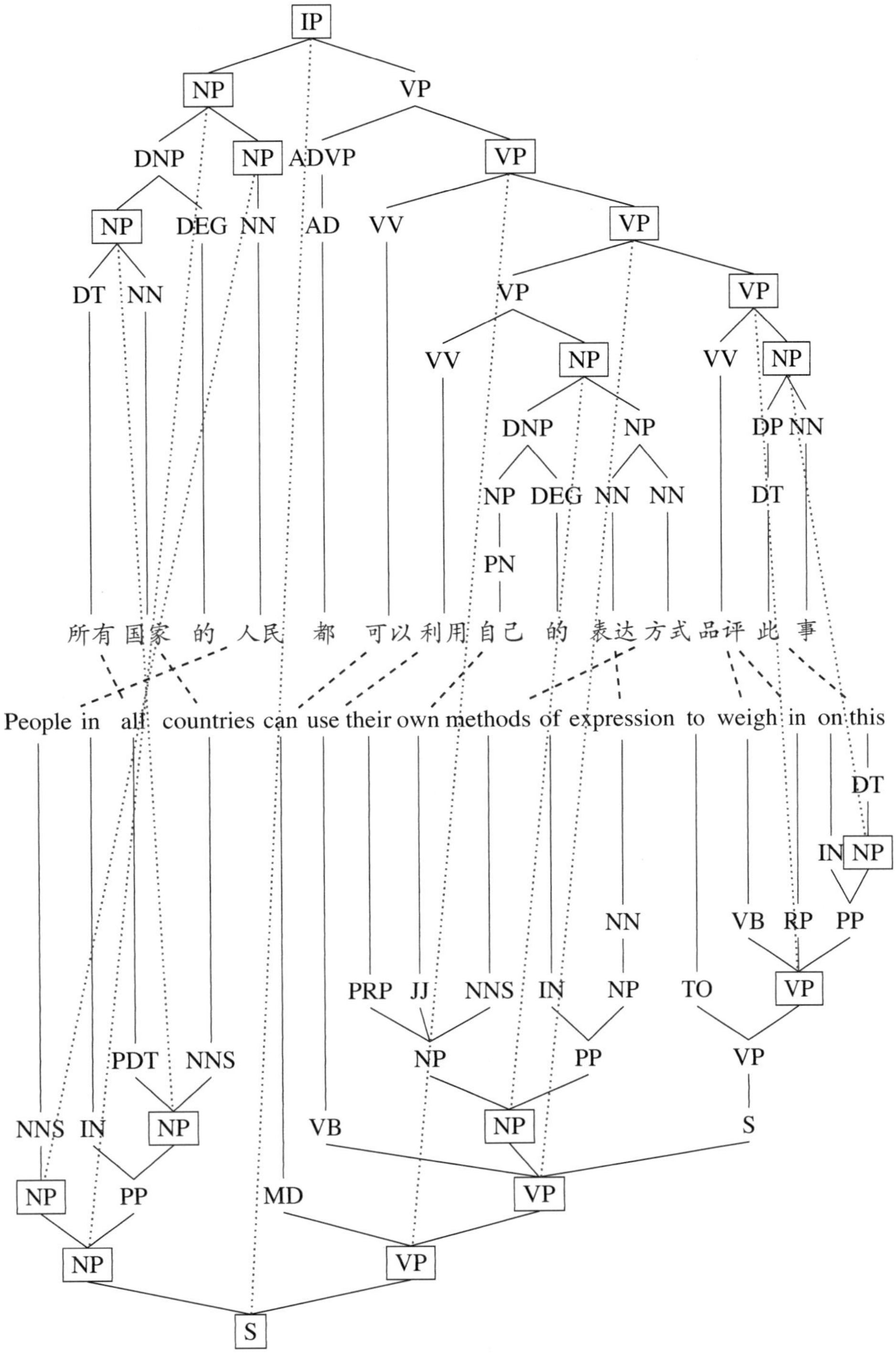

Figure 1: A hierarchically aligned sentence pair

string to 品评/weigh in since *to weigh in* is not even a constituent in the English parse tree. For a more comprehensive and detailed description of the HACEPT project, see (Deng and Xue, 2014).

A natural question arises for our approach: cross-linguistic divergences between languages may cause parse tree incompatibilities to arise, which calls into question the possibility of doing phrase alignments to a useful extent. The fact is that we did find incompatibilities between parse trees in our annotation. In the next section, we report three types of parse tree incompatibilities we have encountered.

3 Three types of parse tree incompatibilities

During the annotation process, we encountered three types of parse tree incompatibilities that make some phrase alignments impossible. The three types are distinguished by the sources of their occurrence and are listed below:

Three types of incompatibilities between parallel parse trees:

a. Incompatibilities caused by lexical-semantic differences between the two languages

b. Incompatibilities caused by translation-related reasons

c. Incompatibilities caused by different annotation standards

Let us look at the first type. On the lexical level, languages differ in terms of whether or not a piece of semantic information is encoded in a lexical item. For instance, Chinese does not have a verb that expresses the meaning of the English verb *prioritize*, which needs to be translated using a phrase. This does not necessarily cause problems for phrase alignments. Taking *prioritize* for instance, the English phrase *prioritize transportation projects* is translated as 安排/arrange 交通/transportation 项目/project 的 优先/priority 顺序/order (literally *arrange transportation projects' priority order*, i.e., *prioritize transportation projects*). Note that a phrase alignment can be made between the two VPs and also the two NPs *transportation projects* and 交通/transportation 项目/project despite the fact that the meaning of *prioritize* is expressed by a discontinuous phrase in Chinese (安排/arrange ... 的 优先/priority 顺序/order, i.e., *arrange the priority order of* ...). The most extreme case in this category which usually causes incompatibilities and makes phrase-level alignment impossible is idiomatic expressions. An idiom is a single lexical item just like a word and its meaning generally has to be expressed literally in another language. For instance, the idiomatic part in *Markets function best so long as* ***no one has a finger on the scale*** is translated as (只要/so long as) 大家/everyone 公正/justly 行事/act (市场/market 运作/function 最/most 好/good), which literally is *everyone justly acts*. The parse tree for both the English idiom and its Chinese translation is given in Figure 2. No phrase alignment is possible between the idiom and its translation except that between the two root nodes that dominate each string. Phrase alignments are reduced to a minimal extent in cases like this.

Now let us discuss the second type. Consider this example, where the Chinese sentence 他/he 没有/not 提到/mention 这/this 一/one 点/point (*He did't mention this point*) is translated as *There was no mention made of this by him*. Given this particular translation, it is impossible to make a phrase alignment between the Chinese VP 没有/not 提到/mention 这/this 一/one 点/point and *no mention made of this* although the two strings match in meaning. This is because, as shown in Figure 3, the NP node that dominates the English string also dominates the PP *by him*. Note that *him* in the PP corresponds to 他/he, which is outside the Chinese VP. The issue here is caused by the translation. Note that the Chinese sentence is in active voice, but the given translation is in passive voice, which is why the PP *by him* appears at the end of the sentence and causes the problem. If the more literal translation *He didn't mention this point* were provided, 没有/not 提到/mention 这/this 一/one 点/point could be aligned with *didn't mention this point*, and 提到/mention 这/this 一/one 点/point could be aligned with *mention this point*, which is also impossible with the given translation. Phrase alignments are reduced by some extent in cases like this.

For the first two types of incompatibilities already discussed, the negative impact of them on phrase alignments can be reduced by the enlargement of the corpus, which currently has $8,932$ sentence pairs.

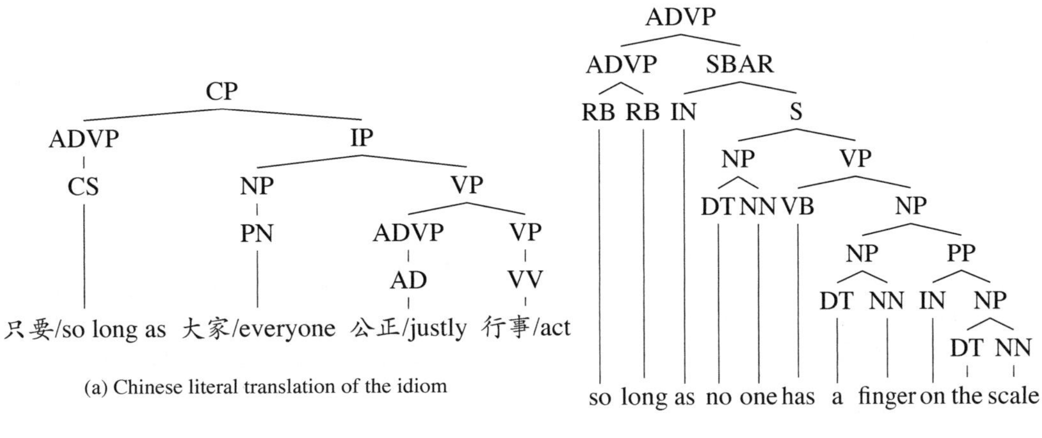

(a) Chinese literal translation of the idiom

(b) An English idiom

Figure 2: Structural divergence caused by idiomatic expressions

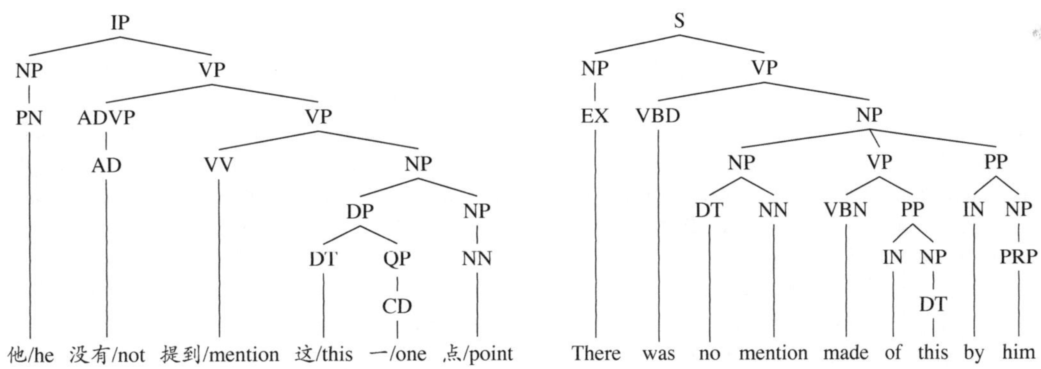

(a) Chinese sentence

(b) Non-literal English translation

Figure 3: Structural divergence caused by non-literal translations

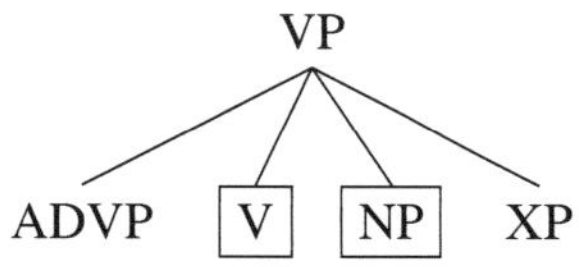

(a) PTB structure for VP

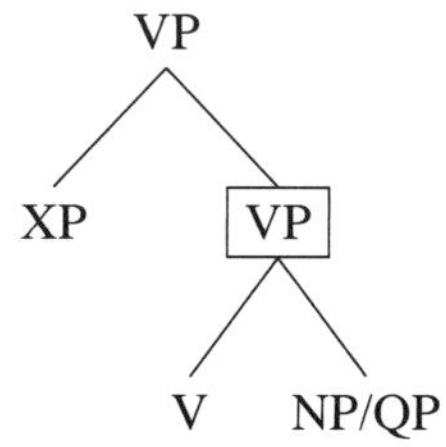

(b) CTB structure for VP

Figure 4: Bracketing decisions for VP made by PTB and CTB. XP = {PP, ADVP, S}

Idioms which make phrase-level alignment impossible are rare in our corpus. On average, there are about 5 cases in a file of 500 sentence pairs. As for the incompatibilities caused by translation, it is possible for the phrase alignments missed in those cases to be made up if the phrases involved reappear in a more literal translation. These two issues do not pose a real threat to our approach. As annotators, we cannot do much about these two issues, especially the latter one, since our data is got as is. Due to these two reasons, we will not discuss them further in this paper.

Next let us turn to the last type of incompatibility. Use the sentence pair in Figure 1 for instance. Note that the Chinese VP 利用/use 自己/own 的 表达/expression 方式/method matches the English string *use their own methods of expression* in terms of both grammaticality and meaning. However, the English parse tree has no phrasal node for the string that could form an alignment to the Chinese VP. Similarly, the Chinese NP 表达/expression 方式/method corresponds to the English string *methods of expression*, but again, no phrasal node is present in the English parse tree that could be aligned with the Chinese NP. Our statistics shows that, in a file with 500 sentence pairs, there are approximately 50 instances of the incompatibility in VPs illustrated here and 20 in NPs (an instance is a case where a legitimate phrase alignment cannot be made). These are both quite high frequency. In the next section, we discuss the reason for the incompatibility and give a solution to fix the issue.

4 A common incompatibility pattern and its solution

There is a pattern for the incompatibility illustrated at the end of Section 3. The cause for the incompatibility is the bracketing annotation of the complement-adjunct distinction made by the Penn Treebank (PTB) bracketing guidelines (Bies et al., 1995). The pattern is found in both VPs and NPs.

Let us discuss VPs first. To see the pattern, we need some background information about the internal composition of both English and Chinese VPs and how VPs are parsed according to PTB and CTB annotation standards. Let us start with the English VP. Besides the verb, there can be both preverbal and postverbal constituents in an English VP. Preverbal constituents are much more restricted than postverbal constituents in terms of both phrase types and the number of constituents allowed. Most commonly seen in our corpus, an ADVP is present before the verb if there is a preverbal constituent at all. By contrast, various kinds of constituents (NP, PP, ADVP, S) can appear post-verbally and more than one of these phrases can co-occur. When there is more than one post-verbal constituent, quite often one of them is the complement of the verb and the others are adjuncts. Due to engineering considerations, the PTB bracketing guidelines decided on a flat structure for the English VP, where preverbal and postverbal constituents and the verb are treated as sisters that are directly attached to the VP-node (Bies et al., 1995). A general structure for the English VP is given in Figure 4a, where it can be seen that the complement-adjunct distinction is not made.

Now let us turn to the Chinese VP. In a Chinese VP, there can also be both preverbal and postverbal constituents, but the situation is quite different from that in English. Unlike in English VPs where postverbal constituents are freer, postverbal constituents in Chinese VPs are restricted and can only be the complement of the verb or one particular kind of phrase, namely QP, which includes counting phrases such as *three times* as in *went there three times*, and duration phrases such as *for three years* as in *lived there for three years*. Adjuncts including ADVP, PP, and different kinds of adverbial clauses come before the verb. The second difference is that Chinese strongly favors no more than one constituent after the verb. In theory, a complement phrase and a QP can co-occur after the verb, but in reality, if the two co-occur in a sentence, the complement will most likely be preposed to the left of the verb by either topicalization or the introduction of the function word 把, leaving QP the only post-verbal element. The structure of a Chinese VP stipulated by the CTB bracketing standards (Xue and Xia, 2000) is provided in Figure 4b.

Now let us compare the two structures in Figure 4. Note that in the English VP there is no phrasal node that dominates the verb and its immediate sister on the right, which, in many cases, is the complement of the verb. By contrast, there is a node in the Chinese VP (the boxed VP) that groups together the verb and a post-verbal constituent, which could be either the complement or a QP (some QPs are complements and some others are adjuncts, an issue that does not need to bother us here). This is where the incompatibility arises: the boxed VP-node in the Chinese tree has no node-counterpart to align with in the English tree, but the string dominated by that boxed VP has a match in the English sentence. The example in Figure 1 illustrates the issue, where the Chinese VP dominating the string 利用/use 自己/own 的 表达/expression 方式/method has no possible phrase alignment although the string corresponds in meaning to the English string *use their own methods of expression*.

To eliminate the incompatibility, an extra layer of projection is needed in the English tree. To be specific, we need to combine the verb and its complement to create a VP node, which then can be aligned to the boxed VP in the Chinese tree. Still using the example in Figure 1 for instance, we need to create a VP node by combining the English verb *use* and its object NP *their own methods of expression*, so that the Chinese VP 利用/use 自己/own 的 表达/expression 方式/method can be aligned with the resultant VP. This can be done through binarization.

Now let us turn to the pattern in NPs. We will look at the English NP first. There can be constituents both before and after the head in an English NP. Post-nominal constituents can be either a PP or an S whereas pre-nominal constituents can be one or more than one of the following kinds of elements: determiners (*the/a/an*), demonstratives (*this/that* etc.), quantifiers (*some*, *many* etc.), numerals and adjectives. The PTB bracketing guidelines make the decision that all pre-nominal elements and the head be grouped together using a flat structure to form a NP, which then is treated as a sister of a post-nominal constituent, be it a complement or an adjunct. As for the Chinese NP, the major difference between a Chinese NP and an English one is that there can only be pre-nominal constituents in Chinese NPs. In other words, the head noun is the rightmost element in a Chinese NP and nothing comes after it.

The incompatibility has to do with the complement-adjunct distinction. The complement of an English noun can be either a PP or an S, which always comes after the noun. Due to space limit, we only discuss PP below. An English noun and its PP complement, because of the close semantic relationship between the two, are usually translated as a compound noun in Chinese. For instance, *student of linguistics* is translated as the N-N compound 语言学/linguistics 学生/student. A compound is treated by the CTB bracketing standard as an NP dominating all its components. Unfortunately, the English head noun and its complement do not form a constituent, which, if present, can be aligned with the node for the Chinese compound. This causes incompatibility to arise. Take Figure 1 for instance, the English string *methods of expression* is translated as the Chinese compound noun 表达/expression 方式/method. As shown by the structure, the noun *method* and its PP complement do not form a constituent. As a result, the Chinese compound noun has no alignment.

To remove the incompatibility, we need to change the existing structure of the English NP. Still using the example in Figure 1 for instance, if the English noun phrase has the structure in Figure 5, then we can align the English NP *methods of expression* with the Chinese NP 表达/expression 方式/method. The structure in Figure 5 is different from what is given by the PTB standards in that the head noun (such as

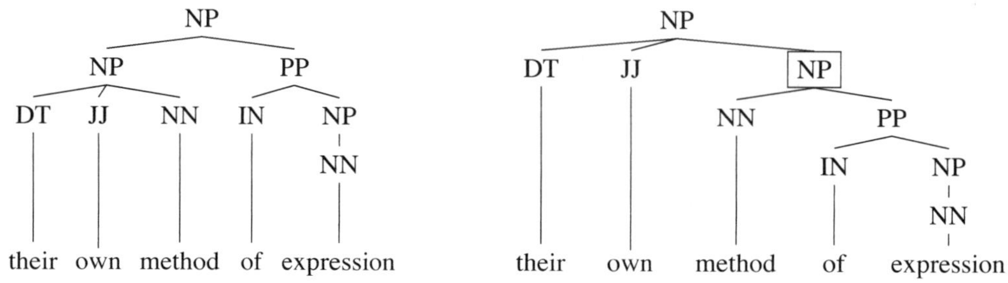

(a) Current structure

(b) Proposed new structure

Figure 5: A proposed revision for the existing structure of English NPs

method) is combined with its complement (such as the PP *of expression*) first to create an NP, which then is modified by, say, an adjective (such as *own*) and a determiner (such as *their*). From the semantic point of view, a pre-nominal adjective is an adjunct to the head noun that is not as closely related to the head noun as its complement. The new structure given in Figure 5b reflects this semantic fact by combining the complement with the head before the adjective.

5 Conclusion

In this paper, we argue that it is feasible to align Chinese-English parallel parse trees despite incompatibility issues. We show that the most common incompatibility is caused by bracketing guideline design, which can be fixed by changing the existing structures stipulated by the current annotation standards. The revised structures we proposed to avoid the incompatibility are deeper than the existing PTB structures and respect the complement-adjunct distinction, which is a well-established notion in linguistics that has been shown to manifest itself in different kinds of phenomena cross-linguistically. In syntax, the distinction is made by combining the head and its complement first to form a constituent, which then is combined with an adjunct. This way of representing the distinction is standard and gives arise to a structure that is binary-branching and deep. In syntactic annotation, linguistic sophistication which requires the parse tree to reflect well-established linguistic notions such as the complement-adjunct distinction is an important consideration and generally gives arise to deeper structures. In addition to linguistic sophistication, another important consideration in syntactic annotation is engineering economy, which requires the annotation to be economical in the sense that it can be carried out in a convenient and efficient manner to save annotation effort and time. This means that the parse tree needs to be as flat as possible since shallow structures are much easier to annotate than deep ones. These two competing considerations interact to influence the establishment of bracketing standards.

Due to engineering pressure caused by the fact that it is not easy to make a consistent distinction between complements and adjuncts in annotation, the PTB bracketing guidelines chose a shallow structure for both VPs and NPs as shown above. The decision is understandable since no incompatibility ever arises in the construction of a monolingual treebank like PTB. With the advent of new use cases of monolingual treebanks such as hierarchically aligned parallel treebanks, new issues like incompatibility emerge and call for adjustments to some decisions that have been made without such issues. As shown in Section 4, some decisions made in existing bracketing annotation cause incompatibilities and make legitimate phrase alignments impossible. For the purpose of aligning parallel parse trees, deeper and linguistically motivated structures are needed. This raises the interesting question whether we should have a deeper and linguistically motivated structure to start with when constructing a monolingual treebank. Based on what we have seen in this paper, a positive answer to the question seems reasonable at least in some cases such as VPs and NPs for the sake of better serving uses cases like constructing parallel treebanks with hierarchical alignments.

Acknowledgements

The HACEPT project, under which the work presented in this paper is done, is supported by the IBM subcontract No. 4913014934 under DARPA Prime Contract No. 0011-12-C-0015 entitled "Broad Operational Language Translation". We would like to thank Libin Shen and Salim Roukos for their inspiration and discussion during early stages of the project, Abe Ittycheriah and Niyu Ge for their help with setting up the data, Loretta Bandera for developing and maintaining the annotation tool, and three anonymous reviewers for their helpful comments. We are grateful for the hard work of our four annotators: Hui Gao, Shiman Guo, Tse-ming Wang and Lingya Zhou. Any opinions, findings, conclusions or recommendations expressed in this material are those of the authors and do not necessarily reflect those of the sponsor or any of the people mentioned above.

References

Ann Bies, Mark Ferguson, Karen Katz, Robert MacIntyre, Victoria Tredinnick, Grace Kim, Mary Ann Marcinkiewicz, and Britta Schasberger. 1995. Bracketing guidelines for Treebank II style Penn Treebank project. Technical report, University of Pennsylvania.

David Chiang. 2010. Learning to translate with source and target syntax. In *Proceedings of the 48th Annual Meeting of the Association for Computational Linguistics*, pages 1443--1452.

Dun Deng and Nianwen Xue. 2014. Building a Hierarchically Aligned Chinese-English Parallel Treebank. In *Proceedings of the 25th International Conference on Computational Linguistics (COLING 2014).*

Daniel Gildea. 2003. Loosely tree-based alignment for machine translation. In *Proceedings of the 41st Annual Meeting on Association for Computational Linguistics-Volume 1*, pages 80--87.

Xuansong Li, Niyu Ge, and Stephanie Strassel. 2009. Tagging guidelines for Chinese-English word alignment. Technical report, Linguistic Data Consortium.

Yang Liu, Yajuan Lü, and Qun Liu. 2009. Improving tree-to-tree translation with packed forests. In *Proceedings of the Joint Conference of the 47th Annual Meeting of the ACL and the 4th International Joint Conference on Natural Language Processing of the AFNLP*, pages 558--566.

Mitchell P. Marcus, Beatrice Santorini, and Mary Ann Marcinkiewicz. 1993. Building a Large Annotated Corpus of English: The Penn Treebank. *Computational Linguistics*, 19(2):313--330.

Jun Sun, Min Zhang, and Chew Lim Tan. 2010. Exploring syntactic structural features for sub-tree alignment using bilingual tree kernels. In *Proceedings of the 48th Annual Meeting of the Association for Computational Linguistics*, pages 306--315.

Tong Xiao and Jingbo Zhu. 2013. Unsupervised sub-tree alignment for tree-to-tree translation. *Journal of Artificial Intelligence Research*, 48:733--782.

Nianwen Xue and Fei Xia. 2000. The bracketing guidelines for Penn Chinese Treebank project. Technical report, University of Pennsylvania.

Nianwen Xue, Fei Xia, Fu dong Chiou, and Martha Palmer. 2005. The Penn Chinese Treebank: Phrase Structure Annotation of a Large Corpus. *Natural Language Engineering*, 11(2):207--238.

Sentence diagrams: their evaluation and combination

Jirka Hana and **Barbora Hladká** and **Ivana Lukšová**
Charles University in Prague, Faculty of Mathematics and Physics
Institute of Formal and Applied Linguistics
Prague, Czech Republic
{hana,hladka,luksova} (at) ufal.mff.cuni.cz

Abstract

The purpose of our work is to explore the possibility of using sentence diagrams produced by schoolchildren as training data for automatic syntactic analysis. We have implemented a sentence diagram editor that schoolchildren can use to practice morphology and syntax. We collect their diagrams, combine them into a single diagram for each sentence and transform them into a form suitable for training a particular syntactic parser. In this study, the object language is Czech, where sentence diagrams are part of elementary school curriculum, and the target format is the annotation scheme of the Prague Dependency Treebank. We mainly focus on the evaluation of individual diagrams and on their combination into a merged better version.

1 Introduction

Syntactic parsing has been an attractive topic for both theoretical and computational linguists for many years. In combination with supervised machine learning techniques, several corpus-based parsers have been implemented (e.g., (Nivre et al., 2007), (de Marneffe et al., 2006), (McDonald et al., 2005)), combined (e.g., (Surdeanu and Manning, 2010)), and adapted (e.g., (McClosky et al., 2010),(Zhang and Wang, 2009)). The performance of such techniques directly correlates with the size of training data: the more annotated data, the better. However, the annotation process is very resource consuming, thus we have been seeking for alternative ways of faster and cheaper annotation. Namely, we have been inspired by the solution of crowdsourcing, see e.g. (Brabham, 2013).

In Czech schools, practicing morphology and syntax is an obligatory part of the curriculum. Schoolchildren draw sentence diagrams similar to syntactic trees in dependency grammar theories (Hudson, 1984; Sgall et al., 1986; Mel'čuk, 1988), with labeled nodes and edges. Our goal is to collect such diagrams and transform them into the annotation scheme of the Prague Dependency Treebank (Hajič et al., 2006). Thereby we enlarge training data for taggers and parsers of Czech. Traditionally, diagrams that we need are only in students' notebooks so they are not accessible to us at all. Since we require diagrams electronically, we have been developing a sentence diagram editor *Čapek*. We have designed it both as a CALL (Computer-Assisted Language Learning) system for practicing morphology and dependency-based syntax and as a crowdsourcing system for getting annotated data. In addition, the editor can be used for drawing sentence diagrams in any natural language. On the other hand, transformation rules have to be specified with respect to a particular target annotation scheme. We introduced this approach in (Hana and Hladká, 2012).

Data quality belongs to the most important issues related to crowdsourcing, see e.g. (Sabou et al., 2012), (Wang et al., 2010), (Hsueh et al., 2009). We discuss the data quality from two aspects: (i) evaluation of students' diagrams against teachers' and/or other students' diagrams, i.e. we consider how diagrams are similar; (ii) combination of students' diagrams of one sentence to get a better diagram, i.e. we deal with multiple, possibly noisy, annotations and we study if they are useful.

Our paper is organized as follows: in Section 2, we describe Czech sentence diagrams and how they differ from the PDT annotation scheme. We introduce the Čapek editor in Section 3. Section 4 introduces

LAW VIII - The 8th Linguistic Annotation Workshop, pages 38–47,
Dublin, Ireland, August 23-24 2014.

a tree edit distance metric we use to quantify the difference between diagrams. Section 5 discusses an algorithm combining alternative diagrams into a single structure. Finally, some initial evaluation and other statistics are presented in Section 6.

2 Czech sentence diagrams

In the Czech sentence diagrams (hence SDs), a sentence is represented as a type of dependency structure.[1] The structure is a directed acyclic graph (roughly a tree) with labeled nodes. The nodes correspond to words: one (most common), multiple (auxiliary words are considered markings on their heads, e.g. preposition and noun, or a complex verb form share a single node) or none (in case of dropped subjects). The edges capture the dependency relation between nodes (e.g., between an object and its predicate). The node label expresses the type of dependency, or syntactic function.

Formally, a sentence diagram over a sentence $s = w_1 \ w_2 \ \ldots \ w_n$ is a directed acyclic graph $D = (Nodes, Edges)$, where $Nodes$ is a partition of s. Moreover, the $Nodes$ set might contain a dummy node corresponding to a dropped subject. The first node N_1 of an edge $E = (N_1, N_2)$ is a child node of the second node N_2.

For illustration, let's consider the sentence in (1) and its diagram in Figure 1:

(1) (—) Ráno půjdu se svým kamarádem na houby.
I in the morning will go with my friend mushrooming.
'I will go mushrooming with my friend in the morning.'

Since our goal is to get more data annotated according to the PDT schema (the so-called a-layer or surface syntax), we characterize certain aspects of SD with respect to the PDT conventions depicted in Figure 2:

- **Tokenization.** There is a 1:1 correspondence between tokens and nodes in PDT; all punctuation marks have their corresponding nodes. Cf. 8 tokens and 8 nodes in Example 1 and Figure 2. In SDs, there is an N:1 correspondence between tokens and nodes (N can be 0 for dropped subjects); punctuation is mostly ignored. Cf. 8 tokens and 6 nodes in Example 1 and Figure 1.

- **Multi-token nodes.** SDs operate on both single-token (*půjdu* 'will go') and multi-token nodes (*se kamarádem* 'with friend', *na houby* 'for mushrooms'). The tokens inside each multi-token node are ordered in accordance with their surface word order. Auxiliary words, auxiliary verbs, prepositions, modals etc. do not have their own nodes and are always part of a multi-token node. PDT handles single-token nodes only.

- **Subject and predicate.** In PDT, predicate is the root and the subject depends on it; in Figure 1, they are on the same level; cf. the nodes for *(já) půjdu* 'I will go'.

- **PRO subject.** SDs introduce nodes for elided subjects (see the --- node in Figure 1), which are common in Czech. PDT does not represent them explicitly.

- **Morphological tags.** We adopt the system of positional tags used in PDT to capture morphological properties of words. Tags are assigned to each token in the sentence, not to the nodes.

- **Syntactical tags (functors)**. Our SDs use 14 syntactical tags (Subject, Predicate, Attribute, Adverbial of time/place/manner/degree/means/cause/reason/condition/opposition, Verbal Complement). PDT distinguishes significantly higher number of functors, but most of the additional tags are used in rather specific situations that are captured by different means in school syntax (parenthesis, ellipsis), are quite technical (punctuation types), etc. In the vast majority of cases, it is trivial to map SD functors to PDT functors.

[1]For expository reasons, in this paper, we ignore complex sentences consisting of multiple clauses. Their SD is a disconnected graph where each component is an SD of a single clause. Such sentences and graphs are however part of the evaluation in Section 6.

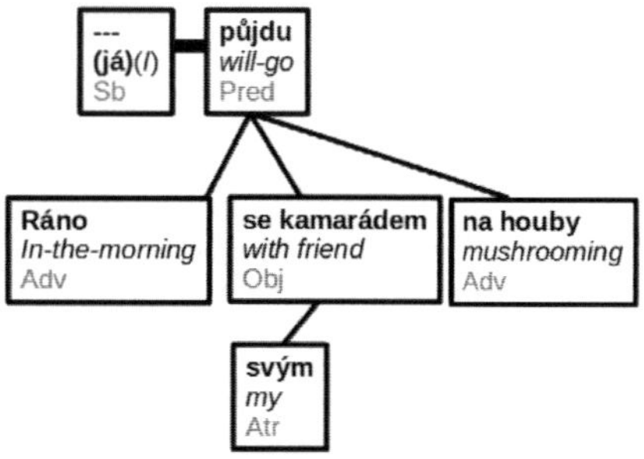

Figure 1: A sample of sentence diagram

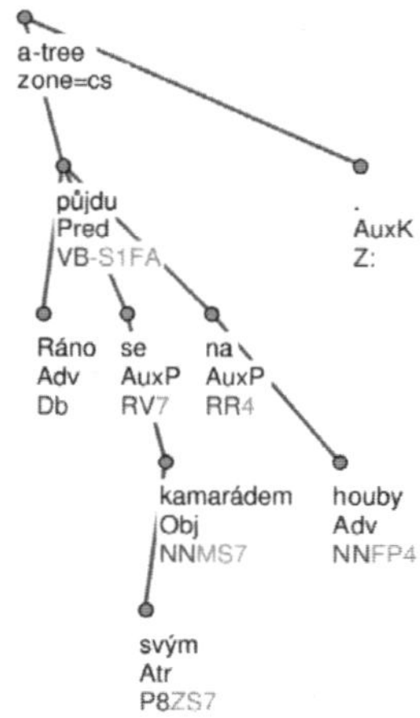

Figure 2: A sample of PDT tree

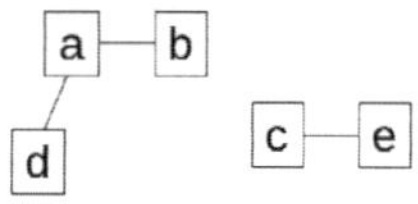

Figure 3: A possible sentence diagram draw in Čapek

3 Čapek editor

Since we wanted to provide students with a sentence diagram editor that is easy to use, we have decided not to use the TrEd editor,[2] a versatile, flexible but also complex tool, which is used as the main annotation tool of the Prague Dependency Treebanks. Instead, we decided to implement *Čapek*, a new system. It exists as a desktop application, written in Java on top of the Netbeans Platform, [3] and as a web application.[4]

Students use the editor in a similar way as they are used to use chalk/pen at school. A simple and intuitive GUI supports the following operations:

- **JOIN** Merge two nodes into a single multi-token node.
- **SPL** Divide a multi-token into nodes corresponding to single tokens.
- **INS** Create a node for elided subject.
- **LINK** Link a node to its governing parent node.
- **LAB** Label a node with syntactic function.
- **MLAB** Label a token with morphological function.

Intentionally, we did not make Čapek to perform any consistency checks, except acyclicity of the graph. Thus students can create a graph with several components, all nodes can be a subject, etc.

4 Similarity of sentence diagrams

We compute the similarity between sentence diagrams using a tree edit distance. Our definition is based on a tree edit distance in (Bille, 2005). It assumes two trees T_1, T_2 and three edit operations: relabeling a node, deleting a non-root node, and inserting a node. T_1 is transformed into T_2 by a sequence of edit

[2] http://ufal.mff.cuni.cz/tred
[3] http://platform.netbeans.org
[4] http://capek.herokuapp.com/

operations S. Each operation has a particular cost, the cost of the sequence S is simply the sum of the cost of individual operations. Then *tree edit distance* between two trees is the cost of a cheapest sequence of operations turning one tree into another.

Our situation is similar, however:

- the compared sentence diagrams are always over the same sentence, i.e. over the same set of tokens
- diagrams are not trees: they are acyclic graphs but unlike trees they might consist of several components (either because they capture complex sentences, or because the students did not finish them). In addition, a diagram usually has two "roots": one for the subject and one for predicate. However, it is trivial to transform them into the corresponding tree, considering the subject to be the daughter of the predicate.

Thus, we modify the distance from (Bille, 2005). For an example, see Figure 4 with nodes of two particular diagrams over a 6-token sentence. The arrows show a token-node mapping specified by the annotator of D_1:

- Let D_1 and D_2 be sentence diagrams; we are turning D_2 into D_1.
- We consider the following operations:
  - `SPL` – detaching a token from a node
  - `JOIN` – adding a token to a node
  - `INS` – adding an empty node (used for elided subjects)
  - `LINK` – linking a node with its parent and removing all inconsistent edges. If manipulating a non-root node, relink the node to its new parent and remove the edge to its former parent. If manipulating a root node, like *a* in Figure 5 a), link the node to its new parent, e.g. to *e*, see Figure 5 b). Then the diagram consists of a single cycle. Thus remove the edge from *e* to its former parent *c* and *e* becomes a root, see Figure 5 c).
  - `SLAB` – change node syntactic label

  All operations are assumed to have the cost of 1. Without loss of generality, we can assume that operations are performed in stages: first all `SPL`s, then all `JOIN`s, etc. In Figure 4, first we apply `SPL` twice on the nodes $[b, c]$, $[d, e, f]$ and then `JOIN` also twice on the nodes $[a]$, $[b]$ and $[e]$, $[f]$.

- Finally, the measure is normalized by sentence length. Thus, we redefine the tree edit distance $TED(D_1, D_2, n)$ for diagrams D_1, D_2 and sentence of n tokens as follows:

$$TED(D_1, D_2, n) = (\#SPL + \#JOIN + \#INS + \#LINK + \#SLAB)/n$$

.

- We define the tree edit distance for annotators A_1, A_2 and a set of sentences S ($s_i \in S$) as the average tree distance over those sentences:

$$\overline{TED}(A_1, A_2, S) = \frac{1}{|S|}\sum_{i=1}^{|S|} TED(D^i_{A_1}, D^i_{A_2}, |s_i|)$$

.

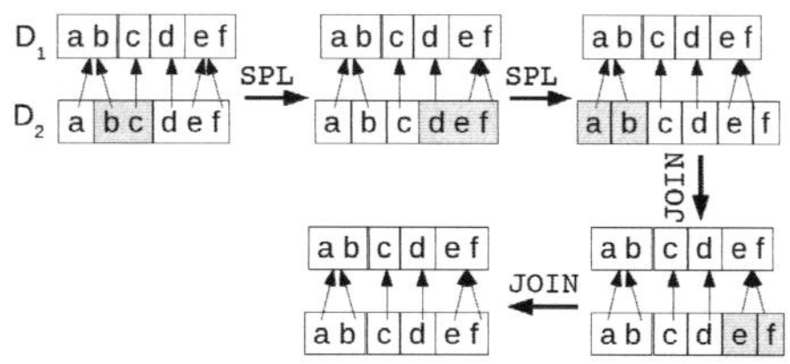

Figure 4: Turning nodes of D_2 into nodes of D_1

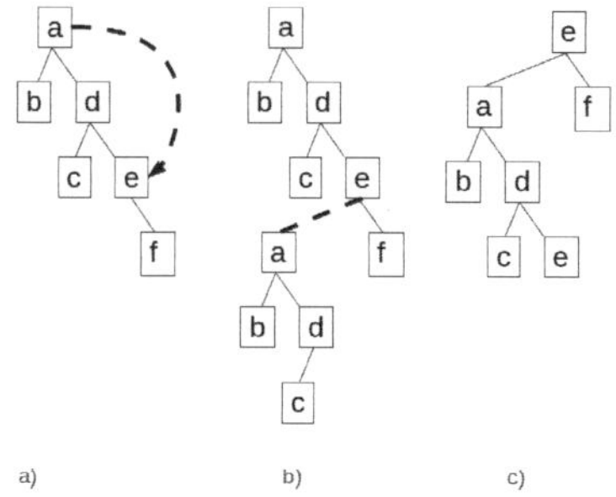

Figure 5: Linking a root node

5 Combination of sentence diagrams

We deal with sentence diagrams and their differences before transformation into a target annotation scheme. We propose a majority-voting method to combine m multiple diagrams $D_1, \ldots, D_m$ created by m different users over the sentence $s = w_1\ w_2\ \ldots\ w_n$. In some sense, our task is similar to the task of combination independently-trained syntactic parsers. However, at least to our knowledge, the experiments performed so far, e.g. (Surdeanu and Manning, 2010), are based on the assumption that all input parsers build syntactic structures on the same set of nodes. Given that, we address a significantly different task. We approach it using the concept of assigning each candidate node and edge a score based on the number of votes it received from the input diagrams. The votes for edges are weighted by a specific criterion.

To build a final diagram, we first create its set of nodes $FinalNodes$, then its set of edges $FinalEdges$ linking nodes in $FinalNodes$, and finally extend the set of nodes by any empty nodes. The method can produce both nodes and edges that do not occur in any of the input diagrams.

Building $FinalNodes$

1. $\forall t, u \in s\ .\ v(t,u) = \sum_{k=1}^{m} \delta([t,u], D_k)$, where $\delta([t,u], D) = 1$ if the tokens t and u are in the same node in the diagram D, and 0 otherwise. We compute the number of votes $v(t,u)$ to measure user preferences for having token pair t, u in one node. In total, there are $\binom{|s|}{2}$ token pairs.

2. The set $FinalNodes$ is formed as a partition over tokens induced by the $v(t,u)$ equivalence relation:

$$FinalNodes = s/eq \text{ where } eq(t,u) \Leftrightarrow v(t,u) > m/2$$

For illustration, we start with the sentence $a\ b\ c\ d$ and three diagrams with nodes displayed in Figure 6. All of them consist of two nodes, namely $Nodes_1 = \{[a,b,c],[d]\}$, $Nodes_2 = \{[a],[b,c,d]\}$, $Nodes_3 = \{[a,b],[c,d]\}$. First, we calculate the votes for each possible token pairs, see Table 1. There are two candidates with a majority of votes, namely (a,b) and (b,c), both with two votes. Thus, $FinalNodes = \{[a,b,c],[d]\}$. A final diagram consists of n nodes $[w_1], \ldots, [w_n]$ if there is no candidate with majority of votes, see Figure 7 and Table 2.

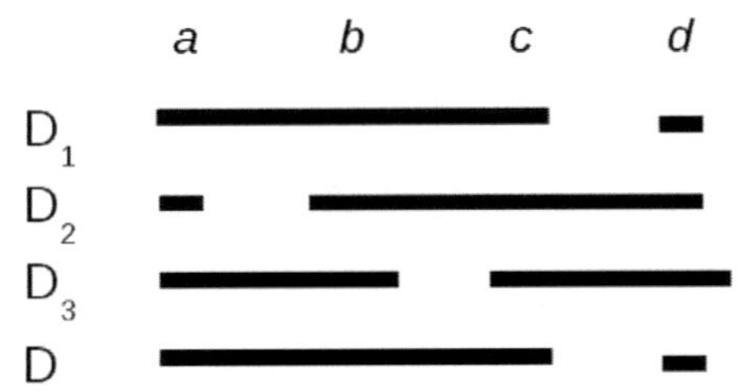

Figure 6: Sentence $a\ b\ c\ d$ and nodes in three diagrams

	a	b	c	d
a	x	2	1	0
b	x	x	2	1
c	x	x	x	1
d	x	x	x	x

Table 1: Two candidates for joining

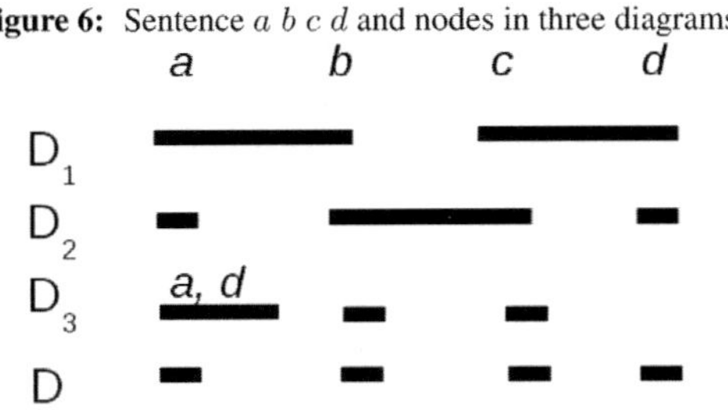

Figure 7: Sentence $a\ b\ c\ d$ and nodes in three other diagrams

	a	b	c	d
a	x	1	0	1
b	x	x	1	0
c	x	x	x	1
d	x	x	x	x

Table 2: No candidates with the great majority of votes

Building $FinalEdges$

1. $fn = |FinalNodes|$

2. $\forall D_{k=1,\dots,m}$, $\forall E = (N_1, N_2) \in Edges_k$, $\forall (t,u) \in tokens(N_1) \times tokens(N_2) : v^k(t,u) = 1/(|tokens(N_1)||tokens(N_2)|)$. We compute $v^k(t,u)$ to measure user preference for having token t in a node dependent on a node containing u. We take it proportionally to the number of tokens in two particular nodes.

3. We initialize a set of potential edges as a set of all possible edges over the final nodes. I.e. $PotentialEdges$ is formed as a variation of fn nodes choose 2. Let $p = |PotentialEdges| = fn(fn-1)$. Then weights are assigned to the potential edges:

   $\forall E = (N_1, N_2) \in PotentialEdges : v_E = \sum_{k=1}^{m} v^k(t,u), (t,u) \in tokens(N_1) \times tokens(N_2)$

4. Sort $PotentialEdges$ so that $v_{E_1} \geq v_{E_2} \geq \dots \geq v_{E_p}$

5. $FinalEdges := \emptyset$

6. until $PotentialEdges = \emptyset$

   - $FinalEdges := FinalEdges \cup E_1$
   - $PotentialEdges := PotentialEdges \setminus E_1$
   - $PotentialEdges := PotentialEdges \setminus -E_1$
   - $PotentialEdges := PotentialEdges \setminus \{E : E \cup FinalEdges \text{ has a cycle}\}$

For illustration, we assume three diagrams D_1, D_2, D_3 displayed in Figure 8. We compute weights of token pairs proportionally to the number of tokens in nodes identifying a given edge, e.g. the edge $([a,b],[c])$ in D_1 determines two token pairs (a,c) and (b,c), each of them with the weight $1/2$. See Table 3 for other weights. Let $FinalNodes = \{[a,b],[c],[d]\}$. There are six possible edges connecting the final nodes, namely $([a,b],[c])$,$([c],[a,b])$,$([a,b],[d])$,$([d],[a,b])$,$([c],[d])$,$([d],[c])$. For each of them, we compute its weight, see Table 4. Then we sort them – $([a,b],[c])$, $([c],[d])$, $([a,b],[d])$, $([c],[a,b])$, $([d],[a,b])$, $([d],[c])$. Table 5 traces the algorithm for adding edges into a final diagram. Finally, we get the diagram D in Figure 8.

	([a, b], [c])	([c], [a, b])	([a, b], [d])	([d], [a, b])	([c], [d])	([d], [c])
weight	13/6	0	1/2	0	1	0

Table 4: Computing weights of edges-candidates to be added into a final diagram

1st	$FinalEdges$						
	$PotentialEdges$	([a, b], [c])	([c], [d])	([a, b], [d])	([c], [a, b])	([d], [a, b])	([d], [c])
2nd	$FinalEdges$	([a, b], [c])					
	$PotentialEdges$		([c], [d])	([a, b], [d])	~~([c], [a, b])~~	([d], [a, b])	([d], [c])
3rd	$FinalEdges$	([a, b], [c])	([c], [d])				
	$PotentialEdges$			~~([a, b], [d])~~		~~([d], [a, b])~~	~~([d], [c])~~

Table 5: Adding edges into a final diagram

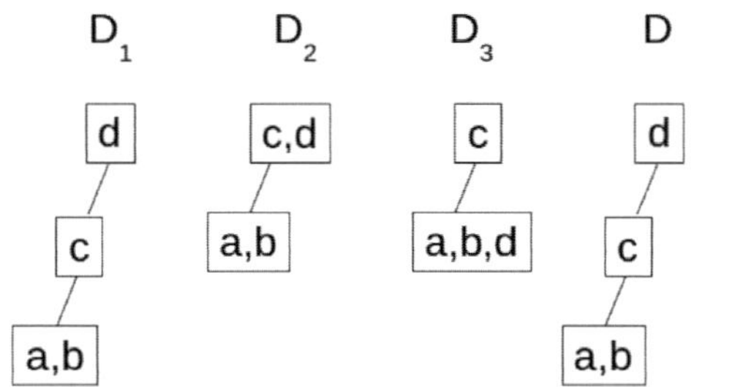

Figure 8: Input diagrams D_1, D_2, D_3 and final diagram D

D_1		D_2		D_3	
token pair	weight	token pair	weight	token pair	weight
(a, c)	1/2	(a, c)	1/4	(a, c)	1/3
(b, c)	1/2	(a, d)	1/4	(b, c)	1/3
(c, d)	1	(b, c)	1/4	(d, c)	1/3
		(b, d)	1/4		

Table 3: Assigning weights to token pairs

6 Data and initial experiments

We randomly selected a workbench of 101 sentences from a textbook of Czech language for elementary schools (Styblík and Melichar, 2005) with the average length of 8.5 tokens, for details see Figure 9. These sentences were manually analysed according to the school system with the emphasis placed on syntactic analysis. Namely, elementary school teachers T1 and T2 and secondary school students S1 and S2 drew school system diagrams using Čapek 1.0. Teachers T1 and T2 are colleagues from the same school but they were drawing diagrams separately. Students S1 and S2 study at different schools and they are students neither of T1 nor T2. In Table 6, we present $\overline{TED}$ for pairs of teachers and students. As we expected, the teachers' diagrams are the most similar ones and on the other hand, the students' diagrams are the most different one. Taking teacher T1 as a gold-standard data, student S1 made less errors that student S2. We analyzed differences in details considering two aspects:

- Do nodes closer to the root node cause more differences? A diagram D2 is transformed into a diagram D1 by a sequence of operations (`SPL`, `JOIN`, `INS`, `LINK`, `SLAB`) where the first operation

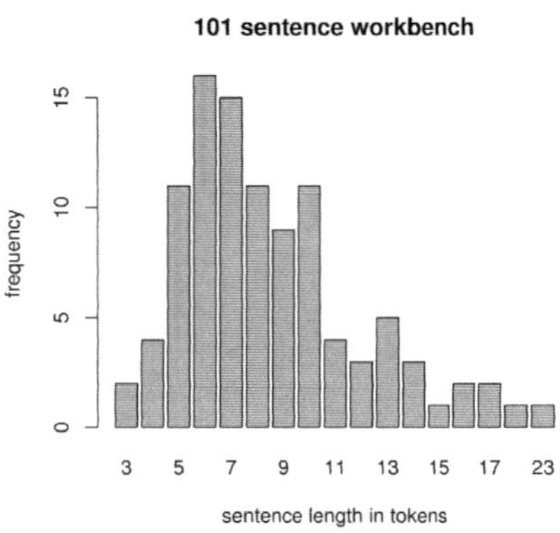

Figure 9: Length of sentences in the workbench

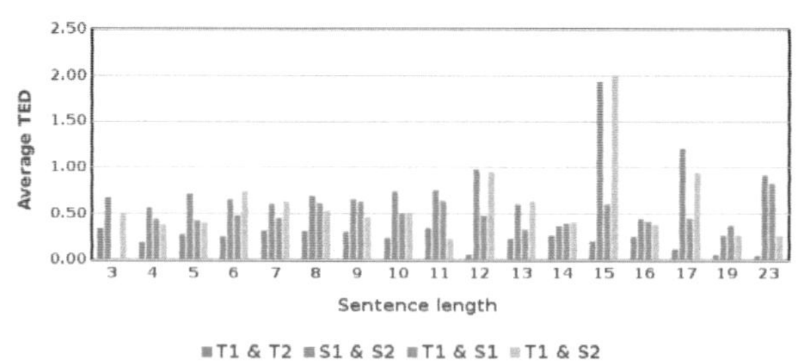

Figure 10: $\overline{TED}$ vs. Sentence length

	(T1,T2)	(T1,S1)	(T1,S2)	(S1,S2)	U1	U2	U3	U4	U5	U6	U7	MV
# of sentences	101	91	101	91	10	10	10	10	10	10	10	10
$\overline{TED}$	0.26	0.49	0.56	0.69	0.78	0.63	0.56	0.76	0.38	0.62	1.21	0.40

Table 6: $\overline{TED}$ for pairs of teachers and students, for pairs of teacher T1 and users U1,...,U7 and their combination MV

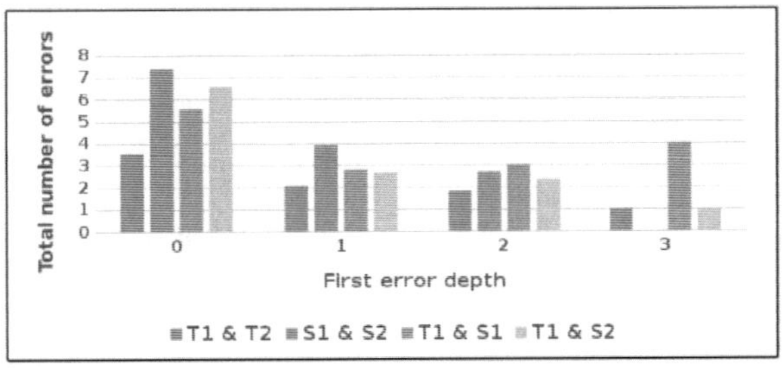

Figure 11: First Error Depth

is applied on the node in some depth of D2 (where the depth of a node is the length of the path from the root to that node). Figure 11 illustrates this depth for pairs of teachers and students. We observe that the very first operation is applied in the root nodes mostly. So we can suppose that recognizing predicate and its dependent nodes is the most difficult step for users.

- Do longer sentences cause more difficulties? In Figure 10, we observe that the sentence length does not influence discrepancies between teachers at all (measured by $\overline{TED}$). For students, we can see peaks for sentences of 12, 15, 17, 23 tokens. However, we suppose that longer sentences do not cause obstacles for them.

A group of 7 users U1, ..., U7, graduate and undergraduate students, drew diagrams for 10 (S_{10}) sentences randomly selected from the workbench using Čapek 2.0. We merged their analyses using the MV algorithm. When the final diagrams are compared to the diagrams by the T1 teacher, we get $\overline{TED}(T_1, MV(U1, \ldots, U8), S_{10}) = 0.4$. To see whether we built a better final diagram, we computed $\overline{TED}(T_1, U_i, S_{10})$ for each user – see columns U1,...,U7 in Table 6. One can see that only one user (U5) has a slightly better agreement with the T1 diagrams. The user U7 actually managed to have more than one error (differences from T1) per annotated token.

7 Conclusion

In this paper, we have shown our motivation for getting more syntactically annotated data by sentence diagrams transformation. We have implemented Čapek, a diagram editor, which allows students to perform sentence analysis electronically. We can then collect their diagrams easily. The editor is designed as both a CALL and crowdsourcing system for practicing morphology and syntax and for collecting diagrams over a given set of sentences. Both aspects have to deal with a quantitative measure of agreement, therefore we designed a tree edit distance metric comparing two or multiple diagrams. In addition, we have formulated an algorithm combining multiple crowdsourced diagrams into a single better diagram. Finally, we presented the results of a pilot study with promising results.

In the near future, to get more statistically significant results, we plan to address the following issues:

- evaluating the combination algorithm on complex sentences
- specifying the practice of crowdsourcing: how to distribute tasks, and how to assign voting weights to users based on their past results
- getting more diagrams

Acknowledgements

The authors would like to thank numerous persons for their sentence diagrams drawn using Čapek. We gratefully acknowledge support from the Charles University Grant Agency (grant no. 1568314), Charles University in Prague, Faculty of Mathematics and Physics. This work has been using language resources developed and/or stored and/or distributed by the LINDAT/CLARIN project of the Ministry of Education, Youth and Sports of the Czech Republic (project LM2010013).

References

Philip Bille. 2005. A survey on tree edit distance and related problems. *Theoretical computer science*, 337(1):217–239.

Daren C. Brabham. 2013. *Crowdsourcing*. MIT Press.

Marie-Catherine de Marneffe, Bill MacCartney, and Christopher D. Manning. 2006. Generating typed dependency parses from phrase structure parses. In *Proceedings of the 8th International Conference on Language Resources and Evaluation (LREC 2006)*, pages 449–454.

Jan Hajič, Eva Hajičová, Jarmila Panevová, Petr Sgall, Petr Pajas, Jan Štěpánek, Jiří Havelka, and Marie Mikulová. 2006. Prague Dependency Treebank 2.0. Number LDC2006T01. Linguistic Data Consortium.

Jirka Hana and Barbora Hladká. 2012. Getting more data: Schoolkids as annotators. In *Proceedings of the 8th International Conference on Language Resources and Evaluation (LREC 2012)*, pages 4049–4054, İstanbul, Turkey. European Language Resources Association.

Pei-Yun Hsueh, Prem Melville, and Vikas Sindhwani. 2009. Data quality from crowdsourcing: A study of annotation selection criteria. In *Proceedings of the NAACL HLT 2009 Workshop on Active Learning for Natural Language Processing*, HLT '09, pages 27–35, Stroudsburg, PA, USA. Association for Computational Linguistics.

Richard Hudson. 1984. *Word Grammar*. Blackwell.

David McClosky, Eugene Charniak, and Mark Johnson. 2010. Automatic domain adaptation for parsing. In *Human Language Technologies: The 2010 Annual Conference of the North American Chapter of the Association for Computational Linguistics*, HLT '10, pages 28–36, Stroudsburg, PA, USA. Association for Computational Linguistics.

Ryan McDonald, Fernando Pereira, Kiril Ribarov, and Jan Hajič. 2005. Non-projective dependency parsing using spanning tree algorithms. In *Proceedings of the Conference on Human Language Technology and Empirical Methods in Natural Language Processing*, HLT '05, pages 523–530, Stroudsburg, PA, USA. Association for Computational Linguistics.

Igor Mel'čuk. 1988. *Dependency syntax: theory and practice*. State University of New York Press.

Joakim Nivre, Johan Hall, Jens Nilsson, Atanas Chanev, Glsen Eryigit, Sandra Kübler, Svetoslav Marinov, and Erwin Marsi. 2007. Maltparser: A language-independent system for data-driven dependency parsing. *Natural Language Engineering*, 13(2):95–135.

Marta Sabou, Kalina Bontcheva, and Arno Scharl. 2012. Crowdsourcing research opportunities: Lessons from natural language processing. In *Proceedings of the 12th International Conference on Knowledge Management and Knowledge Technologies*, i-KNOW '12, pages 17:1–17:8, New York, NY, USA. ACM.

Petr Sgall, Eva Hajičová, and Jarmila Panevová. 1986. *The Meaning of the Sentence and Its Semantic and Pragmatic Aspects*. Academia/Reidel Publishing Company, Prague, Czech Republic/Dordrecht, Netherlands.

Vlastimil Styblík and Jiří Melichar. 2005. *Český jazyk - Přehled učiva základní školy*. Fortuna.

Mihai Surdeanu and Christopher D. Manning. 2010. Ensemble models for dependency parsing: Cheap and good? In *Human Language Technologies: The 2010 Annual Conference of the North American Chapter of the Association for Computational Linguistics*, HLT '10, pages 649–652, Stroudsburg, PA, USA. Association for Computational Linguistics.

Aobo Wang, Cong Duy Vu Hoang, and Min-Yen Kan. 2010. Perspectives on crowdsourcing annotations for natural language processing.

Yi Zhang and Rui Wang. 2009. Cross-domain dependency parsing using a deep linguistic grammar. In *Proceedings of the Joint Conference of the 47th Annual Meeting of the ACL and the 4th International Joint Conference on Natural Language Processing of the AFNLP: Volume 1 - Volume 1*, ACL '09, pages 378–386, Stroudsburg, PA, USA. Association for Computational Linguistics.

Finding your "inner-annotator": An experiment in annotator independence for rating discourse coherence quality in essays

Jill Burstein
Educational Testing Service
666 Rosedale Road
Princeton, NJ 08541
jburstein@ets.org

Swapna Somasundaran
Educational Testing Service
666 Rosedale Road
Princeton, NJ 08541
ssomasundaran@ets.org

Martin Chodorow
Hunter College, CUNY
695 Park Avenue
New York, NY
martin.chodorow@hunter.cuny.edu

Abstract

An experimental annotation method is described, showing promise for a subjective labeling task – discourse coherence quality of essays. Annotators developed personal protocols, reducing front-end resources: protocol development and annotator training. Substantial inter-annotator agreement was achieved for a 4-point scale. Correlational analyses revealed how unique linguistic phenomena were considered in annotation. Systems trained with the annotator data demonstrated utility of the data.

1 Introduction[1]

Systems designed to evaluate discourse coherence quality often use supervised methods, relying on human annotation that requires significant front-end resources (time and cost) for protocol development and annotator training (Burstein et al., 2013). Crowd-sourcing (e.g., Amazon Mechanical Turk) has been used to collect annotation judgments more efficiently than traditional means for tasks requiring little domain expertise (Beigman Klebanov et al., 2013; Louis & Nenkova, 2013). However, proprietary data (test-taker essays) may preclude crowd-sourcing use. In the U.S., the need for automated writing evaluation systems to score proprietary test-taker data is likely to increase when Common Core[2] assessments are administered to school-age students beginning in 2015 (Shermis, in press), increasing the need for data annotation. This paper describes an experimental method for capturing discourse coherence quality judgments for test-taker essays. Annotators developed personal protocols reflecting their intuitions about essay coherence, thus reducing standard front-end resources. The paper presents related work (Section 2), the experimental annotation (Section 3), system evaluations (Section 4), and conclusions (Section 5).

2 Related Work

Even after extensive training, subjective tasks may yield low inter-annotator agreement (Burstein & Wolska, 2003; Reidsma & op den Akker, 2008; Burstein et al., 2013). Front-end annotation activities may require significant resources (protocol development and annotator training) (Miltsakaki and Kukich, 2000; Higgins, et al., 2004; Wang et al., 2012; Burstein et al., 2013). Burstein et al (2013) reviewed coherence features as discussed in cognitive psychology (Graesser et al., 2004), reading research (Van den Broek, 2012), and computational linguistics, and concluded that evaluating text coherence is *highly personal* , relying on a *variety of features*, including adherence to standard writing conventions (e.g., grammar), and patterns of rhetorical structure and vocabulary usage. They describe an annotation protocol that uses a 3-point coherence quality scale (3 (*high*), 2 (*somewhat*,) and 1 (*low*)) applied by 2 annotators to label 1,500 test-taker essays from 6 task types (Table 1). Protocol development took several weeks, and offered extensive descriptions of the 3-point scale, including illustrative test-taker responses; rigorous annotator training was also conducted. Burstein et al, 2013 collapsing the 3-point scale to a 2-point scale (i.e., *high* (3), *low* (1,2)). Results for a *binary* discourse coherence quality system (*high* and *low* coherence) for essays achieved only *borderline modest*

[2] See http://www.corestandards.org/.

LAW VIII - The 8th Linguistic Annotation Workshop, pages 48–53,
Dublin, Ireland, August 23-24 2014.

Essay-Writing Item Type	Test-Taker Population
1. K-12 expository	Students[3], ages 11-16
2. Expository	NNES-Univ
3. Source-based, integrated (reading and listening)	NNES-Univ
4. Expository	Graduate school applicants
5. Critical argument	Graduate school applicants
6. Professional licensing, content/expository	Certification for a business-related profession

Table 1. Six item types & populations in the experimental annotation task. NNES-Univ = non-native English speakers, university applicants

performance (κ=0.41)[4]. Outcomes reported in Burstein et al are consistent with discussions that text coherence is a complex and individual process (Graesser et al, 2004; Van den Broek, 2012), motivating our experimental method. In contrast to training annotators to follow an annotation scheme pre-determined by others, annotators devised their own scoring protocols, capturing their independent impressions – *finding their "inner-annotator.*" The practical outcomes of success of the method would be reduced front-end resources in terms of time required to (a) develop the annotation protocol and (b) train annotators. As a practical end-goal, another success criterion would be to achieve inter-annotator agreement such that classifiers could be trained, yielding *substantial* annotator-system agreement.

3 Experimental Annotation Study

Annotation scoring protocols from 2 annotators for coherence quality are evaluated and described.

3.1 Human Annotators

Two high school English teachers (employed by a company specializing in annotation) performed the annotation. Annotators never met each other, did not know about each other's activities, and only communicated about the annotation with a facilitator from the company.

3.2 Data

A random sample of 250 essays for 6 different item types (*n*=1500) and test-taker populations (Table 1) was selected. The sample was selected across 20 different prompts (test questions) for each item type in order to ensure topic generalizability in the resulting systems. Forty essays were randomly selected for a small pilot study; the remaining data (1460 essays) were used for the full annotation study. For the full study, 20% of the essays (*n*=292) had been randomly selected for double annotation to measure inter-annotator agreement; the remaining 1168 essays were evenly divided, and each annotator labeled half (*n*=584 per annotator). Each annotator labeled a total of 876 essays across the 6 task types.

3.3 Experimental Method Description

A one-week pilot study was conducted. To provide some initial grounding, annotators received a 1-page task description that offered a high-level explanation of "coherence" describing the end-points of a potential protocol. (This description was written in about an hour.) It indicated that high coherence is associated with an essay that can be *easily understood*, and low coherence is associated with an *incomprehensible* essay. Each annotator developed her own protocol: for each score point she wrote descriptive text illustrating a set of defining characteristics for each score point of coherence quality (e.g., "*The writer's point is difficult to understand.*"). Annotator 1 (A1) developed a 4-point scale;

[3] Note that this task type was administered in an instructional setting; all other tasks were completed in high-stakes assessment settings.

[4] Kappa was not reported in the paper, but was accessed through personal communication.

Feature Type	A1 (*r*)	A2 (*r*)
Grammar errors (e.g., subject verb agreement)	0.42	0.35
Word usage errors (e.g., determiner errors)	0.46	0.44
Mechanics errors (e.g., spelling, punctuation)	0.58	0.52
EGT -- best 3 features (out of 112 features): F1, F2, F3	F1. -0.30 F2. -0.28 F3. 0.27	F1. -0.14 F2. -0.15 F3. 0.11
RST features-- best 3 features (out of 100 features): F1, F2, F3	F1. -0.27 F2. 0.15 F3. 0.19	F1. -0.19 F2. 0.08 F3. 0.06
LDSP	0.19	0.06

Table 2. Pearson r between annotator discourse coherence scores and features. All correlations are significant at $p < .0001$, except for A2's long-distance sentence-pair similarity at $p < .05$.

Annotator 2 (A2) developed a 5-point scale. Because the two scales were different, κ could not be used to measure agreement, so a Spearman rank-order correlation (r_S) was used, yielding a promising value (r_S=0.82). Annotator protocols were completed at the end of the pilot study.

A full experiment was conducted. Each annotator used her protocol to assign a coherence quality score to each essay. Annotators assigned a score and wrote brief comments as explanation (drawing from the protocol). Comments provided a score supplement that could be used to support analyses beyond quantitative measures (Reidsma & Carletta, 2008). The data were annotated in 12 batches (by task) composed of 75 essays (50 unique; 25 for double annotation). A Spearman rank-order correlation was computed on the double-scored essays for completed batches. If the correlation fell below 0.70 (which was infrequent), one of the authors reviewed the annotator scores and comments to look for inconsistencies. Agreement was re-computed when annotator revisions were completed to ensure inter-rater agreement of 0.70. Annotations were completed over approximately 4 weeks to accommodate annotator schedules. While a time log was not strictly maintained, we estimate the total time for communication to resolve inconsistency issues was about 4-6 hours. One author communicated *score-comment inconsistencies* (e.g., high score with critical comments) to the company's facilitator (through a brief e-mail); the facilitator then relayed the inconsistency information to the annotator(s). The author's data review and communication e-mail took no longer than 45 minutes for the few rounds where agreement fell below 0.70. Communication between the facilitator and the annotator(s) involved a brief discussion, essentially reviewing the points made in the e-mail.

3.4 Results: Inter-annotator agreement

Using the Spearman rank-order correlation, inter-rater agreement on the double-annotated data was r_S=0.71. In order to calculate Kappa statistic, A2's 5-point scale assignments were then mapped to a 4-point scale by collapsing the two lowest categories (1,2) into one (1), since there were very few cases of 1's; this is consistent with low frequencies of very low-scoring essays. Using quadratic weighted kappa (QWK), post-mapping indicated *substantial* agreement between the two annotators (κ=0.61).

3.5 Correlational Analysis: Which Linguistic Features Did Annotators Consider?

A1 and A2 wrote brief comments explaining their coherence scores. Comments were shorthand notation drawn from their protocols (e.g., *There are significant grammatical errors...thoughts do not connect.*). Both annotators included descriptions such as "*word patterns*," "*logical sequencing*," and "*clarity of ideas*"; however, A2 appeared to have more comments related to grammar and spelling. Burstein et al., (2013) describe the following features in their binary classification system: (1) grammar, word usage, and mechanics errors (GUM), (2) rhetorical parse tree features (Marcu, 2000) (RST), (3) entity-grid transition probabilities to capture local "topic distribution" (Barzilay & Lapata, 2008) (EGT), and (4) a long-distance sentence pair similarity measure using latent semantic analysis (Foltz, 1998) to capture "long distance, topical distribution. (LDSP). Annotated data from this study were processed with the Burstein et al (2013) system to extract the features above in (1) – (4). To quantify the observed differences in the annotators' comments and potential effects for system score assignment (Section 4), we computed Pearson (*r*) correlations between the system features (on our annotated data set), and the discourse coherence scores of A1 and A2 (using the 4-point scale mapping for A2). There are 112 entity-transition probability features and 100 Rhetorical Structure Theory (RST) features. In Table 2, the correlations of the three best predictors from the EGT and RST sets, and the GUM features and the LDSP feature are shown. Correlations in Table 2 are significantly correlated between the feature sets and annotator coherence scores. However, we observed that the EGT, RST, and LDSP feature correlation values for A2 are notably smaller than A1's. This suggests that A2 may have had a strong reliance on GUM features, or that the system feature set did not capture all linguistic phenomena that A2 considered.

4 System Evaluation[5]

To evaluate the utility of the annotated data, two evaluations were conducted: one built classifiers with all system features (Sys_All), and a second with the GUM features (Sys_GUM). Using 10-fold cross-validation with a gradient boosting regression learner, four classifiers were trained to predict coherence quality ratings on a 4-point scale, using the respective annotator data sets: A1 and A2 Sys_All, and A1 and A2 Sys_GUM systems.

4.1 Results

Sys-All trained with A1 data consistently outperformed Sys-All trained with A2 data. Results are reported for averages across the 10-folds, and showed *substantial* system-human agreement for A1 (κ = 0.68) and *modest* system-human agreement for A2 (κ = 0.55). When Sys_GUM was trained with A1 data, system-human agreement dropped to a *modest* range (κ = 0.60); when Sys_GUM was trained with A2 data, however, human agreement was essentially unchanged, staying in the *modest* agreement range (κ = 0.50). Consistent with the correlational analysis, this finding suggests that A2 has strong reliance on GUM features, or the system may have been less successful in capturing A2 features beyond GUM.

5 Discussion and Conclusions

Our experimental annotation method significantly reduced front-end resources for protocol development and annotator training. Analyses reflect one genre: essays from standardized assessments. Minimal time was required from the authors or the facilitator (about two hours) for protocol development; the annotators developed personal protocols over a week during the pilot; in Burstein et al (2013), this process was report to take about one month. Approximately 4-6 hours of additional discussion from one author and the facilitator was required during the task; Burstein et al (2013) required two researchers and two annotators participated in several 4-hour training sessions, totaling about 64-80 hours of person-time across the 4 participants (personal communication). In addition to its efficiency, the experimental method was *successful* per criteria in Section 2. The method captures annotators' subjective judgments about coherence quality, yielding *substantial* inter-annotator agreement (κ=0.61) across a 4-point scale. Second, classifiers trained with annotator data showed that the systems showed *substantial* and *modest* agreement (A1 and A2, respectively) – demonstrating annotation utility, especially for A1. Correlational analyses were used to analyze effects of features that annotators may have considered in making their decisions. Comment patterns and results from the correlation analysis suggested that A2's decisions were either based on narrower considerations (GUM errors), or not captured by our feature set.

The experimental task facilitated the successful collection of subjective coherence judgments with substantial inter-annotator agreement on test-taker essays. Consistent with conclusions from Reidsma & Carletta (2008), outcomes show that quantitative measures of inter-annotator agreement should not be used exclusively. Descriptive comments were useful for monitoring *during* annotation, interpreting annotator considerations and system evaluations *during* and *after* annotation, and informing system development. In the future, we would explore strategies to evaluate intra-annotator reliability (Beigman-Klebanov, Beigman, & Diermeier, 2008) which may have contributed to lower system performance with A2 data.

---

[5] Many thanks to Binod Gywali for engineering support.

References

Beata Beigman-Klebanov, Nitin Madnani,, and Jill Burstein. 2013. Using Pivot-Based Paraphrasing and Sentiment Profiles to Improve a Subjectivity Lexicon for Essay Data, *Transactions of the Association for Computational Linguistics*, Vol.1: 99-110.

Beata Beigman-Klebanov, Eyal Beigman, and Daniel Diermeier. 2008. Analyzing Disagreements. In Proceedings of the workshop on Human Judgments in Computational Linguistics, Manchester: 2-7.

Jill Burstein, Joel Tetreault and Martin Chodorow. 2013. Holistic Annotation of Discourse Coherence Quality in Noisy Essay Writing. In the *Special issue of Dialogue and Discourse on: Beyond semantics: the challenges of annotating pragmatic and discourse phenomena* Eds. S. Dipper, H. Zinsmeister, and B. Webber. Discourse & Dialogue 42, 34-52.

Jill Burstein and Magdalena Wolska..2003. Toward Evaluation of Writing Style: Overly Repetitious Word Use. In *Proceedings of the 11th Conference of the European Chapter of the Association for Computational Linguistics*. Budapest, Hungary.

Jacob Cohen. 1960. "A coefficient of agreement for nominal scales". Educational and Psychological Measurement 20 1: 37–46.

Joseph Fleiss and Jacob Cohen 1973. "The equivalence of weighted kappa and the intraclass correlation coefficient as measures of reliability" in *Educational and Psychological Measurement*, Vol. 33:613–619.

Peter Foltz, Walter Kintsch, & Thomas Landuaer. 1998. Textual coherence using latent semantic analysis. *Discourse Processes*, 252&3: 285–307.

Arthur Graesser, Danielle McNamara, Max Louwerse. and Zhiqiang Cai, Z. 2004. Coh-metrix: Analysis of text on cohesion and language. *Behavior Research Methods, Instruments, & Computers,* 36(2), 193-202.

Derrick Higgins, Jill Burstein, Daniel Marcu &. Claudia Gentile. 2004. Evaluating Multiple Aspects of Coherence in Student Essays. In *Proceedings of 4th Annual Meeting of the Human Language Technology and North American Association for Computation Linguistics*:185–192, Boston, MA

J. Richard Landis,. & G. Koch. 1977. "The measurement of observer agreement for categorical data". *Biometrics* **33** 1: 159–174.

Annie Louis and Ani Nenkova. 2013. A Text Quality Corpus for Science Journalism. In the *Special Issue of Dialogue and Discourse on: Beyond semantics: the challenges of annotating pragmatic and discourse phenomena* Eds. S. Dipper, H. Zinsmeister, and B. Webber, 42: 87-117.

Eleni Miltsakaki and Karen Kukich. 2000. Automated evaluation of coherence in student essays. In *Proceedings of the Language Resources and Evaluation Conference*, Athens, Greece.

Daniel Marcu. 2000. *The Theory and Practice of Discourse Parsing and Summarization.* Cambridge, MA: The MIT Press.

Dennis Reidsma, and Rieks op den Akker. 2008. Exploiting `Subjective' Annotations. In *Proceedings of the Workshop on Human Judgments in Computational Linguistics*, Coling 2008, 23 August 2008, Manchester, UK.

Dennis Reidsma, and Jean Carletta. 2008. Reliability measurements without limits. *Computational Linguistics*, 343: 319-336.

Mark Shermis. to appear. State-of-the-art automated essay scoring: Competition, results, and future directions from a United States demonstration. *Assessing Writing.*

Y. Wang, M. Harrington, and P. White. 2012. Detecting Breakdowns in Local Coherence in the Writing of Chinese English Speakers. The *Journal of Computer Assisted Learning*. 28: 396–410.

Paul Van den Broek. 2012. Individual and developmental differences in reading comprehension: Assessing cognitive processes and outcomes. In: Sabatini, J.P., Albro, E.R., O'Reilly, T. (Eds.), *Measuring up: Advances in how we assess reading ability.*, pp. 39-58. Lanham: Rowman & Littlefield Education.

Optimizing annotation efforts to build reliable annotated corpora for training statistical models

Cyril Grouin[1] Thomas Lavergne[1,2] Aurélie Névéol[1]
[1] LIMSI–CNRS, 91405 Orsay, France [2] Université Paris Sud 11, 91400 Orsay, France
firstname.lastname@limsi.fr

Abstract

Creating high-quality manual annotations on text corpus is time-consuming and often requires the work of experts. In order to explore methods for optimizing annotation efforts, we study three key time burdens of the annotation process: (i) multiple annotations, (ii) consensus annotations, and (iii) careful annotations. Through a series of experiments using a corpus of clinical documents annotated for personally identifiable information written in French, we address each of these aspects and draw conclusions on how to make the most of an annotation effort.

1 Introduction

Statistical and Machine Learning methods have become prevalent in Natural Language Processing (NLP) over the past decades. These methods sucessfully address NLP tasks such as part-of-speech tagging or named entity recognition by relying on large annotated text corpora. As a result, developping high-quality annotated corpora representing natural language phenomena that can be processed by statistical tools has become a major challenge for the scientific community. Several aspects of the annotation task have been studied in order to ensure corpus quality and affordable cost. Inter-annotator agreement (IAA) has been used as an indicator of annotation quality. Early work showed that the use of automatic pre-annotation tools improved annotation consistency (Marcus et al., 1993). Careful and detailed annotation guideline definition was also shown to have positive impact on IAA (Wilbur et al., 2006).

Efforts have investigated methods to reduce the human workload while annotating corpora. In particular, active learning (Settles et al., 2008) sucessfully selects portions of corpora that yield the most benefit when annotated. Alternatively, (Dligach and Palmer, 2011) investigated the need for double annotation and found that double annotation could be limited to carefully selected portions of a corpus. They produced an algorithm that automatically selects portions of a corpus for double annotation. Their approach allowed to reduce the amount of work by limiting the portion of doubly annotated data and maintained annotation quality to the standard of a fully doubly annotated corpus. The use of automatic pre-annotations was shown to increase annotation consistency and result in producing quality annotation with a time gain over annotating raw data (Fort and Sagot, 2010; Névéol et al., 2011; Rosset et al., 2013). With the increasing use of crowdsourcing for obtaining annotated data, (Fort et al., 2011) show that there are ethic aspects to consider in addition to technical and monetary cost when using a microworking platform for annotation. While selecting the adequate methods for computing IAA is important (Artstein and Poesio, 2008) for interpreting the IAA for a particular task, annotator disagreement is inherent to all annotation tasks. To address this situation (Rzhetsky et al., 2009) designed a method to estimate annotation confidence based on annotator modeling. Overall, past work shows that creating high-quality manual annotations is time-consuming and often requires the work of experts. The time burden is distributed between the sheer creation of the annotations, the act of producing multiple annotations for the same data and the subsequent analysis of multiple annotations to resolve conflicts, viz. the creation of a consensus. Research has addressed methods for reducing the time burden associated to these annotation

LAW VIII - The 8th Linguistic Annotation Workshop, pages 54–58,
Dublin, Ireland, August 23-24 2014.

activities (for example, adequate annotation tools such as automatic pre-annotations can reduce the time burden of annotation creation) with the final goal of producing the highest quality of annotations.

In contrast, our hypothesis in this work is that annotations are being developed for the purpose of training a machine learning model. Therefore, our experiments consist in training a named entity recognizer on a training set comprising annotations of varying quality to study the impact of training annotation quality on model performance. In order to explore methods for optimizing annotation efforts for the development of training corpora, we revisit the three key time burdens of the annotation process on textual corpora: (i) careful annotations, (ii) multiple annotations, and (iii) consensus annotations. Through a series of experiments using a corpus of French clinical documents annotated for personally identifiable information (PHI), we address each of these aspects and draw conclusions on how to make the most of an annotation effort.

2 Material and methods

2.1 Annotated corpus

Experiments were conducted with a corpus of clinical documents in French annotated for 10 categories of PHI. The distribution of the categories over the corpus varies with some categories being more prevalent than others. In addition, the performance of entity recognition for each type of PHI also varies (Grouin and Névéol, 2014). The datasets were split to obtain a training corpus (200 documents) and a test corpus (100 documents). For all documents in the training corpus, three types of human annotations are available: annotations performed independently by two human annotators and consensus annotations obtained after adjudication to resolve conflicts between the two annotators. Inter-annotator agreement on the training corpus was above 85% F-measure, which is considered high (Artstein and Poesio, 2008).

The distribution of annotations over all PHI categories on both corpora (train/dev) is: address (188/100), zip code (197/97), date (1025/498), e-mail (119/57), hospital (448/208), identifier (135/76), last name (1855/855), first name (1568/724), telephone (802/386) and city (450/217).

2.2 Automatic Annotation Methods

We directly applied the MEDINA rule-based de-identification tool (Grouin, 2013) to obtain baseline automatic annotations. We used the CRF toolkit Wapiti (Lavergne et al., 2010) to train a series of models on the various sets of annotations available for the training corpus.

Features set For each CRF experiment, we used the following set of features with a $l1$ regularization:

- Lexical features: unigram and bigram of tokens;
- Morphological features: (i) the token case *(all in upper/lower case, combination of both)*, (ii) the token is a digit, (iii) the token is a punctuation mark, (iv) the token belongs to a specific list *(first name, last name, city)*, (v) the token was not identified in a dictionary of inflected forms, (vi) the token is a trigger word for specific categories *(hospital, last name)*;
- Syntactic features: (i) the part-of-speech (POS) tag of the token, as provided by the Tree Tagger tool (Schmid, 1994), (ii) the syntactic chunk the token belongs to, from a home made chunker based upon the previouses POS tags;
- External features: (i) we created 320 classes of tokens using Liang's implementation (Liang, 2005) of the Brown clustering algorithm (Brown et al., 1992), (ii) the position of the token within the document *(begining, middle, end)*.

Design of experiments The models were built to assess three annotation time-saving strategies:

1. Careful annotation: (i) AR=based on automatic annotations from the rule-based system, (ii) AR∩H2=intersection of automatic annotations from the rule-based system with annotations from annotator 2. This model captures a situation where the human annotator would quickly revise the automatic annotations by removing errors: some annotations would be missing (average recall), but the annotations present in the set would be correct (very high precision), (iii) ARH2=automatic annotations from the rule-based system, with replacement of the three most difficult categories by

annotations from annotator 2. This model captures a situation where the human annotator would focus on revising targeted categories, and (*iv*) ARHC=automatic annotations from the rule-based system, with replacement of the three most difficult categories by consensus annotations;

2. Double annotation: (*i*) H1=annotations from annotator 1, (*ii*) H2=annotations from annotator 2, (*iii*) H12=first half of the annotations from annotator 1, second half from annotator 2, and (*iv*) H21=first half of the annotations from annotator 2, second half from annotator 1;
3. Consensus annotation: (*i*) H1∪H2=all annotations from annotator 1 and 2 (concatenation without adjudication), and (*ii*) HC=consensus annotations (after adjudication between annotator 1 and 2).

3 Results

Table 1 presents an overview of the global performance of each annotation run (H12 and H21 achieved similar results) across all PHI categories in terms of precision, recall and F_1-measure (Manning and Schütze, 2000). Table 2 presents the detailed performance of each annotation run for individual PHI categories in terms of F-measure.

	Baseline	AR	AR∩H2	ARH2*	ARHC	H1*	H12	H1∪H2	H2	HC
Precision	.820	.868	.920	.942	.943	.959	.962	.969	.974	.974
Recall	.806	.796	.763	.854	.854	.927	.934	.935	.936	.942
F-measure	.813	.830	.834	.896	.896	.943	.948	.951	.955	.958

Table 1: Overall performance for all automatic PHI detection. A star indicates statistically significant difference in F-measure over the previous model (Wilcoxon test, $p<0.05$)

Category	Baseline	AR	AR∩H2	ARH2	ARHC	H1	H12	H1∪H2	H2	HC
Address	.648	.560	.000	.800	.800	.716	.744	.789	.795	.791
Zip code	.950	.958	.947	.964	.958	.974	.984	.974	.984	.990
Date	.958	.968	.962	.963	.967	.965	.963	.963	.959	.970
E-mail	.937	.927	.927	.927	.927	1.000	1.000	1.000	1.000	1.000
Hospital	.201	.248	.039	.856	.868	.789	.809	.856	.861	.867
Identifier	.000	.000	.000	.762	.797	.870	.892	.823	.836	.876
Last name	.816	.810	.834	.832	.828	.953	.957	.954	.961	.963
First name	.849	.858	.900	.901	.902	.960	.956	.961	.965	.960
Telephone	1.000	.980	.978	.983	.980	.987	.994	.999	.999	1.000
City	.869	.874	.883	.887	.887	.948	.972	.962	.965	.972

Table 2: Performance per PHI category (F-measure)

4 Discussion

4.1 Model performance

Overall, the task of automatic PHI recognition has been well studied and the rule-based tool provides a strong baseline with .813 F-measure on the test set. Table 1 shows that there are three different types of models, in terms of performance: the lower-performing category corresponds to models with no human input. The next category corresponds to models with some human input, and the higher-performing models correspond to models with the most human input. This reflects the expectation that model performance increases with training corpus quality. However, it also shows that, within the two categories that include human input, there is no statistical difference in model performance with respect to the type of human input. We observed that the model trained on annotations from the H2 human annotator performed better (F=0.955) than the model trained on annotations from the H1 annotator (F=0.943). This observation reflects the agreement of the annotators with consensus annotations, where H2 had higher agreement than H1 (Grouin and Névéol, 2014). This is also true at the category level: H2 achieved higher agreement with the consensus compared to H1 on categories "address" (F=0.985>0.767) and "hospital" (F=0.947>0.806) but H2 had lower agreement with the consensus on the category "identifier" (F=0.840<0.933).

4.2 Error Analysis

The performance of CRF models depends on the size of the training corpus and the level of diversity of the mentions. Error analysis on our test data shows that a few specific mentions are not tagged in the test corpus, even though they occur in the training corpus. For example, some hospital names occur in the clinical narratives either as acronyms or as full forms (e.g. "GWH" for "George Washington Hospital" in *transfer patient from GWH*). The acronyms are overall much less prevalent than the full forms and also happen to be difficult to identify for human annotators (depending on the context, a given acronym could refer to either a medical procedure, a physician or a hospital). We observed that the only hospital acronym present in the test corpus was not annotated by any of the CRF models. Nevertheless, only five occurrences of this acronym were found in the training corpus which is not enough for the CRF to learn.

Other errors occur in recognizing sequences of doctors' names that appear without separators in signatures lines at the end of documents (e.g. "*Jane BROWN John DOE Mary SMITH*"). In our test set we observed that models trained on automatic annotations correctly predicted the beginning of such sequences and then produced erroneous predictions for the rest of the sequence (models AR, AR∩H2, ARHC and ARH2). In contrast, models built on human annotations produced correct predictions on the entire sequence (models H1, H12, H1∪H2, H2 and HC). Similarly, for last names containing a nobiliary particle, the models trained on automatic annotations only identified part of the last name as a PHI. We also observed that spelling errors (e.g. "*Jhn DOE*") only resulted in correct predictions from the models trained on the human annotations. We did not find cases where the models built on the automatic annotations performed better than the models built on the human annotations.

4.3 Annotation strategy

Table 1 indicates that for the purpose of training a machine learning entity recognizer, all types of human input are equivalent. In practice, this means that double annotations or consensus annotations are not necessary. The high inter-annotator agreement on our dataset may be a contributing factor for this finding. Indeed, (Esuli et al., 2013) found that with low inter-annotator agreement, models are biased towards the annotation style of the annotator who produced the training data. Therefore, we believe that inter-annotator should be established on a small dataset before annotators work independently. Table 2 shows that using human annotations for selected categories results in strong improvement of the performance over these categories ("address", "hospital" and "identifier" categories in ARHC and ARH2 vs. AR) with little impact on the performance of the model on other categories. Therefore, careful human annotations are not necessarily needed for the entire corpus. Targeting "hard" categories for human annotations can be a good time-saving strategy. While the difference between the models using some human input vs. all human input is statistically significant, the performance gain is lower than between models without human input and some human input. Using data with partial human input for training statistical models can cut annotation cost.

5 Conclusion and future work

Herein we have shown that full double annotation of a corpus is not necessary for the purpose of training a competitive CRF-based model. Our results suggest that a three-step annotation strategy can optimize the annotation effort: (i) double annotate a small subset of the corpus to ensure human annotators understand the guidelines; (ii) have annotators work independently on different sections of the corpus to obtain wide coverage; and (iii) train a machine-learning based model on the human annotations and apply this model on a new dataset.

In future work, we plan to re-iterate these experiments on a different type of entity recognition task where inter-annotator agreement may be more difficult to achieve, and may vary more between categories in order to investigate the influence of inter-annotator-agreement on our conclusions.

Acknowledgements

This work was supported by the French National Agency for Research under grant CABeRneT[1] ANR-13-JS02-0009-01 and by the French National Agency for Medicines and Health Products Safety under grant Vigi4MED[2] ANSM-2013-S-060.

References

Ron Artstein and Massimo Poesio. 2008. Inter-coder agreement for computational linguistics. *Computational Linguistics*, 34(4):555–596.

Peter F Brown, Vincent J Della Pietra, Peter V de Souza, Jenifer C Lai, and Robert L Mercer. 1992. Class-based n-gram models of natural language. *Computational Linguistics*, 18(4):467–79.

Dmitriy Dligach and Martha Palmer. 2011. Reducing the need for double annotation. In *Proc of Linguistic Annotation Workshop (LAW)*, pages 65–73. Association for Computational Linguistics.

Andrea Esuli, Diego Marcheggiani, and Fabrizio Sebastiani. 2013. An enhanced CRFs-based system for information extraction from radiology reports. *J Biomed Inform*, 46(3):425–35, Jun.

Karën Fort and Benoît Sagot. 2010. Influence of pre-annotation on POS-tagged corpus development. In *Proc of Linguistic Annotation Workshop (LAW)*, pages 56–63. Association for Computational Linguistics.

Karën Fort, Gilles Adda, and Kevin Bretonnel Cohen. 2011. Amazon Mechanical Turk: Gold Mine or Coal Mine? *Computational Linguistics*, pages 413–420.

Cyril Grouin and Aurélie Névéol. 2014. De-identification of clinical notes in french: towards a protocol for reference corpus development. *J Biomed Inform.*

Cyril Grouin. 2013. *Anonymisation de documents cliniques : performances et limites des méthodes symboliques et par apprentissage statistique*. Ph.D. thesis, University Pierre et Marie Curie, Paris, France.

Thomas Lavergne, Olivier Cappé, and François Yvon. 2010. Practical very large scale CRFs. In *Proceedings the 48th Annual Meeting of the Association for Computational Linguistics (ACL)*, pages 504–513. Association for Computational Linguistics.

Percy Liang. 2005. Semi-supervised learning for natural language. Master's thesis, MIT.

Chiristopher D. Manning and Hinrich Schütze. 2000. *Foundations of Statistical Natural Language Processing*. MIT Press, Cambridge, Massachusetts.

Mitchell P Marcus, Mary Ann Marcinkiewicz, and Beatrice Santorini. 1993. Building a large annotated corpus of English: the Penn TreeBank. *Computational Linguistics*, 19(2):313–330.

Aurélie Névéol, Rezarta Islamaj Doğan, and Zhiyong Lu. 2011. Semi-automatic semantic annotation of PubMed queries: a study on quality, efficiency, satisfaction. *J Biomed Inform*, 44(2):310–8.

Sophie Rosset, Cyril Grouin, Thomas Lavergne, Mohamed Ben Jannet, Jérémy Leixa, Olivier Galibert, and Pierre Zweigenbaum. 2013. Automatic named entity pre-annotation for out-of-domain human annotation. In *Proc of Linguistic Annotation Workshop (LAW)*, pages 168–177. Association for Computational Linguistics.

Andrey Rzhetsky, Hagit Shatkay, and W John Wilbur. 2009. How to get the most out of your curation effort. *PLoS Comput Biol*, 5(5):e1000391.

Helmut Schmid. 1994. Probabilistic part-of-speech tagging using decision trees. In *Proc of International Conference on New Methods in Language*.

Burr Settles, Mark Craven, and Lewis Friedland. 2008. Active learning with real annotation costs. In *Proc of the NIPS Workshop on Cost-Sensitive Learning*.

W John Wilbur, Andrey Rzhetsky, and Hagit Shatkay. 2006. New directions in biomedical text annotation: definitions, guidelines and corpus construction. *BMC Bioinformatics*, 25(7):356.

[1]CABeRneT: Compréhension Automatique de Textes Biomédicaux pour la Recherche Translationnelle
[2]Vigi4MED: Vigilance dans les forums sur les Médicaments

A Web-based Geo-resolution Annotation and Evaluation Tool

Beatrice Alex, Kate Byrne, Claire Grover and Richard Tobin
School of Informatics
University of Edinburgh
{balex,kbyrne3,grover,richard}@inf.ed.ac.uk

Abstract

In this paper we present the Edinburgh Geo-annotator, a web-based annotation tool for the manual geo-resolution of location mentions in text using a gazetteer. The annotation tool has an inter-linked text and map interface which lets annotators pick correct candidates within the gazetteer more easily. The geo-annotator can be used to correct the output of a geoparser or to create gold standard geo-resolution data. We include accompanying scoring software for geo-resolution evaluation.

1 Introduction

Many kinds of digitised content have an important geospatial dimension. However not all geospatial information is immediately accessible, particularly in the case where it is implicit in place names in text. The process of geo-resolution (also often referred to as geo-referencing, geoparsing or geotagging) links instances of textual geographic information to location coordinates, enabling searching and linking of digital content using its geospatial properties.

Geo-resolution tools can never be completely accurate and their performance can vary significantly depending on the type and quality of the input texts as well as on the gazetteer resources they consult. For this reason, users of text collections are frequently disappointed in the results of geo-resolution and, depending on their application and dataset size, they may decide to take remedial action to improve the quality. The tool we describe here is a web-based, manual annotation tool which can be used to correct the output of geo-resolution. It has been developed in step with our geo-resolution system, the Edinburgh Geoparser (Grover et al., 2010), but it could also be used to correct the output of other tools. In our work, we use the geo-annotator to create gold-standard material for geo-resolution evaluation and have produced accompanying scoring software.[1]

2 Related Work

Within the field of NLP, SpatialML is probably the best known work in the area of geo-referencing. SpatialML is an annotation scheme for marking up natural language references to places and grounding them to coordinates. The SpatialML corpus (Mani et al., 2008) instantiates this annotation scheme and can be used as an evaluation corpus for geo-resolution (Tobin et al., 2010). Other researchers develop their own geo-annotated corpora and evaluate against these, e.g. Clough (2005), Leidner (2007).

Within the field of Information Retrieval, there is an ACM special interest group on spatially-related information, SIGSPATIAL[2], with regular geographic IR conferences (GIR conferences) where geo-referencing research is presented, see for example Purves et al. (2007).

There are currently several geoparsing tools available, such as GeoLocate[3], and CLAVIN[4], as well as our own tool, the Edinburgh Geoparser. All of these enable users to geo-reference text collections but do

[1] The Edinburgh Geo-annotator will be available at http://www.ltg.ed.ac.uk.
[2] http://www.sigspatial.org/
[3] http://www.museum.tulane.edu/geolocate/
[4] http://clavin.bericotechnologies.com/

LAW VIII - The 8th Linguistic Annotation Workshop, pages 59–63,
Dublin, Ireland, August 23-24 2014.

not address the question of how to interact with the geo-annotations in order to correct them, nor do they assist in creating evaluation materials for particular text collections.

The Edinburgh Geo-annotator has been developed in tandem with the Edinburgh Geoparser and earlier versions have been used in the GeoDigRef project (Grover et al., 2010) to create evaluation data for historical text collections as well as in the botanical domain (Llewellyn et al., 2012; Llewellyn et al., 2011) where we adapted it to allow curators to geo-reference the textual metadata associated with herbarium specimens. The current version has also been used to create gold standard data for Trading Consequences, a historical text mining project on mining location-centric trading information relevant to the nineteenth century (Klein et al., 2014). The Pelagios project, which deals with texts about the ancient world, has recently developed Recogito[5], a geo-resolution correction tool similar to our own.

3 Annotation Tool

The Edinburgh Geo-annotator is a geo-resolution annotation tool which can be used to correct geo-resolution output or to create manually annotated gold standard data for evaluating geo-resolution algorithms and tools. The geo-annotator has a web-based interface allowing easy off-site annotation in inter-disciplinary projects by domain experts (who are not always necessarily the developers of the geo-referencing software).[6] The interface allows users to select documents from a collection of prepared files containing annotated location entity mentions. By selecting and loading a document, the user can see its textual content and the location mentions highlighted within it.

The current tool is set up to select locations from a set of location candidates retrieved from GeoNames and visualised by pins on a Google Maps (v3) window. However, it can be configured to use candidates from a different location gazetteer. There are two files associated with each document: (1) an HTML file which contains the text of the document and (2) an XML file which contains the candidates for each location mention in the text and in which the annotations are stored. Candidates are linked to location mentions via identifiers.

All location mentions displayed in the text interface are highlighted in colour (see Figure 1). Those in red (e.g. Dublin) have one or more potential candidates in the gazetteer, while those in blue (e.g. British Empire) do not have candidate entries in the gazetteer. There are a number of reasons why a mention does not have a gazetteer entry. For example, the mention might be an old name of a location which is not stored in the gazetteer, or the mention contains a misspelling. During the annotation phase, the user is instructed to go through the red location mentions in the text and select the appropriate candidate.

In some cases there is only one candidate that can be selected (see Figure 2). The user can zoom to the correct location pin which when selected shows a popup with the relevant gazetteer information for that entry. The user can choose this candidate by pressing either "Select for this mention" if the choice is specific to the selected mention or "Select for all mentions" if the selection can be propagated for all mentions with the same string in the document. Once a pin is selected, it and the location mention in the text turn green. To undo a selection, the user can click on a green pin and press either "Deselect for this mention" or "Deselect for all mentions".

In other cases, there are many candidates to choose from. For example, when clicking on the first location mention (Dublin) shown in Figure 1, the map adjusts to the central point of all 42 candidate locations. When reading a piece of text, human beings can often easily understand which location a place name refers to based on the context it appears in, which means that choosing between multiple candidates manually is not expected to be a difficult task. However, the number of location candidates that are suggested by GeoNames and consequently displayed in the interface can be limited in the data files, if for example the user only wants to choose between a small number of candidates.

In the case of Dublin (see Figure 1), the user would then zoom into the correct Dublin to select a candidate and discover that there are two pins which are relevant, *Dublin* – the capital, and *Baile Átha Cliath* – the Gaelic name for Dublin and its gazetteer entry referring to the administrative division (see Figure 3). The gazetteer information in the popup can assist the user to make a choice. In this case, it is clear from the context that the text refers to the capital. It might not always be as clearcut to choose

[5] http://pelagios-project.blogspot.co.at/2014/01/from-bordeaux-to-jerusalem-and-back.html

[6] The geo-annotator is run via a javascript programme which calls an update.cgi script on the server side to write the saved data to file. We have tested it in Safari, Firefox and Chrome.

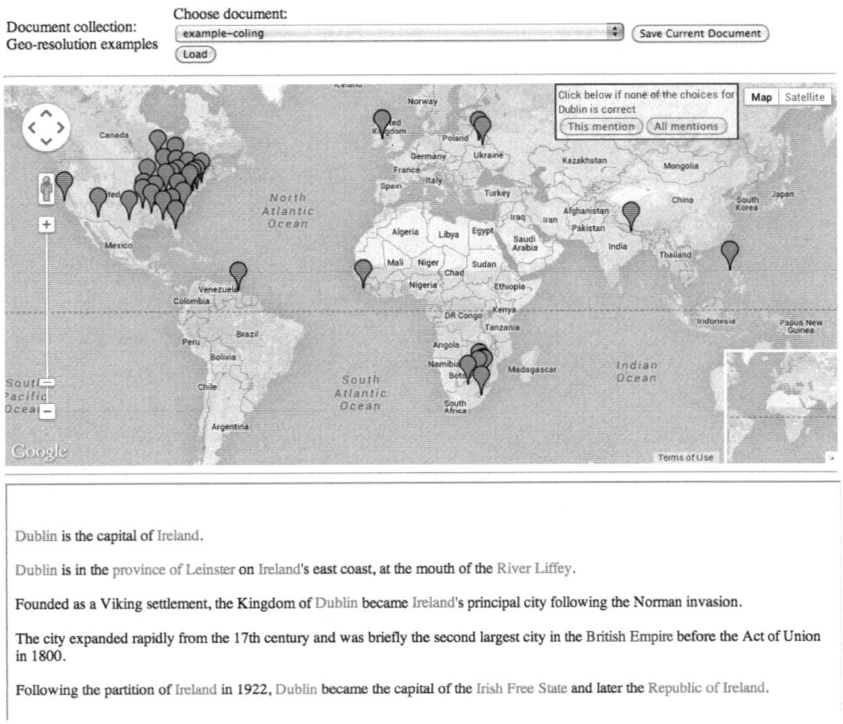

Figure 1: When an example location mention (e.g. Dublin) is clicked the map adjusts to show all potential location candidates that exist in the gazetteer for this place name.

between multiple candidates. In such cases, it is important that the annotation guidelines provide detailed instruction as to which type of gazetteer entry to prefer.

If none of the candidates displayed on the map are correct, then the user must mark this by pressing "This mention" (or "All mentions") in the box located at the top of right corner of the map (see Figure 1). Once there are only green or blue location mentions left in the text, the annotation for the selected document is complete and the user should press "Save Current Document" and move to the next document in the collection.

4 Geo-resolution Evaluation

It is important to be able to report the quality of a geo-resolver's performance in concrete and quantifiable terms. Along with the annotation tool, we are therefore also releasing an evaluation script which compares the manually geo-resolved locations to those predicted by an automatic geoparser.[7] We follow standard practice in comparing system output to hand-annotated gold standard evaluation data. The script evaluates the performance of the geo-resolution independently from geo-tagging, meaning that it only considers named entities which were tagged in the input to the manual geo-resolution annotation but not those that were missed. It is therefore preferable to use input data which contains manually annotated or corrected location mentions.

The evaluation script computes the number of correctly geo-resolved locations and accuracy in percent. Both figures are presented for a strict evaluation of exact match against gazetteer identifier and for a lax evaluation where the grid references of the gold and the system choice have to occur within a small distance of one another to count as a match. For a pair of location candidates (gold vs. system), we compute the Great-circle distance using a special case of the Vincenty formula which is most accurate for all distances.[8] The lax evaluation is provided as even with clear annotation guidelines, annotators

[7]We provide Mac and Linux binaries of the evaluation scripts.

[8]For the exact formula, see: `http://en.wikipedia.org/wiki/Great-circle_distance`

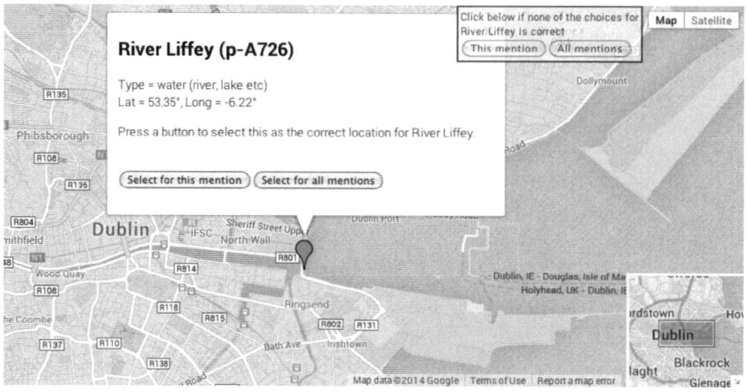

Figure 2: Example candidate for the location mention *River Liffey* and its gazetteer entry information shown in a popup.

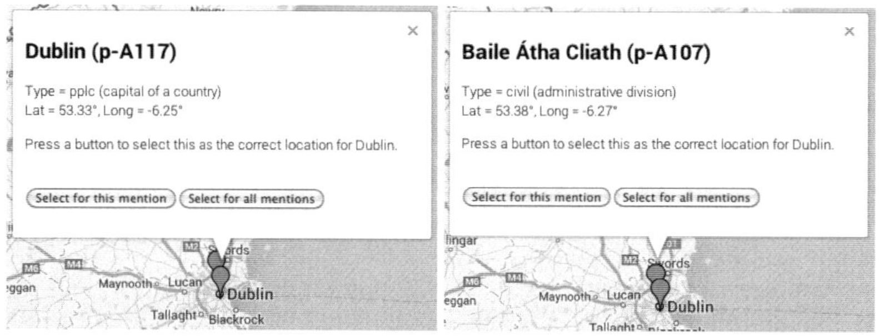

Figure 3: Choosing between multiple candidates for the same location mention.

can find it difficult to chose between different location types for essentially the same place (e.g. see the example for Dublin in Figure 3).

During the manual annotation, three special cases can arise. Some location mentions do not have a candidate in the gazetteer (those appearing in blue), while others do have candidates in the gazetteer but the annotator does not consider any of them correct. Occasionally there are location mentions with one or more candidates in the gazetteer but an annotator neither chooses one of them nor selects "none". The latter cases are considered to be annotation errors, usually because the annotator has forgotten to resolve them. The evaluation excludes all three cases when computing accuracy scores but notes them in the evaluation report in order to facilitate error analysis (see sample output in Figure 4).

```
total: 11    exact: 10 (90.9\%)    within 6.0km 11 (100.0\%)
note: no gold choice for British Empire
note: annotator selected "none" for Irish Free State
```

Figure 4: Sample output of the geo-resolution evaluation script. When setting the lax evaluation to 6km, one candidate selected by the system was close enough to the gold candidate to count as a match.

5 Summary

We have presented a web-based manual geo-resolution annotation and evaluation tool which we are releasing to the research community to facilitate correction of automatic geo-resolution output and evaluation of geo-resolution algorithms and techniques. In this paper we introduce the annotation tool and its main functionalities and describe two geo-resolution evaluation metrics with an example, namely strict and lax accuracy scoring. The release will contain more detailed documentation of the configuration and installation process and the document formats for the textual input and candidate gazetteer entries.

References

Paul Clough. 2005. Extracting metadata for spatially-aware information retrieval on the internet. In *Proceedings of Workshop on Geographic Information Retrieval (GIR'05)*.

Claire Grover, Richard Tobin, Kate Byrne, Matthew Woollard, James Reid, Stuart Dunn, and Julian Ball. 2010. Use of the Edinburgh geoparser for georeferencing digitised historical collections. *Phil. Trans. R. Soc. A*.

Ewan Klein, Beatrice Alex, Claire Grover, Richard Tobin, Colin Coates, Jim Clifford, Aaron Quigley, Uta Hinrichs, James Reid, Nicola Osborne, and Ian Fieldhouse. 2014. Digging Into Data White Paper: Trading Consequences.

Jochen L. Leidner. 2007. *Toponym Resolution in Text: Annotation, Evaluation and Applications of Spatial Grounding of Place Names*. Ph.D. thesis, School of Informatics, University of Edinburgh.

Clare Llewellyn, Elspeth Haston, and Claire Grover. 2011. Georeferencing botanical data using text analysis tools. In *Proceedings of the Biodiversity Information Standards Annual Conference (TDWG 2011)*.

Clare Llewellyn, Claire Grover, Jon Oberlander, and Elspeth Haston. 2012. Enhancing the curation of botanical data using text analysis tools. In Panayiotis Zaphiris, George Buchanan, Edie Rasmussen, and Fernando Loizides, editors, *Theory and Practice of Digital Libraries*, volume 7489 of *Lecture Notes in Computer Science*, pages 480–485. Springer Berlin Heidelberg.

Inderjeet Mani, Janet Hitzeman, Justin Richer, Dave Harris, Rob Quimby, and Ben Wellner. 2008. SpatialML: Annotation scheme, corpora, and tools. In *Proceedings of the Sixth International Language Resources and Evaluation (LREC'08)*.

Ross S. Purves, Paul Clough, Christopher B. Jones, Avi Arampatzis, Benedicte Bucher, David Finch, Gaihua Fu, Hideo Joho, Awase Khirni Syed, Subodh Vaid, and Bisheng Yang. 2007. The design and implementation of SPIRIT: a spatially-aware search engine for information retrieval on the internet. *International Journal of Geographic Information Systems (IJGIS)*, 21(7).

Richard Tobin, Claire Grover, Kate Byrne, James Reid, and Jo Walsh. 2010. Evaluation of georeferencing. In *Proceedings of Workshop on Geographic Information Retrieval (GIR'10)*.

Annotating Uncertainty in Hungarian Webtext

Veronika Vincze[1,2], Katalin Ilona Simkó[1], Viktor Varga[1]
[1]University of Szeged
Department of Informatics
[2]MTA-SZTE Research Group on Artificial Intelligence
`vinczev@inf.u-szeged.hu`
`{kata.simko,viktor.varga.1991}@gmail.com`

Abstract

Uncertainty detection has been a popular topic in natural language processing, which manifested in the creation of several corpora for English. Here we show how the annotation guidelines originally developed for English standard texts can be adapted to Hungarian webtext. We annotated a small corpus of Facebook posts for uncertainty phenomena and we illustrate the main characteristics of such texts, with special regard to uncertainty annotation. Our results may be exploited in adapting the guidelines to other languages or domains and later on, in the construction of automatic uncertainty detectors.

1 Background

Detecting uncertainty in natural language texts has received a considerable amount of attention in the last decade (Farkas et al., 2010; Morante and Sporleder, 2012). Several manually annotated corpora have been created, which serve as training and test databases of state-of-the-art uncertainty detectors based on supervised machine learning techniques. Most of these corpora are constructed for English, however, their domains and genres are diverse: biological texts (Medlock and Briscoe, 2007; Kim et al., 2008; Settles et al., 2008; Shatkay et al., 2008; Vincze et al., 2008; Nawaz et al., 2010), clinical texts (Uzuner et al., 2009), pieces of news (Saurí and Pustejovsky, 2009; Wilson, 2008; Rubin et al., 2005; Rubin, 2010), encyclopedia texts (Ganter and Strube, 2009; Farkas et al., 2010; Szarvas et al., 2012; Vincze, 2013), reviews (Konstantinova et al., 2012; Cruz Díaz, 2013) and tweets (Wei et al., 2013) have been annotated for uncertainty, just to mention a few examples.

The diversity of the resources also manifests in the fact that the annotation principles behind the corpora might slightly differ, which led Szarvas et al. (2012) to compare the annotation schemes of three corpora (BioScope, FactBank and WikiWeasel) and they offered a unified classification of semantic uncertainty phenomena, on the basis of which these corpora were reannotated, using uniform guidelines. Some other uncertainty-related linguistic phenomena are described as discourse-level uncertainty in Vincze (2013). As a first objective of our paper, we will carry out a pilot study and investigate how these unified guidelines can be adapted to texts written in a language that is typologically different from English, namely, Hungarian.

As a second goal, we will also focus on annotating texts in a new domain: social media texts – apart from Wei et al. (2013) – have not been extensively investigated from the uncertainty detection perspective. As the use and communication through the internet is becoming more and more important in people's lives, the huge amount of data available from this domain is a valuable source of information for computation linguistics. However, processing texts from the web – especially social media texts from blogs, status updates, chat logs and comments – revealed that they are very challenging for applications trained on standard texts. Most studies in this area focus on English, for instance, sentiment analysis from tweets has been the focus of recent challenges (Wilson et al., 2013) and Facebook posts have been analysed from the perspective of computational psychology (Celli et al., 2013). A syntactically

LAW VIII - The 8th Linguistic Annotation Workshop, pages 64–69,
Dublin, Ireland, August 23-24 2014.

annotated treebank of webtext has been also created for English (Bies et al., 2012). However, methods developed for processing English webtext require serious alterations to be applicable to other languages, for example Hungarian, which is very different from English syntactically and morphologically. Thus, in our pilot study we will annotate Hungarian webtext for uncertainty and examine the possible effects of the domain and the language on uncertainty detection.

In the following, we will present the uncertainty categories that were annotated in Hungarian webtext and we will illustrate the difficulties of both annotating Hungarian webtext and annotating uncertainty phenomena in them.

2 Uncertainty Categories

Here we just briefly summarize uncertainty categories that we applied in the annotation, based on Szarvas et al. (2012) and Vincze (2013).

Linguistic uncertainty is related to modality and the semantics of the sentence. For instance, the sentence *It may be raining* does not contain enough information to determine whether it is really raining (semantic uncertainty). There are several phenomena that are categorized as semantic uncertainty. A proposition is **epistemically** uncertain if its truth value cannot be determined on the basis of world knowledge. **Conditionals** and **investigations** also belong to this group – the latter is characteristic of research papers, where research questions usually express this type of uncertainty. Non-epistemic types of modality are also be listed here such as **doxastic** uncertainty, which is related to beliefs.

However, there are other linguistic phenomena that only become uncertain within the context of communication. For instance, the sentence *Many people think that Dublin is the best city in the world* does not reveal who exactly think that, hence the source of the proposition about Dublin remains uncertain. This is a type of discourse-level uncertainty, more specifically, it is called **weasel** (Ganter and Strube, 2009). On the other hand, **hedges** make the meaning of words fuzzy: they blur the exact meaning of some quality/quantity. Finally, **peacock** cues express unprovable evaluations, qualifications, understatements and exaggerations.

The above categories proved to be applicable to Hungarian texts as well. However, the morphologically rich nature of Hungarian required some slight changes in the annotation process. For instance, modal auxiliaries like *may* correspond to a derivational suffix in Hungarian, which required that in the case of *jöhet* "may come" the whole word was annotated as uncertain, not just the suffix *-het*.

3 Annotating Hungarian Webtext

Annotating uncertainty in webtexts comes with the usual difficulties of working with this domain. We annotated Hungarian posts and comments from Facebook, which made the uncertainty annotation more challenging than on standard texts. Texts were randomly selected from the public posts available at the Facebook-sites of some well-known brands (like mobile companies, electronic devices, nutrition expert companies etc.) and from the comments that users made on these posts. For our pilot annotation, we used 1373 sentences and 18,327 tokens (as provided by magyarlanc, a linguistic preprocessing toolkit developed for standard Hungarian texts (Zsibrita et al., 2013)).

One fundamental property of social media texts is their similarity to oral communication despite their written form. The communication is online and multimodal; its speed causing a number of possibilities for error. The quick typing makes typos, abbreviations and lack of capitalization, punctuation and accentuated letters more common in these texts. Accentuated and unaccentuated vowels represent different sounds in Hungarian that can change the meaning of words (*kerek* "round", *kerék* "wheel" and *kérek* "I want"). Other types of linguistic creativity are also common, such as the use of emoticons and English words and abbreviations in Hungarian texts. However, these attributes do not characterize social media texts homogeneously. For instance, blog posts are closer to standard texts since they are usually written by a PR expert from the side of the brand, who presumably spends more time with elaborating on the text of the posts than an average user. On the other hand, comments and chat texts are closer to oral communication because users here want to react as quickly as possible, making them harder to analyze.

Our corpus of Facebook posts and comments exhibited a number of these properties. It contained a lot of typos, abbreviations and letters that should have been accentuated. These sometimes caused interpretation problems even for the human annotators; especially as these posts and comments were annotated without broader context. Lack of capitalization and punctuation was more common in the comment section of the corpus than in the posts. Emoticons were also frequent in both parts of the corpus.

Example 1: Typos in our corpus.

ugya ilynem *van csak fekete* ***elől*** *és szürke* ***hátúl*** – original

ugyanilyenem van csak fekete **elöl** és szürke **hátul** – standardized

(same.kind-POSS1SG have but black front and grey back)

"I have the same kind but its front is black and its back is grey."

Example 2: Abbreviation in our corpus.

Amúgy meg ***sztem*** *Nektek nem kellene a Saját oldalatokon magyarázkodni!* – original

Amúgy meg **szerintem** Nektek nem kellene a saját oldalatokon magyarázkodni! – standardized

(by.the.way PART according.to-POSS1SG you-DAT not should the own site-POSS3PL-SUP explain.yourselves-INF)

"By the way I think you should not be explaining yourselves on your own site."

Example 3: Lack of accentuation in our corpus.

es Marai Sandornak is ma van a szuletesnapja. – original

és Márai Sándornak is ma van a születésnapja. – standardized

(and Márai Sándor-GEN also today has the birthday-POSS3SG)

"And today is also Márai Sándor's birthday"

4 Uncertainty in Hungarian Webtext

Apart from the above mentioned usual problems when dealing with webtext, other difficulties emerged during their uncertainty annotation. Uncertainty is often related to opinions, but writers of these texts do not usually express these as opinions, but as factual elements. Linguistic uncertainty is not annotated in these cases, as these sentences do not hold uncertain meanings semantically, even if certain facts in them are clearly not true or at least the writers obviously lack evidence to back them up.

Example 4: Information without evidence in our corpus.

Új megfigyelés, hogy az elektronok úgy viselkednek, mint az antioxidánsok.

(new observation that the electrons that.way behave as the antioxidants)

"It is a new observation that electrons behave as antioxidants."

The uncertainty annotation of this text differed greatly from our corpus of Hungarian Wikipedia articles and news (Vincze, 2014), which domains are much closer to standard language use. Table 1 shows the distribution of the different types of uncertainty cues in these domains. Comparing this new subcorpus with the other two shows certain domain specific characteristics. Unlike Facebook posts and comments, the other two domains should not contain subjective opinions according to the objective nature of news media and encyclopedias. This is consistent with the difference in the proportion of peacock cues in each subcorpus: Facebook posts abound in them but their number is low in the other types of texts.

The relatively small number of hedges and epistemic uncertainty may be attributed to the previously mentioned observation that the writers of these posts and comments often make confident statements, even if these are not actual facts.

The resemblance of Facebook posts and comments to oral communication also means that elements that could also signify uncertainty can have different uses in this context. Certain phrases may indicate politeness or other pragmatic functions that in a different domain would mean and be annotated as linguistic uncertainty.

Example 5: The use of uncertain elements for politeness reasons in our corpus.

sajnos úgy tűnik a futáraink valamiért valóban nem érkeztek meg hozzátok szombaton

(unfortunately that.way seems the carriers-POSS1PL something-CAU really not arrive-PAST-3PL you-ALL Saturday-SUP)

"Unfortunately it seems like our carriers did not get to you on Saturday for some reason."

The phrase *úgy tűnik* "it seems" can express uncertainty in some contexts, but in the above example, it is used as a marker of politeness, in order to apologize for and mitigate the inconvenience they caused to their customers by not delivering some package in time.

Uncertainty cue	**Wikipedia**		**News**		**Webtext**	
	#	%	#	%	#	%
Weasel	1801	32.02	258	10.93	50	9.72
Hedge	2098	37.3	799	33.86	147	28.59
Peacock	787	14	94	3.98	192	37.35
Discourse-level total	4686	83.3	1151	48.77	389	75.6
Epistemic	439	7.8	358	15.16	21	4.08
Doxastic	315	5.6	710	30.08	44	8.56
Conditional	154	2.74	128	5.42	59	11.47
Investigation	31	0.55	13	0.55	1	0.19
Semantic total	939	16.69	1209	51.22	125	24.3
Total	5625	100	2360	100	514	100

Table 1: Uncertainty cues.

5 Conclusions

In this paper, we focused on annotating Hungarian Facebook posts and comments for uncertainty phenomena. We adapted guidelines proposed for uncertainty annotation of standard English texts to Hungarian, and we also showed that this domain exhibit certain characteristics which are not present in other domains that are more similar to standard language use. First, users usually express their opinions as facts, thus relatively less markers of hedges or epistemic uncertainty occur in the corpus. Second, uncertainty cue candidates can fulfill politeness functions, and apparently they do not signal uncertainty in these contexts. Third, the characteristics of webtext may cause difficulties in annotation since in some cases, the meaning of the text is vague due to typos or other errors.

Our pilot study of annotating Hungarian webtext for uncertainty leads us to conclude that the annotation guidelines are mostly applicable to Hungarian as well and webtexts also exhibit the same uncertainty categories as more standard texts, although the distribution of uncertainty categories differ among different types of text. Besides, politeness factors should get more attention in this domain. Our results may be employed in adapting annotation guidelines of uncertainty to other languages or domains as well. Later on, we would like to extend our corpus and we would like to implement machine learning methods to automatically detect uncertainty in Hungarian webtext, for which these findings will be most probably fruitfully exploited.

Acknowledgements

This research was funded in part by the European Union and the European Social Fund through the project FuturICT.hu (grant no.: TÁMOP-4.2.2.C-11/1/KONV-2012-0013). Veronika Vincze was partially funded by the National Excellence Program TÁMOP-4.2.4.A/2-11/1-2012-0001 of the State of Hungary, co-financed by the European Social Fund.

References

Ann Bies, Justin Mott, Colin Warner, and Seth Kulick. 2012. English Web Treebank. Linguistic Data Consortium, Philadelphia.

Fabio Celli, Fabio Pianesi, David Stilwell, and Michal Kosinski. 2013. Extracting evaluative conditions from online reviews: Toward enhancing opinion mining. In *Workshop on Computational Personality Recognition*, Boston, July.

Noa P. Cruz Díaz. 2013. Detecting negated and uncertain information in biomedical and review texts. In *Proceedings of the Student Research Workshop associated with RANLP 2013*, pages 45–50, Hissar, Bulgaria, September. RANLP 2013 Organising Committee.

Richárd Farkas, Veronika Vincze, György Móra, János Csirik, and György Szarvas. 2010. The CoNLL-2010 Shared Task: Learning to Detect Hedges and their Scope in Natural Language Text. In *Proceedings of the Fourteenth Conference on Computational Natural Language Learning (CoNLL-2010): Shared Task*, pages 1–12, Uppsala, Sweden, July. Association for Computational Linguistics.

Viola Ganter and Michael Strube. 2009. Finding Hedges by Chasing Weasels: Hedge Detection Using Wikipedia Tags and Shallow Linguistic Features. In *Proceedings of the ACL-IJCNLP 2009 Conference Short Papers*, pages 173–176, Suntec, Singapore, August. Association for Computational Linguistics.

Jin-Dong Kim, Tomoko Ohta, and Jun'ichi Tsujii. 2008. Corpus annotation for mining biomedical events from literature. *BMC Bioinformatics*, 9(Suppl 10).

Natalia Konstantinova, Sheila C.M. de Sousa, Noa P. Cruz, Manuel J. Mana, Maite Taboada, and Ruslan Mitkov. 2012. A review corpus annotated for negation, speculation and their scope. In Nicoletta Calzolari (Conference Chair), Khalid Choukri, Thierry Declerck, Mehmet Ugur Dogan, Bente Maegaard, Joseph Mariani, Jan Odijk, and Stelios Piperidis, editors, *Proceedings of the Eight International Conference on Language Resources and Evaluation (LREC'12)*, Istanbul, Turkey, may. European Language Resources Association (ELRA).

Ben Medlock and Ted Briscoe. 2007. Weakly Supervised Learning for Hedge Classification in Scientific Literature. In *Proceedings of the ACL*, pages 992–999, Prague, Czech Republic, June.

Roser Morante and Caroline Sporleder. 2012. Modality and negation: An introduction to the special issue. *Computational Linguistics*, 38:223–260, June.

Raheel Nawaz, Paul Thompson, and Sophia Ananiadou. 2010. Evaluating a meta-knowledge annotation scheme for bio-events. In *Proceedings of the Workshop on Negation and Speculation in Natural Language Processing*, pages 69–77, Uppsala, Sweden, July. University of Antwerp.

Victoria L. Rubin, Elizabeth D. Liddy, and Noriko Kando. 2005. Certainty identification in texts: Categorization model and manual tagging results. In J.G. Shanahan, J. Qu, and J. Wiebe, editors, *Computing attitude and affect in text: Theory and applications (the information retrieval series)*, New York. Springer Verlag.

Victoria L. Rubin. 2010. Epistemic modality: From uncertainty to certainty in the context of information seeking as interactions with texts. *Information Processing & Management*, 46(5):533–540.

Roser Saurí and James Pustejovsky. 2009. FactBank: a corpus annotated with event factuality. *Language Resources and Evaluation*, 43:227–268.

Burr Settles, Mark Craven, and Lewis Friedland. 2008. Active learning with real annotation costs. In *Proceedings of the NIPS Workshop on Cost-Sensitive Learning*, pages 1–10.

Hagit Shatkay, Fengxia Pan, Andrey Rzhetsky, and W. John Wilbur. 2008. Multi-dimensional classification of biomedical text: Toward automated, practical provision of high-utility text to diverse users. *Bioinformatics*, 24(18):2086–2093.

György Szarvas, Veronika Vincze, Richárd Farkas, György Móra, and Iryna Gurevych. 2012. Cross-genre and cross-domain detection of semantic uncertainty. *Computational Linguistics*, 38:335–367, June.

Özlem Uzuner, Xiaoran Zhang, and Tawanda Sibanda. 2009. Machine Learning and Rule-based Approaches to Assertion Classification. *Journal of the American Medical Informatics Association*, 16(1):109–115, January.

Veronika Vincze, György Szarvas, Richárd Farkas, György Móra, and János Csirik. 2008. The BioScope Corpus: Biomedical Texts Annotated for Uncertainty, Negation and their Scopes. *BMC Bioinformatics*, 9(Suppl 11):S9.

Veronika Vincze. 2013. Weasels, Hedges and Peacocks: Discourse-level Uncertainty in Wikipedia Articles. In *Proceedings of the Sixth International Joint Conference on Natural Language Processing*, pages 383–391, Nagoya, Japan, October. Asian Federation of Natural Language Processing.

Veronika Vincze. 2014. Uncertainty detection in Hungarian texts. In *Proceedings of Coling 2014*.

Zhongyu Wei, Junwen Chen, Wei Gao, Binyang Li, Lanjun Zhou, Yulan He, and Kam-Fai Wong. 2013. An empirical study on uncertainty identification in social media context. In *Proceedings of the 51st Annual Meeting of the Association for Computational Linguistics (Volume 2: Short Papers)*, pages 58–62, Sofia, Bulgaria, August. Association for Computational Linguistics.

Theresa Wilson, Zornitsa Kozareva, Preslav Nakov, Sara Rosenthal, Veselin Stoyanov, and Alan Ritter. 2013. SemEval-2013 Task 2: Sentiment Analysis in Twitter. In *Proceedings of the International Workshop on Semantic Evaluation*, SemEval '13, June.

Theresa Ann Wilson. 2008. *Fine-grained Subjectivity and Sentiment Analysis: Recognizing the Intensity, Polarity, and Attitudes of Private States*. Ph.D. thesis, University of Pittsburgh, Pittsburgh.

János Zsibrita, Veronika Vincze, and Richárd Farkas. 2013. magyarlanc: A Toolkit for Morphological and Dependency Parsing of Hungarian. In *Proceedings of RANLP-2013*, pages 763–771, Hissar, Bulgaria.

A Corpus Study for Identifying Evidence on Microblogs

Paul Reisert[1] **Junta Mizuno**[2] **Miwa Kanno**[1] **Naoaki Okazaki**[1,3] **Kentaro Inui**[1]

[1] Gradute School of Information Sciences, Tohoku University / Miyagi, Japan

[2] Resilient ICT Research Center, NICT / Miyagi, Japan [3] Japan Science and Technology Agency (JST) / Tokyo, Japan

preisert@ecei.tohoku.ac.jp junta-m@nict.go.jp {meihe, okazaki, inui}@ecei.tohoku.ac.jp

Abstract

Microblogs are a popular way for users to communicate and have recently caught the attention of researchers in the natural language processing (NLP) field. However, regardless of their rising popularity, little attention has been given towards determining the properties of discourse relations for the rapid, large-scale microblog data. Therefore, given their importance for various NLP tasks, we begin a study of discourse relations on microblogs by focusing on evidence relations. As no annotated corpora for evidence relations on microblogs exist, we conduct a corpus study to identify such relations on Twitter, a popular microblogging service. We create annotation guidelines, conduct a large-scale annotation phase, and develop a corpus of annotated evidence relations. Finally, we report our observations, annotation difficulties, and data statistics.

1 Introduction

Microblogs have become a popular method for users to express their ideas and communicate with other users. Twitter[1], a popular microblogging service, has recently been the attraction of many natural language processing (NLP) tasks ranging from flu epidemic detection (Aramaki et al., 2011) to gender inference for its users (Ciot et al., 2013). While various tasks are available, despite its daily, rapid large-scale data, evidence relation studies have yet to be explored using Twitter data. Previous research exists for determining the credibility of information on Twitter (Castillo et al., 2011); however, the focus of this work is to determine and annotate evidence relations on microblogs.

Our primary motivation behind focusing on evidence relations includes the possibility of discovering support for a claim which can support the debunking of false information. During the March 2011 Great East Japan Earthquake and Tsunami disaster, victims turned to the Internet in order to obtain information on current conditions, such as family member whereabouts, refuge center information, and general information (Sakaki et al., 2011). However, false information, such as the popular *Cosmo Oil explosion causing toxic rain*, interfered with those looking to find correct information on the status of the disaster areas (Okazaki et al., 2013). This is a scenario in which identification of potentially false information is necessary in order to provide accurate information to victims and others relying on and trusting in the Internet. Therefore, as a start to find support for counterclaims for false information such as the Cosmo Oil explosion, we focus on dialogue between two individuals: a *topic starter*, or a post with no parent; and a *respondent* who provides either an agreeing or disagreeing claim and support for their claim. An example is provided in Figure 1.

We note that our task can appear similar to the field of Why-QA (Verberne, 2006; Oh et al., 2013; Mrozinski et al., 2008), which attempts to discover the answer for *Why* questions. Given our task of discovering agreeing or conflicting claims, and finding specific reasoning to support the claim, we end up with a *Why* question similar to *Why is it true/not true that X*, where *X* is the contents of the claim found in the parent post. However, we consider source mentions or hyperlinks, which can either stand alone or be contained in a statement, question, or request, as a way to answer the above question.

To the best of our knowledge, no corpora for evidence relations on microblogs currently exists. In terms of argumentation corpora, the Araucaria Argumentation Corpus [2] exists which utilizes various argumentation schemes (Walton, 1996; Katzav and Reed, 2004; Pollock, 1995). In this work, we

[1] https://twitter.com

[2] http://araucaria.computing.dundee.ac.uk/doku.php

LAW VIII - The 8th Linguistic Annotation Workshop, pages 70–74,
Dublin, Ireland, August 23-24 2014.

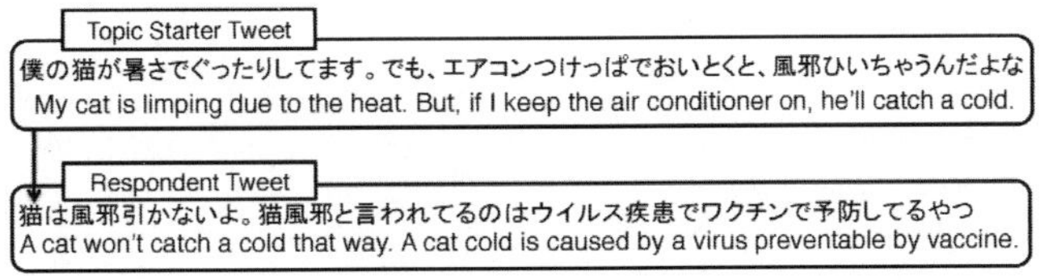

Figure 1: topic starter post and respondent post on the microbloging service Twitter.

manually annotate evidence relation claim and support. We conduct a corpus study that uses both current data and March 2011 data from Twitter, manually observing its structure and evidence, and devising guidelines based on our findings. We utilize these guidelines for conducting a large-scale annotation stage and develop a corpus with our results. We present our findings, challenges in annotation, and also the result statistics in the later sections. The corpora and annotation guidelines are currently available at: http://www.cl.ecei.tohoku.ac.jp/index.php?Open%20Resources%2FEvidence%20Relation%20Corpusw

2 Annotation Method

In this section, we describe evidence relation structure, target data, and our annotation method outline.

Evidence relations, defined by Mann and Thompson (1988) consist of a **claim**, or something that an author wishes for a reader to believe, and **support**, or something that increases the believability of the claim, and it can be understood by the following: *The program as published for calendar year 1980 really works. In only a few minutes, I entered all the figures from my 1980 tax return and got a result which agreed with my hand calculations to the penny.*, where the latter is support to the former claim.

With this in mind, we aim to explore what type of claims and support units exist on microblogs. Our microblog choice is Twitter, where users post *tweets* containing up to 140 characters. Tweets may then be replied to by other users. Each pair in our corpus consists of, what we refer to as, a *topic starter's* tweet and all of its direct reply tweets, or *respondent's* tweets. The topic starter's tweet is a top-level tweet not in response to another tweet, and the respondent tweet consists of a tweet directly in reply to the topic starter's tweet. We then discover respondent claims that agree or disagree with the topic starter. In addition, we target only pairs which contain an evidence relation.

The outline for annotation is as follows: 1) Given two tweets (topic starter and respondent), detect relation at agreeing or disagreeing level 2) Mark the claim and support in the respondent tweet

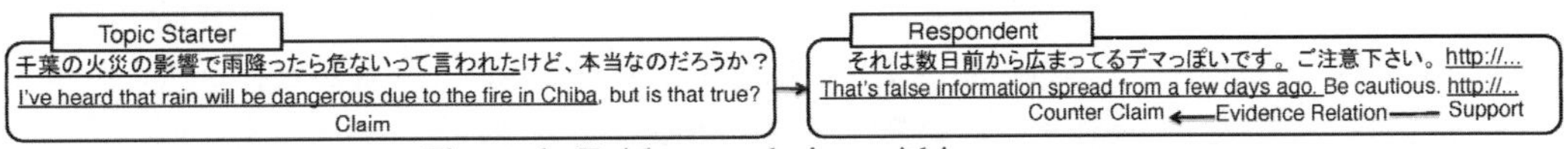

Figure 2: Evidence relation within a response.

We target this scenario because: 1) we assume that a topic will be presented in a topic starter's tweet and a respondent's direct reply will be responding to the topic content, and 2) it is possible to lose important information, such as topic keywords, for a reply tweet not in reply to a topic starter tweet.

Using this outline, we utilized Japanese Twitter data from the 2011 Great Eastern Tohoku Earthquake, specifically hottolink[3] data, and created a list of guidelines to use for our large-scale annotation in the next section by manually observing roughly 6,000 tweet pairs.

3 Large-scale Annotation

In order to obtain and observe more evidence relations, we conducted a large-scale annotation stage. We discuss the data and our statistics and observations.

3.1 Data

Using the guidelines in the previous section, we composed a list of 56,033 filtered tweets from various time periods, shown in the table below.

[3]http://www.hottolink.co.jp/press/936

Table 1: Data for large-scale annotation phase (A = Agree, D = Disagree, P = Partly A/D, O = Other)

#	Set	Pairs	Evidence	A	D	P	O
1	3-11 False Rumor topic starter Data	5753	1029	177	637	74	141
2	Togetter Controversial Category Data	2410	283	164	105	12	2
3	Togetter Negative Tag Data	1233	129	51	71	7	0
4	Twitter Random Controversial Topic Filtered Data	6918	277	168	94	14	1
5	3-11 Random Data	13064	381	241	115	21	4
6	3-11 Negative respondent Keyword Data	26655	1543	836	521	126	60
	Total	**56033**	**3642**	**1637**	**1543**	**254**	**208**

For Sets 1, 5, 6, we utilize the hottolink corpus mentioned briefly in the previous section. Set 1 consists of filtered pairs containing a well-known rumored topic from a list of 10 topics, such as Cosmo Oil Toxic Rain and Drinking Isodine for Radiation Prevention, and also contained a negative keyword in the respondent's tweet. We also included all other direct replies for the topic starter's tweet. Similarly, Set 5 contains random data from the hottolink corpus, unfiltered, and Set 6 contains pairs filtered via a negative keyword in the reply only.

Set 2 consists of crawled data from Togetter[4]. Togetter offers a summarization of popular, and potentially controversial, tweets for various categories, such as news, society, and sports. We first crawled all popular categories around January 2014 and obtained unique tweet IDs. We then used the Twitter API[5] to extract the tweet information from its ID in order to determine if it was a direct respondent tweet. If so, we obtained its topic starter tweet and thus created our pairs.

For Set 3, we appended negative keywords to the Togetter hyperlink (e.g. *http://togetter.com/t/デマ*) in order to obtain tweets that had been tagged with a negative keyword. We then used the same procedure as Set 2 in order to obtain topic starter and respondent tweet pairs.

Finally, Set 4 consists of 6,918 tweet pairs randomly selected from a collection of tweet pairs from Togetter, where each topic starter tweet is filtered by a topic from a list of around 300 controversial topics.

3.2 Statistics and Observations

In this section, we summarize the results of the annotated large-scale corpus by first providing information on the discovered evidence relations. Of 56,033 pairs, 3,642, or roughly 6.5%, were labeled as containing an evidence relation. Shown in Table 1 are the specific amount of evidence relations found in each set, along with the exact amount of claims that either agree, disagree, partly agree and disagree, and other. Also shown in Table 1 is the number of agreeing, disagreeing, partly agreeing/disagreeing, and other statistics for pairs labeled as evidence for each set.

3.2.1 Type Distribution

Since an important goal of this paper was to determine *what types* of claims and support we would discover, we classified random annotated tweet pairs by claim type and support type.

attitude Claim contains only reply user attitude (e.g., "I agree with you" or "It's false information")

request Claim requests some action (e.g., "Please delete and correct your tweet immediately")

question Claim is a question regarding the original tweet (e.g., "Why do you think so?" or only "?")

statement Claim is an opinion of a reply user (e.g., "Radiation cannot be reduced by a normal filter.")

Table 2: Type distribution results

Claim Type	Support Type	Disaster	General
attitude	causality	36	27
	elaboration	45	40
	source	35	7
request	causality	13	9
	elaboration	4	8
	source	15	0
statement	causality	21	22
	elaboration	49	31
	source	12	7
question	causality	1	2
	elaboration	3	9
	source	2	0
summary		**236**	**162**

[4]http://togetter.com

[5]https://dev.twitter.com/docs/api

Each of the three types of support (below) are in square brackets.
causality Support is a reason of a claim (e.g., "Isodine is no good because [it will ruin your health]")
elaboration Support is not a reason of a claim, but an elaboration (e.g., "topic starter: I definitely do not ride side by side with a car when I'm on my bicycle. respondent: Me too. [I do not ride side by side even when I ride a motorbike]")
source Support contains source information of the claim, such as hyperlink and name of the media (e.g., "Please read this web site [URL]" or "I saw it on the TV")

From Table 2, we found many source samples during disaster times but not for non-disaster periods. For our second finding, we discovered that attitude and statement were tweeted with support, while request and question were not. This indicates that people require some action without any support. For our third finding, we found that there were many replies which contain a statement and its support, while Twitter allows only 140 characters. This indicates many informative support segments on Twitter.

3.2.2 Annotation Issues

Below we enumerate issues that were encountered during our annotation process.

Reliability For determining annotation reliability, we had 10% of random samples from Set 1 annotated by another annotator and found that the inter-annotator agreement Cohen's kappa value was only .476. Both annotators marked 45 of the same pairs as evidence. Annotator A marked 60 other pairs as evidence, while Annotator B marked 15 other pairs as evidence. We believe this statistic is because tweets with evidence were infrequent and that many examples contained implicit relations, opposed to containing a discourse marker. From Annotator A's results, we found that only 9 examples contained an explicit discourse marker and 96 did not. Prasad et al. (2008) has already recognized that it is difficult to annotate relations when no discourse marker is present. We plan to automatically annotate evidence relations via machine learning and provide a probability that a pair is evidence to help manual annotation.

Multiple Claims With Twitter's character constraints, we expected to discover only one claim per reply with multiple support segments. However, we found that a few of our annotated segments contained multiple claim and multiple support segments.

Range Annotation range was a problem we discovered after observing our annotated data. Although such annotated cases were small (only 2 respondent tweets), most likely due to annotators avoiding such annotations, we still believe this type of annotation is important for future work. The example below was labeled as *unsure*:
{コスモ石油の件は}$_{\text{CLAIM}}${本社HPで}$_{\text{SUPPORT}}${デマだと公表されています。}$_{\text{CLAIM}}$ ({The Cosmo Oil case,}$_{\text{CLAIM}}$ {on the official HP,}$_{\text{SUPPORT}}$ {is publicly announced false.}$_{\text{CLAIM}}$)

4 Conclusion and Future Work

As no corpora exists for evidence relations on microblogs, we conducted a corpus study using the popular microblogging service, Twitter. We created a list of guidelines for evidence relation annotation by observing roughly 6,000 tweet pairs from March 2011 Twitter data, or disaster-specific data. Next, we conducted a large-scale annotation stage, consisting of 56,033 tweets, and discovered 3,642 contained a type of evidence relation. Our annotated data set is available at: http://www.cl.ecei.tohoku.ac.jp/index.php?Open%20Resources%2FEvidence%20Relation%20Corpus

We manually observed that the presence of evidence relations do indeed exist on microblogs; however, their existence is rather infrequent. To address this sparsity issue for future annotation, we plan to increase the number of pairs containing an evidence relation per data set by constructing a model that can automatically annotate evidence relations and provide a probability that a pair contains an evidence relation. In this work, we did not analyze the quality of evidence we discovered. Therefore, we aim towards determining the factuality, or degree of certainty, for a given claim and support in order to determine the evidence relation's overall quality.

Acknowledgments

We would like to acknowledge MEXT (Ministry of Education, Culture, Sports, Science and Technology) for their generous financial support via the Research Student Scholarship. This study was partly supported by Japan Society for the Promotion of Science (JSPS) KAKENHI Grant No. 23240018 and Japan Science and Technology Agency (JST). Furthermore, we would like to also thank Eric Nichols (Honda Research Institute Japan Co., Ltd.) for his discussions on the topic of evidence relations.

References

Eiji Aramaki, Sachiko Maskawa, and Mizuki Morita. 2011. Twitter catches the flu: Detecting influenza epidemics using Twitter. In *Proceedings of the Conference on Empirical Methods in Natural Language Processing*, EMNLP '11, pages 1568–1576.

Carlos Castillo, Marcelo Mendoza, and Barbara Poblete. 2011. Information credibility on Twitter. In *Proceedings of the 20th International Conference on World Wide Web*, WWW '11, pages 675–684.

Morgane Ciot, Morgan Sonderegger, and Derek Ruths. 2013. Gender inference of Twitter users in non-English contexts. In *Proceedings of the 2013 Conference on Empirical Methods in Natural Language Processing*, pages 1136–1145.

Joel Katzav and Chris Reed. 2004. A classification system for arguments. *Technical Report*.

William C. Mann and Sandra A. Thompson. 1988. Rhetorical structure theory: Toward a functional theory of text organization. *Text*, 8(3):243–281.

Joanna Mrozinski, Edward Whittaker, and Sadaoki Furui. 2008. Collecting a why-question corpus for development and evaluation of an automatic QA-system. In *Proceedings of ACL-08: HLT*, pages 443–451.

Jong-Hoon Oh, Kentaro Torisawa, Chikara Hashimoto, Motoki Sano, Stijn De Saeger, and Kiyonori Ohtake. 2013. Why-question answering using intra- and inter-sentential causal relations. In *Proceedings of the 51st Annual Meeting of the Association for Computational Linguistics (Volume 1: Long Papers)*, pages 1733–1743.

Naoaki Okazaki, Keita Nabeshima, Kento Watanabe, Junta Mizuno, and Kentaro Inui. 2013. Extracting and aggregating false information from microblogs. In *Proceedings of the Workshop on Language Processing and Crisis Information*, pages 36–43.

John L. Pollock. 1995. *Cognitive Carpentry: A Blueprint for How to Build a Person*. MIT Press.

Rashmi Prasad, Nikhil Dinesh, Alan Lee, Eleni Miltsakaki, Livio Robaldo, Aravind Joshi, and Bonnie Webber. 2008. The penn discourse treebank 2.0. In *Proceedings of the Sixth International Conference on Language Resources and Evaluation (LREC'08)*.

Takeshi Sakaki, Fujio Toriumi, and Yutaka Matsuo. 2011. Tweet trend analysis in an emergency situation. In *Proceedings of the Special Workshop on Internet and Disasters*, SWID '11, pages 3:1–3:8.

Suzan Verberne. 2006. Developing an approach for why-question answering. In *Proceedings of the Eleventh Conference of the European Chapter of the Association for Computational Linguistics: Student Research Workshop*, EACL '06, pages 39–46.

Douglas N. Walton. 1996. *Argumentation Schemes for Presumptive Reasoning*. Psychology Press.

Semi-Semantic Part of Speech Annotation and Evaluation

Qaiser Abbas
Fachbereich Sprachwissenschaft
Universität Konstanz
78457 Konstanz, Germany
qaiser.abbas@uni-konstanz.de

Abstract

This paper presents the semi-semantic part of speech annotation and its evaluation via Krippendorff's α for the URDU.KON-TB treebank developed for the South Asian language Urdu. The part of speech annotation with the additional subcategories of morphology and semantics provides a treebank with sufficient encoded information. The corpus used is collected from the Urdu Wikipedia and news papers. The sentences were annotated manually to ensure a high annotational quality. The inter-annotator agreement obtained after evaluation is 0.964, which lies in the range of perfect agreement on a scale. Urdu is comparatively an under-resourced language and the development of the treebank with rich part of speech annotation will have significant impact on the state-of-the-art for Urdu language processing.

1 Introduction

Urdu, an invariant of *Hindavi* came into existence during the muslim rule from 1206 AD to 1858 AD (Khan, 2006). They used Persian/Urdu script for Urdu in contrast of the Devanagari script for Hindavi. Urdu became a literary language after existence of an increasing number of literature during 18th and 19th century (McLane, 1970). Hindi/Hindavi is a close language to Urdu except the script writing style and the differences in the formal and informal versions. Urdu is the national language of Pakistan and an official language in India. According to a report by SIL Ethnologue (Lewis, 2013), Urdu/Hindi has 456.2 million speakers in the whole world. Urdu is a morphologically rich language (MRL) and in need of a number of resources to compete in the race of computational resources.

The design of the part of speech (POS) annotation scheme depends upon the need. If the people want to do text processing, text mining, etc., then they might be interested in a limited POS annotation scheme. However, the people who are interested in language parsing, then a POS annotation scheme with rich information is needed. Getting state-of-the-art parsing results for a MRL is a challenge till to date. According to Tsarfaty et. al. (2013; 2010), without proper handling of morphological entities in the sentences, promising results for MRLs can not be achieved and the depth of information encoded in an annotation correlates with the parsing performance. The best broad coverage and robust parsers to date have grammars extracted from the treebanks, which are a collection of syntactically annotated sentences by humans. The problem statement described requires an explicit encoding of morphological information at the POS level and the treebanks with sufficient encoding of morphology, POS, syntactic and functional information are the best candidates to provide the state-of-the-art parsing results in case of MRLs. The work presented here is the part of a large effort made for the construction of the URDU.KON-TB treebank, which was built by considering the parsing needs of Urdu. The annotation scheme of the treebank contains semi-semantic POS (SSP), semi-semantic syntactic (SSS) and functional (F) tag sets, from which only the SSP tag set is presented here along with its annotation evaluation.

The relevant resources of Urdu are now growing but most of the resources lack in morphological and functional information. The initial corpus developed in the EMILLE project (McEnery et al., 2000) comprised multi-lingual corpora for the South Asian languages. Its Urdu part was annotated according to a

LAW VIII - The 8th Linguistic Annotation Workshop, pages 75–81,
Dublin, Ireland, August 23-24 2014.

POS annotation scheme devised by Hardie (2003), which contained 350 morpho-syntactic tags based on the gender, number agreement. It was so detailed that the Urdu computational linguists avoided it to practice in statistical parsing, even it was a good effort. However, now the computational linguists are realizing and attempting morphological information in their annotation (Manning, 2011). In (2007), Urdu ParGram project introduced a resource that lied in the domain of tree-banking. In this project, Urdu lexical functional grammar (LFG) was encoded, which is still in progress. The LFG grammar encoded has rich morphological information, but unfortunately, the annotation scheme is not published yet due to their different motives towards the parallel treebank development. Similarly, in (2009), Sajjad and Schmid presented a new POS annotation scheme, which lacks in morphological, syntactical and functional information. Due to which, it can only be used for the training of POS taggers and is not suitable for the parsing purpose. Moreover, the explicit annotation evaluation was not performed. Another POS tag set was devised by Muaz et. al. in (2009), which contained 32 general POS tags. The devised scheme has the same issues as mentioned in the work of Sajjad and Schmid (2009). In (2009), Abbas et. al. built the first NU-FAST treebank for Urdu with the POS and syntactic labels only. The design of that treebank neither contained detailed morphological and functional information nor any information about the displaced constituents, empty arguments, etc. Another Hindi-Urdu tree-banking (HUTB) (Bhatt et al., 2009; Palmer et al., 2009) effort was done in a collaborative project[1]. However, the Urdu treebank being developed was comparatively small and was being done as a part of a larger effort at establishing a treebank for Hindi. Moreover, many of the issues with respect to Urdu were not quite addressed and the project is still in progress. To continue this effort, another treebank for Urdu was designed by Abbas in (2012), which comprised of 600 annotated sentences and it was done without the annotation evaluation.

The current work presented in this paper, not only enhances the size of the proposed treebank by Abbas (2012), but also resolves the annotation issues along with the complete annotation guidelines and its evaluation. The development of the URDU.KON-TB treebank starts with the collection of a corpus discussed briefly in Section 2. The semi-semantic (partly or partially semantic) POS (SSP) annotation scheme is described in Section 3. Similarly, the evaluation of the SSP annotation is presented in Section 4 along with a brief presentation of annotation issues. Finally, the conclusion is given in Section 5 and the detailed version of the SSP tag set is given in Appendix.

2 Corpus Collection

One thousand (1000) sentences taken from the corpus (Ijaz and Hussain, 2007) are extensively modified to get rid of licensing constraints, because we want to share our corpus freely under a Creative-Commons-Attribution/Share-Alike License 3.0 or higher. The next four hundred (400) sentences are collected from the Urdu Wikipedia[2], which is already under the same license. Thus the size of the corpus is limited to fourteen hundred (1400) sentences. The corpus contains text of local & international news, social stories, sports, culture, finance, history, religion, traveling, etc.

3 Semi-Semantic POS (SSP) Annotation

After the annotation evaluation presented in Section 4, the revised annotation scheme of the URDU.KON-TB treebank has a semi-semantic POS (SSP), semi-semantic syntactic (SSS) and a functional (F) tag set. The term semi-semantic (partly or partially semantic) is used with the POS because the tags are compounded with the semantic tags partially e.g. a noun *house* with spatial semantics tagged as N.SPT, an adjective *previous* in the *previous year* with temporal semantics tagged as ADJ.TMP, etc. The same concept is applied on the SSS annotation. The details of SSS and F labeling is beyond the scope of this paper. At POS level, a dot '.' is used to add morphological and semantical subcategories into the main POS categories displayed in Table 1 of Appendix. The POS, morphological and semantical information all together, make a rich SSP annotation scheme for the URDU.KON-TB treebank. The need for such type of schemes is highly advocated in (Clark et al., 2010; Skut et al., 1997), etc.

[1] http://verbs.colorado.edu/hindiurdu/

[2] http://ur.wikipedia.org/wiki/صفحہ اول

A simple POS tag set was devised first, which had twenty two (22) main POS-tag categories described in Table 1 of Appendix, which includes some non-familiar tags like HADEES and M to represent the Arabic statements of prophets in Urdu text and a phrase or a sentence marker, respectively. The labels for morphological and semantic subcategories are presented in Tables 2 and 3 of Appendix, respectively, which can be added to the 22 main POS tag categories by using a dot '.' symbol in the form of compound tags like N.SPT and ADJ.TMP mentioned earlier. In case of morphology, if a verb V has a perfective morphology, then the compound tag becomes V.PERF. The SSP tag set was refined during the manual annotation process of the sentences and further refined after the annotation evaluation process discussed in Section 4. The final refined form of the SSP tag set depicted in Table 4 of Appendix is the revised form of the POS tag set presented in the initial version of the URDU.KON-TB treebank by Abbas in (2012).

As an example, consider the ADJ (adjective) from the final refined form of the SSP tag set given in Appendix, which is divided into five subcategories of tags DEG (Degree), ECO (Echo), MNR (Manner), SPT (Spatial) and TMP (Temporal). Relevant examples are provided in 1 of Appendix. The example 1(a) of Appendix is a simple case of ADJ, while 1(b) of Appendix is the case of a degree adjective[3] annotated with ADJ.DEG. The example 1(c) of Appendix is the case of reduplication[4] (Abbi, 1992; Bögel et al., 2007). Reduplication has two versions. First *Echo Reduplication* is discussed in the footnote, while the other *Full Word Reduplication* is the repetition of the original word e.g. *sAtH sAtH* 'with/alongwith'. These are adopted in our annotation as ECO (echo) and the REP (repetition), respectively. The example 1(d) of Appendix is the case of adjective having a sense of manner annotated as ADJ.MNR. If an adjective qualifies an action noun, then a sense of action or something is produced, whose behavior or the way to do that action is exploited through ADJ.MNR e.g. *z4AlemAnah t2abdIlIyAN* 'brutal changes'. An exercise of manner adjectives and manner adverbs for English can be seen at Cambridge University[5]. The example 1(e) of Appendix is the case of an adjective having a temporal sense discussed earlier. Finally, the example 1(f) of Appendix is the case of an adjective having a spatial sense. The adjective used here is the derivational form of a city name 'Multan', but it appears here as an adjective and annotated as ADJ.SPT[6] like in this sentence e.g. *voh Ek pAkistAnI laRkA hE* 'He is a pakistani boy'.

Example 1 of Appendix exploited the POS tags for adjectives along with the semantic tagging like TMP, SPT, MNR, etc. However, to give an introduction about morphology and verb functions, another POS category of verb V given in Appendix is presented. It is divided into 11 subcategories, which include COP (copula verb), IMPERF (imperfective morphological form of verb), INF (infinitive form of verb), LIGHT (1st light verb with nouns and adjectives), LIGHTV (2nd light verb with verbs), MOD (modal verb), PERF (perfective morphology), ROOT (root form), SUBTV (subjunctive form), PAST (past tense of a verb) and PRES (present tense of a verb). These tags have further subcategories. All tags represents different morphological forms and the function of a verb that it governs. A few high quality studies were adopted to identify different forms and functions of Urdu verbs (Butt, 2003; Butt, 1995; Butt and Rizvi, 2010; Butt and Ramchand, 2001; Butt, 2010; Abbas and Raza, 2014; Abbas and Nabi Khan, 2009) and some annotated sentences from the URDU.KON-TB treebank are given in example 2 of Appendix.

The sentence in example 2(a) of Appendix is the case of adjective-verb complex verb predicate. These adjective/noun-verb complex predicates were first proposed by Ahmed and Butt (2011). The adjective *dubHar* 'hard' and the verb *kiyA* 'did' with a perfective morphology *yA* at the end are annotated as a ADJ and a V.LIGHT.PERF, respectively. Similarly, a perfective verb *liyA* 'took' after a root form of verb *kar* 'do' is an example of the verb-verb complex predicate depicted in 2(d) of Appendix. This construction is adopted from the studies given in (Butt, 2010). The next sentence in 2(b) of Appendix has a passive construction, which can be inferred from the inflected form of a verb or a verb auxiliary *jAnA* 'to go' preceded by another verb with perfective morphology. To explore some unusual tags, a long sentence

[3]This division is used to represent absolute, comparative and superlative degree in adjectives and adverbs.

[4]In Urdu like other South Asian languages, the reduplication of a content word is frequent. Its effect is only to strengthen the proceeding word or to expand the specific idea of a proceeding word into a general form e.g. *kAm THIk-THAk karnA* 'Do the work right' or *kOI kapRE-vapRE dE dO* 'Give me the clothes or something like those'.

[5]`http://www.cambridge.org/grammarandbeyond/wp-content/uploads/2012/09/Communicative_Activity_Hi-BegIntermediate-Adjectives_and_Adverbs.pdf`

[6]Spatial adjectives are used to describe a place/location, direction or distance e.g. *multAnI* 'Multani', *aglI* 'next', and *dUr* 'far' respectively.

is presented in 2(c) of Appendix. After the name of prophets or righteous religious-personalities, some specific and limited prayers called *s3alAvAt* 'prayers' like *sal-lal-la-ho-a2lEhE-va-AlEhI-salam* 'May Allah grant peace and honor on him and his family', *a2lEh salAm* 'peace be upon him', etc., in Arabic is the most likely in Urdu text and annotated as the PRAY. Similarly, the statements of prophet Muhammad (PBUH) known as *h2adIs2* 'narration' like *In-namal-aa2mAlo-bin-niyAt* 'The deeds are considered by the intensions' in Arabic script is also a tradition in Urdu text and annotated as the HADEES. The phrase markers like comma, double quotes, single quotes, etc. are annotated with the M.P and sentence marker like full-stop, question mark, etc., are annotated with the M.S as presented in the same example.

4 SSP Annotation Evaluation

The SSP annotation evaluation was performed via Krippendorff's α coefficient (Krippendorff, 2004), which is a statistical measure to evaluate the reliability annotation or the inter-annotator agreement (IAA). Krippendorff's α (Krippendorff, 1970; Krippendorff, 2004) satisfies all our needs including random nominal data and five number of annotators in contrast to multi-π (Fleiss, 1971) and multi-κ (Cohen and others, 1960), which can handle only fixed nominal data and they are basically not designed for more than two annotators (Artstein and Poesio, 2008; Carletta et al., 1997). The nominal data given to annotators for the SSP annotation was not fixed. In this situation, the general form of the Krippendorff's α coefficient was selected to meet this requirement.

For the reliability evaluation of the SSP annotation guidelines, it was essential that the annotators should be the native speakers of Urdu along with the linguistics skills. To fulfill this purpose, an undergraduate class of 25 linguistic students was trained at the Department of English, University of Sargodha[7], Pakistan. During this training, thirty two lectures on annotation guidelines with practical sessions were delivered. The duration of each lecture was of 3 hours. The class was further divided into five groups and during their initial practical sessions, one student with a high caliber of understanding from each group was selected (but not informed) secretly for the final annotation. The annotation task of 100 random sentences was divided into 10 home assignments, which were then given to all students (including 5 secret students) periodically with an instruction not to discuss it with each other. The annotation performed by the selected 5 students was then recorded and evaluated. The value of α coefficient obtained after evaluation is 0.964 for the SSP annotation, which is narrated as a good reliability in (Krippendorff, 2004) and lies in the category of perfect agreement according to a scale in (Landis and Koch, 1977). It also means that the IAA is 0.964 and the SSP annotation guidelines are reliable.

The issues found before and after the annotation evaluation concludes the addition, deletion or revision of several tags. For example, the continuous auxiliary *rahA*/VAUX.PROG.PERF and its inflected forms can behave as a copula verb as V.COP.PERF, which was not considered in the initial work. The annotators did not respond well during the annotation of complex predicates, so their identification rules are revised which includes tense, passive, modal, etc., auxiliaries or verbs can not behave as complex predicate e.g. VAUX.LIGHT.MOD is not possible in the updated version. Similarly, the KER tag for identification of a special clause ending with *kar/V.KER kE/KER* 'after doing', was found to be ambiguous and deleted. It was updated with their genuine tags as *kar/V.ROOT kE/CM*.

5 Conclusion

Sufficient rich information in the SSP annotation was encoded to meet the parsing needs of MRL Urdu. The α coefficient value obtained advocates the quality of the SSP annotation along with the complete annotation guidelines for the URDU.KON-TB treebank. Such kind of annotated corpus with rich morphology and semantics is not only useful for the parsing purpose but can be used for the training of POS taggers, text mining, language identification (Abbas et al., 2010) and in many other applications as well.

Acknowledgements

Special thanks to Professor Miriam Butt, due to which linguistically rich the URDU.KON-TB treebank is existing and she participated overwhelmingly in the annotation process of this treebank.

[7] http://uos.edu.pk/

References

Qaiser Abbas and A Nabi Khan. 2009. Lexical Functional Grammar For Urdu Modal Verbs. In *Emerging Technologies, 2009. ICET 2009. International Conference on*, pages 7–12. IEEE.

Qaiser Abbas and Ghulam Raza. 2014. A Computational Classification Of Urdu Dynamic Copula Verb. *International Journal of Computer Applications*, 85(10):1–12, January.

Qaiser Abbas, Nayyara Karamat, and Sadia Niazi. 2009. Development Of Tree-Bank Based Probabilistic Grammar For Urdu Language. *International Journal of Electrical & Computer Science*, 9(09):231–235.

Qaiser Abbas, MS Ahmed, and Sadia Niazi. 2010. Language Identifier For Languages Of Pakistan Including Arabic And Persian. *International Journal of Computational Linguistics (IJCL)*, 1(03):27–35.

Qaiser Abbas. 2012. Building A Hierarchical Annotated Corpus Of Urdu: The URDU.KON-TB Treebank. *Lecture Notes in Computer Science*, 7181(1):66–79.

Anvita Abbi. 1992. *Reduplication In South Asian Languages: An Areal, Typological, And Historical Study*. Allied Publishers New Delhi.

Tafseer Ahmed and Miriam Butt. 2011. Discovering Semantic Classes For Urdu NV Complex Predicates. In *Proceedings of the Ninth International Conference on Computational Semantics*, pages 305–309. Association for Computational Linguistics.

Ron Artstein and Massimo Poesio. 2008. Inter-Coder Agreement For Computational Linguistics. *Computational Linguistics*, 34(4):555–596.

Rajesh Bhatt, Bhuvana Narasimhan, Martha Palmer, Owen Rambow, Dipti Misra Sharma, and Fei Xia. 2009. A Multi-Representational And Multi-Layered Treebank For Hindi/urdu. In *Proceedings of the Third Linguistic Annotation Workshop*, pages 186–189. Association for Computational Linguistics.

Tina Bögel, Miriam Butt, Annette Hautli, and Sebastian Sulger. 2007. Developing A Finite-State Morphological Analyzer For Urdu And Hindi. *Finite State Methods and Natural Language Processing*, page 86.

Miriam Butt and Tracy Holloway King. 2007. Urdu In A Parallel Grammar Development Environment. *Language Resources and Evaluation*, 41(2):191–207.

Miriam Butt and Gillian Ramchand. 2001. Complex Aspectual Structure In Hindi/Urdu. *M. Liakata, B. Jensen, & D. Maillat, Eds*, pages 1–30.

Miriam Butt and Jafar Rizvi. 2010. Tense And Aspect In Urdu. *Layers of Aspect. Stanford: CSLI Publications*.

Miriam Butt. 1995. *The Structure Of Complex Predicates In Urdu*. Center for the Study of Language (CSLI).

Miriam Butt. 2003. The Light Verb Jungle. In *Workshop on Multi-Verb Constructions*.

Miriam Butt. 2010. The Light Verb Jungle: Still Hacking Away. *Complex predicates: cross-linguistic perspectives on event structure*, page 48.

Jean Carletta, Stephen Isard, Gwyneth Doherty-Sneddon, Amy Isard, Jacqueline C Kowtko, and Anne H Anderson. 1997. The Reliability Of A Dialogue Structure Coding Scheme. *Computational linguistics*, 23(1):13–31.

Alexander Clark, Chris Fox, and Shalom Lappin. 2010. *The Handbook Of Computational Linguistics And Natural Language Processing*, volume 57. Wiley. com.

Jacob Cohen et al. 1960. A Coefficient Of Agreement For Nominal Scales. *Educational and psychological measurement*, 20(1):37–46.

Joseph L Fleiss. 1971. Measuring Nominal Scale Agreement Among Many Raters. *Psychological bulletin*, 76(5):378.

Andrew Hardie. 2003. Developing A Tagset For Automated Part-Of-Speech Tagging In Urdu. In *Corpus Linguistics 2003*.

Madiha Ijaz and Sarmad Hussain. 2007. Corpus Based Urdu Lexicon Development. In *the Proceedings of Conference on Language Technology (CLT07), University of Peshawar, Pakistan*.

Abdul Jamil Khan. 2006. *Urdu/Hindi: An Artificial Divide: African Heritage, Mesopotamian Roots, Indian Culture & Britiah Colonialism*. Algora Pub.

Klaus Krippendorff. 1970. Estimating The Reliability, Systematic Error And Random Error Of Interval Data. *Educational and Psychological Measurement*, 30(1):61–70.

Klaus Krippendorff. 2004. Reliability In Content Analysis. *Human Communication Research*, 30(3):411–433.

J Richard Landis and Gary G Koch. 1977. The Measurement Of Observer Agreement For Categorical Data. *biometrics*, pages 159–174.

Gary F. Simons & Charles D. Fennig Lewis, M. Paul. 2013. *Ethnologue: Languages Of The World, 17th Edition*. Dallas: SIL International.

Christopher D Manning. 2011. Part-Of-Speech Tagging From 97% To 100%: Is It Time For Some Linguistics? In *Computational Linguistics and Intelligent Text Processing*, pages 171–189. Springer.

Anthony McEnery, Paul Baker, Rob Gaizauskas, and Hamish Cunningham. 2000. EMILLE: Building A Corpus Of South Asian Languages. *VIVEK-BOMBAY-*, 13(3):22–28.

John R McLane. 1970. *The Political Awakening In India*. Prentice Hall.

Ahmed Muaz, Aasim Ali, and Sarmad Hussain. 2009. Analysis And Development Of Urdu POS Tagged Corpus. In *Proceedings of the 7th Workshop on Asian Language Resources*, pages 24–29. Association for Computational Linguistics.

Martha Palmer, Rajesh Bhatt, Bhuvana Narasimhan, Owen Rambow, Dipti Misra Sharma, and Fei Xia. 2009. Hindi Syntax: Annotating Dependency, Lexical Predicate-Argument Structure, And Phrase Structure. In *The 7th International Conference on Natural Language Processing*, pages 14–17.

Hassan Sajjad and Helmut Schmid. 2009. Tagging Urdu Text With Parts Of Speech: A Tagger Comparison. In *Proceedings of the 12th Conference of the European Chapter of the Association for Computational Linguistics*, pages 692–700. Association for Computational Linguistics.

Wojciech Skut, Brigitte Krenn, Thorsten Brants, and Hans Uszkoreit. 1997. An Annotation Scheme For Free Word Order Languages. In *Proceedings of the fifth conference on Applied natural language processing*, pages 88–95. Association for Computational Linguistics.

Reut Tsarfaty, Djamé Seddah, Yoav Goldberg, Sandra Kuebler, Marie Candito, Jennifer Foster, Yannick Versley, Ines Rehbein, and Lamia Tounsi. 2010. Statistical Parsing Of Morphologically Rich Languages (SPMRL): What, How And Whither. In *Proceedings of the NAACL HLT 2010 First Workshop on Statistical Parsing of Morphologically-Rich Languages*, pages 1–12. Association for Computational Linguistics.

Reut Tsarfaty, Djamé Seddah, Sandra Kübler, and Joakim Nivre. 2013. Parsing Morphologically Rich Languages: Introduction To The Special Issue. *Computational Linguistics*, 39(1):15–22.

Appendix

(1)

(a) *acHA* *laRkA*
ADJ N
'good boy'

(b) *aham* *tarIn* *Saxs2iat*
ADJ ADJ.DEG N
'most important personality'

(c) *burA* *vurA* *kAm*
ADJ ADJ.ECO N
'ugly work'

(d) *jaberaanah* *hakUmat*
ADJ.MNR N
'forceful government'

(e) *guzaStah* *sAl*
ADJ.TMP N
'previous year'

(f) *mUltAnI* *kHUsah*
ADJ.SPT N
'multani shoe'

(2)

(a)

mehangAI	*nE*	*lOgON*	*kA*	*jInA*	*dUbHar*	*kiyA*	*tHA*
N	CM	N	CM	N	ADJ	V.LIGHT.PERF	VAUX.PAST

'The inflation had made the life of people hard'

(b)

giraN-faroSoN	*kE*	*xilAf*	*qAnUn*	*harkat*	*mEN*	*lAyA*	*jAyE*
N	CM	POSTP.MNR	N	N	CM	V.PERF	VAUX.PASS.SUBTV

'The law would be practiced against inflators'

(c) *mUhammad* *sal-lal-la-ho-a2lEhE-va-AlEhl-salam* *nE* *farmAyA* *keh* “
N.PROP PRAY CM V.PERF C.SBORD M.P
al-hUsynON-mInnI-vA-anA-mInal-hUsyn ” *ya2nI* ‘ *hUsyn* *mUjH* *sE* *hE*
HADEES M.P ADV M.P N.PROP P.PERS CM V.COP.PRES
aOr *mEN* *hUsyn* *sE* *hUN* ’ .
C.CORD P.PERS N.PROP CM V.SUBTV M.P M.S

‘Muhammad (May Allah grant peace and honor on him and his family) said that “al-hUsynON-mInnI-vA-anA-mInal-hUsyn” means ‘Hussain is from me and I am from Hussain’ . ’

(d) *tUm* *nE* *haj* *tO* *kar* *liyA* *hO* *gA* *?*
P.PERS CM N PT.EMP V.ROOT V.LIGHTV.PERF VAUX.SUBTV VAUX.FUTR M.S

‘You will have made the pilgrimage?’

Table 1: The main POS-Tag categories

ADJ (Adjective)	PRAY (Specific statements of prayers)
ADV (Adverb)	PREP (Preposition)
C (Conjunction)	PT (Particle)
CM (Case marker)	Q (Quantifier)
DATE (Date)	QW (Question word)
HADEES (Narration of prophets deeds)	SYM (Symbol)
INT (Interjection)	TTL (Title)
M (Marker)	U (Unit)
N (Noun)	V (Verb)
P (Pronoun)	VALA (Vala verb)
POSTP (Postposition)	VAUX (Verb auxiliary)

Table 2: Morphological tag set subcategories

IMPERF (Imperfective form)	PROG (Progressive form)
PERF (Perfective form)	PASS (Passive form)
ROOT (Root form)	FUTR (Future tense)
SUBTV (Subjunctive form)	PAST (Past tense)
INF (Infinite form)	PRES (Present tense)

Table 3: Semantical tagset.

Semantic labels	
CMP (Comparative)	POSS (Possessive)
INST (Instrumental)	SPT (Spatial)
MNR (Manner)	TMP (Temporal)

Table 4: A detailed version of the SSP tagset for the URDU.KON-TB treebank

ADJ (Adjective)	.REL (Relative)	.ROOT (Root)
.DEG (Degree)	.DEM (Demons...)	.SUBTV (Subjunctive)
.ECO (Echo)	.PERS (Personal)	.PAST (Past)
.MNR (Manner)	POSTP (Postposition)	.PRES (Present)
.SPT (Spatial)	.CMP (Comparative)	.LIGHTV (Light Verb)
.TMP (Temporal)	.MNR (Manner)	.IMPERF (Imperfective)
ADV (Adverb)	.POSS (Possessive)	.INF (Infinite)
.DEG (Degree)	.REP (Repeat)	.PERF (Perfective)
.MNR (Manner)	.SPT (Spatial)	.ROOT (Root)
.NEG (Negative)	.TMP (Temporal)	.SUBTV (Subjunctive)
.SPT (Spatial)	PRAY (Pray)	.MOD (Modal)
.TMP (Temporal)	PREP (Preposition)	.IMPERF (Imperfective)
.REL (Relative)	.MNR (Manner)	.PERF (Perfective)
C (Conjunction)	.SPT (Spatial)	.SUBTV (Subjunctive)
.CAUS (Causative)	.TMP (Temporal)	.PERF (Perfective)
.CONS (Concessive)	PT (Particle)	.REP (Repeat)
.CORD (Coordinative)	.ADJ (Adjective)	.ROOT (Root)
.CORR (Co-relative)	.EMP (Emphatic)	.REP (Repeat)
.SBORD (Subordinating)	.INTF (Intensifier)	.SUBTV (Subjunctive)
.COND (Conditional)	.RESULT (Result)	.PAST (Past)
CM (Case Marker)	Q (Quantifier)	.PRES (Present)
DATE (Date)	.ADJ (Adjective)	VALA (Vala)
.D (Day)	.CARD (Cardinal)	VAUX (Verb Auxiliary)
.M (Month)	.FRAC (Fractional)	.IMPERF (Imperfective)
.Y (Year)	.ORD (Ordinal)	.INF (Infinite)
HADEES (Hadees)	QW (Question Word)	.MOD (Modal)
INT (Interjection)	.REP (Repeat)	.IMPERF (Imperfective)
M (Marker)	.TMP (Temporal)	.PERF (Perfective)
.P (Phrase)	.SPT (Spatial)	.SUBTV (Subjunctive)
.S (Sentence)	.MNR (Manner)	.PASS (Passive)
N (Noun)	SYM (Symbol)	.IMPERF (Imperfective)
.ADJ (Adjective)	TTL (Title)	.INF (Infinite)
.MNR (Manner)	.REG (Regard)	.PERF (Perfective)
.REP (Repeat)	U (Unit)	.ROOT (Root)
.PROP (Proper)	V (Verb)	.SUBTV (Subjunctive)
.SPT (Spatial)	.COP (Copula)	.PERF (Perfective)
.TMP (Temporal)	.IMPERF (Imperfective)	.PROG (Progressive)
.REP (Repeat)	.PERF (Perfective)	.ROOT (Root)
.SPT (Spatial)	.ROOT (Root)	.SUBTV (Subjunctive)
.REP (Repeat)	.SUBTV (Subjunctive)	.FUTR (Future)
.TMP (Temporal)	.PAST (Past)	.PAST (Past)
.REP (Repeat)	.PRES (Present)	.PRES (Present)
P (Pronoun)	.IMPERF (Imperfective)	
.DEM (Demonstrative)	.REP (Repeat)	
.INDF (Indefinite)	.INF (Infinite)	
.PERS (Personal)	.LIGHT (Light)	
.POSS (Possessive)	.IMPERF (Impe...)	
.REF (Reflexive)	.INF (Infinite)	
.REP (Repeat)	.PERF (Perfective)	
.REF (Reflexive)	.PROG (Progressive)	

Multiple views as aid to linguistic annotation error analysis

Marilena Di Bari
University of Leeds
mlmdb@leeds.ac.uk

Serge Sharoff
University of Leeds
s.sharoff@leeds.ac.uk

Martin Thomas
University of Leeds
m.thomas@leeds.ac.uk

Abstract

This paper describes a methodology for supporting the task of annotating sentiment in natural language by detecting borderline cases and inconsistencies. Inspired by the co-training strategy, a number of machine learning models are trained on different *views* of the same data. The predictions obtained by these models are then automatically compared in order to bring to light highly uncertain annotations and systematic mistakes. We tested the methodology against an English corpus annotated according to a fine-grained sentiment analysis annotation schema (SentiML). We detected that 153 instances (35%) classified differently from the gold standard were acceptable and further 69 instances (16%) suggested that the gold standard should have been improved.

1 Introduction

This work pertains to the phase of testing the reliability of human annotation. The strength of our approach relies on the fact that we use multiple supervised machine learning classifiers and analyse their predictions in parallel to automatically identify disagreements. Those, in fact, ultimately lead to the discovery of borderline cases in the annotation, an expensive task in terms of time when carried out manually.

Predictions with a number of different labels are manually analysed, since they may indicate inconsistencies in the annotation and cases difficult to annotate. Conversely, cases with high agreement suggest that the annotation schema is reliable. On the one hand, the analysis of those disagreements, in conjunction with the gold annotations, provides fresh insights about the efficacy of the features provided to the classifiers for the learning phase. On the other hand, when all the classifiers agree on a wrong annotation, it is a strong signal of ambiguity in the annotation schema and/or guidelines.

In Section 2 we briefly introduce the data to which we apply the methodology described in Section 3. In Section 4 we report results. In Section 5 we mention studies related to ours and in Section 6 we draw conclusions and identify steps for future work.

2 Data

We tested our methodology on the *SentiML* corpus (Di Bari et al., 2013) for which the annotation guidelines, as well as the original and annotated texts, are publicly available [1]. The corpus consists of 307 English sentences (6987 tokens), taken from political speeches, *TED* talks (Cettolo et al., 2012), and news items from the *MPQA opinion corpus* (Wilson, 2008).

The aim of its annotation is to encapsulate opinions in pairs, by marking the role that each word takes (modifier or target). For example, in

"More of you have lost your homes and even more are watching your home values plummet"

there would be two pairs: *modifier* "lost" and *target* "homes", and *modifier* "values" and *target* "plummet". Such two pairs are called *appraisal groups*.

[1] http://corpus.leeds.ac.uk/marilena/SentiML

LAW VIII - The 8th Linguistic Annotation Workshop, pages 82–86,
Dublin, Ireland, August 23-24 2014.

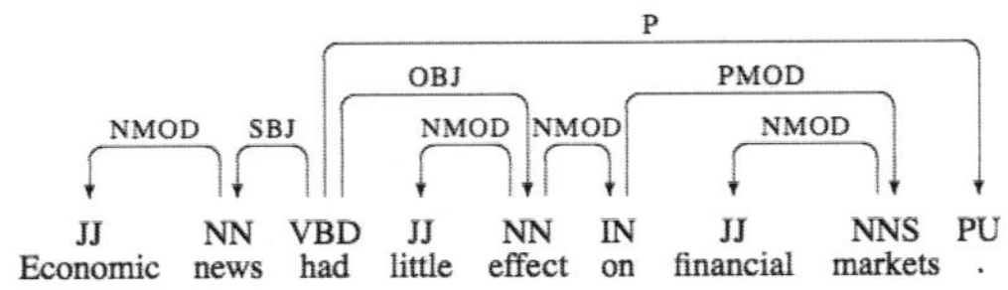

Figure 1: Example of dependency tree. Dependency trees provide features for the machine learning step.

For each of these elements several features are annotated that are believed to improve the task of sentiment analysis. The study presented here relates to the automatic identification of modifiers and targets.

3 Methodology

To test our methodology we selected a corpus for which various types of linguistic information related to appraisal groups were annotated. We started with the identification of modifiers and targets, since this represents the base of all the other levels of annotation.

To test the reliability of annotation we set 10% of our annotated corpus aside, and performed the machine learning part of the study on the remaining 90% of our corpus.

The first step consists of preparing the features for the machine learning phase. The optimal set to model the annotation task varies from problem to problem. We used the following:

- Word features, representing the ordinal identifier, word form, lemma and POS tag of each word.
- Contextual features, representing the lemma and POS tags of the preceding and succeeding words.
- Dependency-based features, representing the reference to the word on which the current token depends in the dependency tree (*head*) along with its lemma, POS tag and relation type (see Figure 1) (Nivre, 2005).
- Number of linked modifiers, representing the number of adjectives and adverbs linked to the current word in the dependency tree.
- Role, representing the predicted role (modifier or target) of the current token in conveying sentiment. The predictions are computed using fixed syntactic rules.
- Gazetteer-based sentiment. We used the *NRC Word-Emotion Association Lexicon* (Mohammad, 2011) to represent the *a-priori* sentiment of each word, i.e. regardless of its context.

Once the features are ready, two or more feature partitions (called *views* in the co-training strategy) have to be defined in order to be as orthogonal as possible (Abney, 2007). We opted for a linguistically-grounded dichotomy: lexical features (word features, role and gazetteer-based sentiment) versus syntactic features (contextual and dependency-based features, number of linked modifiers). The training and test sets are split accordingly.

At this point, machine learning classifiers are chosen. These need to be confidence-rated, i.e. able to provide a confidence rate for each prediction. In our experiments we selected Naïve Bayes, Radial Basis Function Network and Logistic Regression[2]. These models rely on very different strategies, which makes the analysis more reliable. We discarded Support Vector Machines since in our preliminary experiments they achieved high precision (a range between 0.60 and 0.77 across modifiers and targets), but very low recall (a range between 0.05 and 0.06 across modifiers and targets), which resulted in a very low F-measure (a range between 0.09 and 0.11 across modifiers and targets).

A model for each combination of view and classifier is then produced and tested on the test set. We performed a 10-fold cross-validation. In the test phase, we opted for a numerical threshold of 0.67 to consider the predictions reliable. A prediction with a confidence lower than the threshold is considered uncertain.

For each instance we obtained six predictions, which potentially differ from one another. The agreement score is calculated for each class in order to identify the most frequent prediction.

[2]In each case we used the implementation provided by WEKA (`http://www.cs.waikato.ac.nz/~ml/weka/`).

Feature set	Classifier	Modifier			Target		
		Precision	Recall	$F_{\beta=1}$	Precision	Recall	$F_{\beta=1}$
Lexical	Naïve Bayes	**0.71**	0.10	0.48	**0.82**	0.12	0.43
	RBF Network	0.52	**0.56**	**0.54**	0.51	**0.59**	**0.55**
	Logistic regression	0.59	0.42	0.49	0.61	0.48	0.54
Syntactic	Naïve Bayes	0.46	0.48	0.47	**0.82**	0.12	0.43
	RBF Network	0.49	0.35	0.40	0.55	0.50	0.53
	Logistic regression	0.58	0.22	0.32	0.60	0.41	0.49

Table 1: Performance of the classifiers trained on two views, lexical and syntactic. Experiments have been performed using 10-fold cross-validation.

At this point, only the predictions different from the gold annotations are considered: the higher the agreement score, the more the instance is interesting in the context of our analysis.

The final step consists of manually investigating such cases to shed light on the errors. In this experiment we opted for the use of a simple protocol based on the following classification schema:

- W (wrong), where the classifiers disagree with the gold annotation, which we judge to be correct.
- A (ambiguous), where the classifiers disagree with the gold annotation and we judge both to be valid. In such cases, the guidelines need to be clearer or the annotation method could have been simpler.
- M (to modify), where we judge that the gold annotation is incorrect.

This approach has the advantage of yielding a much reduced subset of instances to be examined manually, with respect to the full set.

4 Results

Table 1 shows the performances of the six models obtained from the training of each combination of view and classifier, mentioned in Section 3. F-measures for modifiers range between 0.32 and 0.54 for modifiers, and 0.43 and 0.55 for targets. Overall, the RBF Network trained on the lexical view performs best. However, there is no huge difference in general in performances between the lexical and the syntactic feature sets, which is good in the light of data sparseness.

Performance on the the empty class (no category assigned) was exceptionally good, as 76% was predicted out of the gold 77%, whereas the performance on the modifiers was 4% out of the gold 12% and the performance on the targets was 5% out of the gold 11%. Although the annotation allows each token to be simultaneously annotated as modifier and target, we have not reported the performances for the MT class as the cases were not significant. Finally, there was a 15% of cases in which the classifiers were not confident.

In relation to the manual classification of errors (see final paragraph of Section 3) we found that, out of the total test instances (2066), in 436 cases the most predicted class differed from the gold standard: the label *W* was assigned 214 times (49%), the label *A* was assigned 153 times (35%), the label *M* was assigned 69 times (16%). *W* was mostly assigned when the modifier or the target was correctly identified, but not its counterpart in the pair (e.g., "way forward", "blame society", "wrong side"). It was also assigned when a word was correctly identified as evoking sentiment (e.g., "destroy", "flourish"), but only the first of two or more targets was identified (e.g., "women and children", "the city and the country").

A was assigned when an adverb was annotated as modifier (e.g., "through corruption", "seize gladly", "tragically reminded"): these are cases in which human annotators decide to include the adverb if it is regarded as important for the sentiment. Other cases in which the label has been used is with compound modifiers (e.g., "face to face", "in the face of"), phrasal verbs (e.g., "turn back", "carried forth", "came forth") and difficult couples to link (e.g., "instruments with which we meet them" [challenges]). Finally, this label was also used in cases in which the prediction was sensible, but considered less accurate than the gold one (e.g., in "enjoy relative plenty", the gold standard was "enjoy plenty" and the classifiers predicted “relative plenty”).

M was assigned when another modifier had been wrongly annotated by the annotator, instead of modifying the value of the force of the current one (e.g., in “much more”, only “more”' should have been annotated with *high* force), in the case of couples with no sentiment (e.g., “future generations”, “different form”), of couples not previously identified (e.g., “stairway filled with smoke”, “icy river”) or couples that could have been annotated in an easier way (e.g., “provoke us to step up and do something”, “image resonates with us”).

5 Related work

Evaluating the reliability of human annotation is a challenging and widely studied task (Pustejovsky and Stubbs, 2012). The standard solution is the measurement of an inter-annotator agreement (IAA) coefficient according to a variety of formulae that depend on the characteristics of the annotation setting (Artstein and Poesio, 2008).

For example, in the case of Wilson (2008) and Read and Carroll (2007), it was useful to understand inconsistencies in the selection of the span for attitudes and targets. Since this represents only one of the commonly recognized challenges, some studies have focused on practically testing a methodological framework for schema development for fine-grained and quality semantic annotations. (Bayerl et al., 2003).

Our approach varies from the standard procedure in ways similar to that of Snow et al. (2008). For each expert annotator (six in total) they trained a system using only the judgements provided by these annotators, and then created a test set using the average of the responses of the remaining five labellers on that set. This resulted in six independent expert-trained systems. The difference with our methodology is that we trained six independent classifiers, but based on judgements of only one human annotator, and compared the average of the responses of six classifiers with the gold standard.

Jin et al. (2009) also used the strategy of selecting the labelled sentences agreed upon by their classifiers and achieved good performances in the task of identifying opinion sentences.

Finally, our methodology is also similar to one of those mentioned by Yu (2014). The author used the traditional co-training strategy, i.e. providing a small pool of unlabelled data to two classifiers with confidence rates, in order to obtain automatically labelled examples that would be added to an initial set of labelled ones. Subsequently, this final large set is used to train the the two classifiers and a combination of them (constructed by multiplying their predictions) is eventually the one used to label new documents. Five strategies were applied to obtain the views: (a) using unigrams and bigrams as features, (b) randomly splitting the feature set in two, (c) using two different supervised learning algorithms because they would provide useful examples to each other since based on different learning assumptions; (d) randomly splitting the training set, and (e) applying a character-based language model (CLM) and a bag-of-words model (BOW). We extended the third strategy by using three classifiers and two different views for each of them, and by applying this to the task of annotation validation rather than semi-supervised learning.

6 Conclusions

In this paper we have presented a methodology that makes use of multiple classifiers (based on different views) in order to detect inconsistent annotations and borderline cases. In our test set, we found that in 35% of the wrongly classified cases the predictions were different but acceptable, and in the 16% of them the predictions suggested that the gold standard was wrong. On the other hand, the data resulting from such procedure related to non-disagreeing predictions can be regarded as expression of either the efficacy of the annotation schema and guidelines or the features used for the machine learning step.

Our next goal is to improve the performances of the classifiers over the instances that were incorrectly handled, currently accounting for the 26% in our test set. We will also test the same methodology over the extraction of the link between targets and modifiers (appraisal groups). The machine learning models, the datasets and the error analysis are publicly available in order to ensure reproducibility [3].

[3] http://corpus.leeds.ac.uk/marilena/SentiML/LAW2014_error_analysis.zip

References

Steven Abney. 2007. *Semisupervised Learning for Computational Linguistics*. Chapman & Hall/CRC, 1st edition.

Ron Artstein and Massimo Poesio. 2008. Inter-coder agreement for computational linguistics. *Comput. Linguist.*, 34(4):555–596, December.

Petra S. Bayerl, Harald Lüngen, Ulrike Gut, and Karsten I. Paul. 2003. Methodology for reliable schema development and evaluation of manual annotations. In *Proceedings of the Workshop on Knowledge Markup and Semantic Annotation at the Second International Conference on Knowledge Capture (K-CAP 2003*, pages 17–23.

Mauro Cettolo, Christian Girardi, and Marcello Federico. 2012. Wit^3: Web inventory of transcribed and translated talks. In *Proceedings of the 16th Conference of the European Association for Machine Translation (EAMT)*, pages 261–268, Trento, Italy, May.

Marilena Di Bari, Serge Sharoff, and Martin Thomas. 2013. SentiML: Functional annotation for multilingual sentiment analysis. In *DH-case 2013: Collaborative Annotations in Shared Environments: metadata, vocabularies and techniques in the Digital Humanities*, ACM International Conference Proceedings.

Wei Jin, Hung H. Ho, and Rohini K. Srihari. 2009. Opinionminer: a novel machine learning system for web opinion mining and extraction. In *Proceedings of the 15th ACM SIGKDD international conference on Knowledge discovery and data mining*, KDD '09, pages 1195–1204, New York, NY, USA. ACM.

Saif Mohammad. 2011. From once upon a time to happily ever after: Tracking emotions in novels and fairy tales. In *Proceedings of the 5th ACL-HLT Workshop on Language Technology for Cultural Heritage, Social Sciences, and Humanities*, pages 105–114, Portland, OR, USA, June.

Joakim Nivre. 2005. Dependency grammar and dependency parsing. Technical report, Växjö University.

James Pustejovsky and Amber Stubbs. 2012. *Natural Language Annotation for Machine Learning*. Oreilly and Associate Series. O'Reilly Media, Incorporated.

Jonathon Read, David Hope, and John Carroll. 2007. Annotating expressions of appraisal in English. In *Proceedings of the Linguistic Annotation Workshop*, LAW '07, pages 93–100, Stroudsburg, PA, USA.

Rion Snow, Brendan O'Connor, Daniel Jurafsky, and Andrew Y. Ng. 2008. Cheap and fast—but is it good?: Evaluating non-expert annotations for natural language tasks. In *Proceedings of the Conference on Empirical Methods in Natural Language Processing*, EMNLP '08, pages 254–263, Stroudsburg, PA, USA. Association for Computational Linguistics.

Theresa Ann Wilson. 2008. *Fine-grained Subjectivity and Sentiment Analysis: Recognizing the Intensity, Polarity, and Attitudes of Private States*. Ph.D. thesis, University of Pittsburgh.

Ning Yu. 2014. Exploring co-training strategies for opinion detection. *Journal of the Asssociation for Information Science and Technology*.

Annotating a Large Representative Corpus of Clinical Notes for Parts of Speech

Narayan Choudhary, Parth Pathak, Pinal Patel, Vishal Panchal
ezDI, LLC.
{narayan.c, parth.p, pinal.p, vishal.p}@ezdi.us

Abstract

[We report of the procedures of developing a large representative corpus of 50,000 sentences taken from clinical notes. Previous reports of annotated corpus of clinical notes have been small and they do not represent the whole domain of clinical notes. The sentences included in this corpus have been selected from a very large raw corpus of ten thousand documents. These ten thousand documents are sampled from an internal repository of more than 700,000 documents taken from multiple health care providers. Each of the documents is de-identified to remove any PHI data. Using the Penn Treebank tagging guidelines with a bit of modifications, we annotate this corpus manually with an average inter-annotator agreement of more than 98%. The goal is to create a parts of speech annotated corpus in the clinical domain that is comparable to the Penn Treebank and also represents the totality of the contemporary text as used in the clinical domain. We also report the output of the TnT tagger trained on the initial 21,000 annotated sentences reaching a preliminary accuracy of above 96%.]

1 Introduction

Automated parts of speech (PoS) annotation have been an active field of research for more than 40 years now. Obviously, there are quite a few of tools already available with an impressive accuracy returns (Toutanova et al, 2003; Shen et al., 2007; Spoustov´a et al., 2009; Søgaard, 2010). This is true in the general domain text such as news reports or general domain articles. But when it comes to a niche area like clinical domain, no automated parts of speech taggers are readily available nor has there been any report of any such large corpus developed that meet the standards as set out in the general domain. Interest has grown now as NLP is sought after in the clinical domain, particularly for the task of information extraction from clinical notes.

There have been previous attempts for creating PoS annotated corpus in the clinical domain (Tateisi et al., 2004; Pakhomov et al, 2006; Albright et al., 2013). All of these corpora are relatively small and the PoS taggers trained on them have not been shown to reach above 96% in the clinical domain. Attempts at adapting a general domain PoS tagger to work better for clinical domain include Easy Adapt (Daumé H., 2007) and ClinAdapt (Ferraro et al., 2013). But none of these two adaptation methods enhance the accuracy levels to more than 95%.

Given that the text in clinical notes is radically different from what appears in the general domain, the general domain English PoS tagger models do not perform well on the clinical text. Our experiments with three such general domain taggers, namely Charniak (Charniak and Johnson, 2005), Stanford (Klein and Manning, 2003) and OpenNLP, yielded not more than 95% accuracy. This motivated us to take a radical step of developing a fresh parts of speech annotated corpus comparable to the Penn Treebank. Well, we are aware that it is going to take a lot of money, time and effort. But we also believe that it is necessary if we need better NLP tools for this domain.

2 The Representative Corpus

To ensure that we have a representative corpus, we sampled a corpus of more than 750,000 documents from 119 providers (hospitals and specialty clinics). The biggest challenge was to take a representative sample of documents from various specialties and different work types. Thanks to the metadata information available in our internal repository, this was solved in a rather easier way although we did need to look for information on classification and sub-classification of the domain manually.

LAW VIII - The 8th Linguistic Annotation Workshop, pages 87–92,
Dublin, Ireland, August 23-24 2014.

2.1 Sampling Task

Out of these 750,000 documents, we selected only ten hospitals for document sampling as they were large providers with a greater number of note count and provided a diversity of the specialty doctors/providers dictating the clinical notes. These ten hospitals amounted to a total of 237,110 documents written by 508 doctors of roughly 97 clinical specialties. A summary of this is given in Appendix A.

2.2 Sentence Clustering

We have used 237,110 documents for the process of selecting the sample sentences undergoing the PoS annotation. All of these documents were classified into different categories based on their work types (operative notes, admission notes, discharge summaries etc.), service line (cardiology, oncology, medicine, ambulatory etc.), section headers (History of Present Illness, Chief Complaints, Physical Examination, Laboratory Data etc.). Based on this classification, we have selected a sample of 10,000 documents fairly representing the 237,110 documents selected in the first phase.

These 10,000 documents were parsed using the Charniak's full syntactic parser (Charniak & Johnson, 2005). After some modifications, the Charniak parser on clinical data gives an accuracy of about 95% at the PoS level. A graph based string similarity algorithm was used to find similar sentences from these 10,000 documents. A summary of what it yielded is as follows:

Total Number of Sentences:	704,271
Total Number of Unique Sentences:	365,518
Total Number of Unique Patterns:	234,909

The unique patterns were clustered together using a hierarchical clustering algorithm. Patterns were grouped together by calculating the Euclidean distance with a threshold similarity of 80 or more. Following this method, we got a total of 3,768 patterns that represented all of the unique patterns. We call them pattern heads.

By giving a proportional weightage to each of these pattern heads as per their occurrence in the unique patterns, we derived a total of 56,632 sentences. While no two sentences selected are same, about 41% of the patterns in the sample corpus have a frequency of more than 1.

Appendix B shows example pairs of sentences having the same tag pattern and Appendix C shows example pairs of sentences having similar pattern.

The final selected candidate sentences also contained quite a few junk sentences (which came of course from the clinical notes themselves) or some very frequent smaller patterns (e.g. date patterns), we manually removed them to get a total of 49,278 sentences with a total word count of 491,690 and an average per sentence word count of 9.97. The greatest number of token for a sentence was found to be 221 in the sampled corpus (while the same in the original, actual corpus is 395).

3 Annotation Method

As against the common practice of semi-automatic method of annotating text, we purposely chose to annotate the text from scratch. It has been reported that tools do affect the decisions of the annotators (Marcus et al., 1993). We asked the annotators to use simple notepad and for each of the tokens they had to key in the appropriate PoS label. Tokenization and sentence boundary detection were automatically done before it went to the annotators.

As against the common practice of engaging annotators with a medical background and training them into linguistic annotation (Pakhomov et al., 2006; Fan et al., 2011), we purposely chose to engage linguists and train them into medical language. The annotators were all graduate level researchers in linguistics and had a deep knowledge of theoretical syntax. As next step in linguistics analysis after PoS tagging is syntactic parsing or chunking, the linguists were also motivated to learn about the goals of this task i.e. we informed them about our interests in developing a chunker and a parser afterwards. This information helps the annotators to think in terms of making syntactic tree while assigning a PoS tag. For example, there is always confusion among the tag pairs IN/RP, VBN/JJ and so on. But if one can try drawing a syntactic tree, the confusion gets cleared. While training annotators with medical background in linguistics for the task of PoS tagging may seem rather easy, the same cannot be said for syntactic tree formation. Besides, the linguists always had the choice of consulting medical experts (medical coders, medical transcriptionists with more than 5 years of experience) in case any phrase had to be explained in terms of its meaning.

Training sessions were held for linguists for first 15 days during which differences were brought to fore and a consensus was reached. This period was strictly for training purposes and text annotated during this period was validated more than thrice before getting included in the final corpus. After this training period, an inter-annotator agreement round was run with 10,000 sentences distributed to four annotators in turn. Each file was annotated by at least two annotators. The differences were then compared and arbitrated by a third annotator who discussed the conflicting cases with the initial annotators and brought a consensus among them.

Inter-annotator agreement at the start of this phase was 93% to 95%. This after a month increased to a consistent 97% to 100%. We are at the end of this phase and the accuracy is consistently close to 99%. Also of note is the fact that apart from the initial 5 days of face-to-face training session, the annotators never sit together and they work remotely from the convenience of their location and have a flexible time. We also ensured that they do not work long hours at a stretch doing this job as we know that this is a tedious job and cannot be done in a hurry. For a full-time annotator, the target goal was annotation of 1600 word per day (8 hours) and for the part-time annotators, it was half of that. They were always encouraged to come up with any issues for a weekly discussion on the conflicting or confusing cases.

For the later phases of annotation process, it is ensured that each annotation is validated by at least one other annotator. If disagreements arise, arbitration is done by involving a third annotator following a discussion.

As the text might contain tokenization errors, sentence boundary detection errors and other grammatical or typographical mistakes, the annotators are asked to document them in a separate spreadsheet. The sentences themselves are sacrosanct to the annotators and they can at the most make changes in separating the hyphenated words if they are not properly hyphenated by the tokenizer and document this change.

4 Annotation Guideline

Barring a couple of new tags, the annotation guideline largely follows the Penn Treebank PoS annotation guidelines (Santorini, B., 1990) and takes inputs from various other guidelines such as the Penn Treebank II parsing guidelines (Bies et al., 1995) and MiPACQ guidelines (Warner et al., 2012). A new tag that we have added on top of the Penn tagset looks for marking a difference between the expletive "it" and the pronominal "it" as it helps in tasks like anaphora resolution. The new tag for the expletive use of 'it' is given as "EXP". The tagset contains a total of 41 tags. The other four tags are HYPH, AFX, GW and XX. These tags are well described in the MiPACQ guideline.

As we have also seen the PoS labels given to the Penn Treebank data, we find that we are differing in assigning the tag to some of the words. For example, for the temporal expressions like "today", "yesterday" and "tomorrow", the tag in Penn corpus is invariably NN while we make a difference in their adverbial use and nominal use and assign the tag accordingly as "RB" or "NN".

5 Initial Training Results

After 4 months of annotation, we achieved a total of 21 thousand sentences annotated. For an experimental run, we trained a tagger to test how far we can go with this data. We implemented a modified version of the TnT (Trigram and Tag) (Brants, 2000) algorithm to train a PoS tagger. This tagger was given an input of 17,586 sentences containing a total of 158,330 words and was tested against 3,924 sentences containing a total of 38,143 words.

Without giving any extra features apart from the ones mentioned in Brants, we got a total of 2,621 sentences and 36,234 words annotated correctly. That is the TnT out-of-the-box accuracy was 95.00% as against the Charniak out-of-the-box accuracy of 91.36%.

We also compared the same test data against the Charniak parser (without the resource of tag dictionary and the rules). We find that the current tagger was actually performing better. Results improved by 0.33% if we modified the algorithm to handle unknown words using suffixes from the medical domain. These suffixes were collected specifically from the medical domain and were such for which a single tag could be given.

We also experimented with another method for improvements. This included using a dictionary of unambiguous words (words having single tags invariably, for adjectives and verbs only) and resetting the emission probability to 1 for them. These two improvement techniques combined enhanced the results by 1.24% to push the accuracy to 96.24%.

Given that a fraction of our corpus is giving us 95% accuracy which is at par with or better than reported anywhere else for PoS tagging task in the domain of clinical NLP, we believe that the results should only improve once we increase the training data and apply the improvement techniques available in the book.

6 Conclusion

There is a paucity of good and large enough annotated corpus in the domain of clinical NLP. The existing corpora are small although extensive analysis has been done on them. Our effort through this project is to fill the gap of having a large corpus comparable to the Penn Treebank.

In this paper we described an ongoing effort to create a sample corpus of clinical notes across most of the sub-domains and including all the different types of linguistic styles in this domain. We have also used a novel method for creation of a representative corpus which can be said to represent the whole of the clinical text in current practice across providers within United States.

As compared to semi-automated methods of annotation practiced even in big corpus like the Penn Treebank, we are following a fully manual process of annotation where the annotators are only given contextual information and no other help or props are provided apart from the guidelines to fasten the annotation process. We obtain an inter-annotator agreement of 98.93 and we believe that this is the best approach to go for this task.

Using the basic TnT algorithm we also train a tagger using 30% of our data (17,500 sentences) annotated in the initial 3 months of the project and achieve a baseline accuracy of 95%. We expect that our accuracy should improve to more than 98% once we train the same algorithm on all the 50,000 annotated sentences.

After the completion of the project, we may release this corpus for research use.

Acknowledgements

We acknowledge the contribution of the linguists at JNU, New Delhi namely, Oinam Nganthoibi, Gayetri Thakur, Shiladitya Bhattacharya and Srishti Singh. Thanks also to Suhas Nair and Hiral Dawe for their help in making us understand the nuances of the clinical text. We would also like to thank Prof. Pushpak Bhattacharya and Dr. Girish Nath Jha for their advice.

References

Ann Bies, Mark Ferguson, Karen Katz, Robert MacIntyre, Victoria Tredinnick, Grace Kim, Mary Ann, Marcinkiewicz and Britta Schasberger. 1995. *Bracketing Guidelines for Treebank II Style Penn Treebank Project*. TR, University of Pennsylvania

Daniel Albright, Arrick Lanfranchi, Anwen Fredriksen, William F Styler IV, Colin Warner, Jena D Hwang, Jinho D Choi, Dmitriy Dligach, Rodney D Nielsen, James Martin, Wayne Ward, Martha Palmer, Guergana K Savova. 2013. *Towards Comprehensive Syntactic and Semantic Annotations of the Clinical Narrative*. J. Am. Med. Inform Assoc. 20:922–930

Thorsten Brants. 2000. TnT: A Statistical Part-of-Speech Tagger. In: Proceedings of the Sixth Conference on Applied Natural Language Processing. Pp. 224-231.

Hal Daumé III. 2007. *Frustratingly Easy Domain Adaptation*. In: Proceedings of 45th Ann Meeting of the Assoc Computational Linguistics, 2007; 45:256–63.

Eugene Charniak and Mark Johnson. 2005. *Coarse-to-Fine n-best Parsing and MaxEnt Discriminative Reranking*. ACL'05.

Jung-wei Fan, Rashmi Prasad, Romme M. Yabut, Richard M. Loomis, Daniel S. Zisook, John E. Mattison and Yang Huang. 2011. *Part-of-Speech Tagging for Clinical Text: Wall or Bridge between Institutions?* In: AMIA Annu Symp Proc 2011 22; 2011:382-91.

Jeffrey P Ferraro, Hal Daume III, Scott L DuVall, Wendy W. Chapman, Henk Harkema and Peter J Haug. 2013. *Improving Performance of Natural Language Processing Part-of-Speech Tagging on Clinical Narratives through Domain Adaptation*. Journal of the American Medical Informatics Association. 2013; 20:931–939.

Dan Klein and Christopher D. Manning. 2003. *Accurate Unlexicalized Parsing*. In: Proceedings of the 41st Meeting of the Association for Computational Linguistics, pp. 423-430.

Mitchell P. Marcus, Beatrice Santorini and Mary Ann Marcinkiewicz. 1993. *Building a Large Annotated Corpus of English: The Penn Treebank*. Computational Linguistics 19: 313–330

Serguei V. Pakhomov, Anni Coden and Christopher G. Chute. 2006. *Developing a Corpus of Clinical Notes Manually Annotated for Part of Speech*. International Journal of Medical Informatics. 75(6):418-429

Beatrice Santorini. 1990. *Part-of-Speech Tagging Guidelines for the Penn Treebank Project*. Technical report MS-CIS-90-47, Department of Computer and Information Science, University of Pennsylvania.

Lui Shen, Giorgio Satta and Arvind Joshi, 2007. *Guided Learning for Bidirectional Sequence Classification*. In: ACL 2007.

Anders Søgaard. 2010. *Simple Semi-Supervised Training of Part-of-Speech Taggers*. In: Proceedings of the ACL 2010 Conference Short Papers. 205–208

Drahomira J. Spoustova, Jan Hajic, Jan Raab and Miroslav Spousta. 2009. *Semi-Supervised Training for the Averaged Perceptron POS Tagger*. In: Proceedings of the 12th Conference of the European Chapter of the ACL (EACL 2009). 763–771

Yuka Tateisi and Jun'ichi Tsujii. 2004. *Part-of-Speech Annotation of Biology Research Abstracts*. In: the Proceedings of 4th International Conference on Language Resource and Evaluation (LREC2004). IV. Lisbon, Portugal, pp. 1267-1270

Kristina Toutanova, Dan Klein, Christopher D. Manning and Yoram Singer. 2003. *Feature-rich Part-of-Speech Tag-ging with a Cyclic Dependency Network*. In: NAACL 73. 252–259

Colin Warner, Arrick Lanfranchi, Tim O'Gorman, Amanda Howard, Kevin Gould and Michael Regan. 2012. *Bracketing Biomedical Text: An Addendum to Penn Treebank II Guidelines*. http://clear.colorado.edu/compsem/documents/treebank_guidelines.pdf (accessed 11 May, 2014)

Appendix A: Summary of the Medical Sub-Domains Included in the Sample Corpus of Clinical Notes

Domains	Count	Sub-Specialties	Doctor Count	Top Level Domains	Note Count	Sub-Specialties	Doctor Count
Family Medicine	12515	9	58	Pathology	4901	1	6
Vascular and Thoracic Surgery	2447	7	11	Obstetrics	3771	1	7
IM_Cardiology	11555	6	40	IM_After Hours Care	3072	1	5
IM_Pulmonology	6563	6	21	Urology	2976	1	13
Emergency Medicine	12742	5	28	IM_Neurology	2796	1	12
Oncology	8325	4	11	IM_Hematology	1475	1	1
IM_Nephrology	5684	4	24	IM_General Medicine	1457	1	9
Unclassified	1941	4	4	IM_Pediatrics	1326	1	13
IM_Infectious Diseases	376	4	11	Anesthesiology	1211	1	1
Hospitalist	17767	3	12	IM_Oncology	1138	1	4
IM_Internal Medicine General	15751	3	56	Psychiatry	827	1	5

Surgery	9287	5	33	Neurosurgery	729	1	5
Otorhinolaryngology	605	3	6	IM_Physician Assistant	437	1	4
Radiology	84635	2	16	Podiatry	345	1	10
IM_Gastroenterology	6592	2	23	Opthalmology	321	1	3
IM_Physical Medicnie and Rehabilitation	5495	2	6	Nurse Practitioner	314	1	4
Orthopedics	5480	2	19	IM_Pain Management	305	1	2
Obstetrics & Gynecology	1243	2	16	IM_Occupational Medicine	82	1	1
IM_Geriatrics	103	2	2	IM_Rheumatology	77	1	2
IM_Hospice Care and Palliative Medicine	153	2	2	IM_Endocrinology	31	1	2

Appendix B: Example of Sentences having the same pattern

Sentence	Another Sentence With Same Pattern
ALLERGIES : He is allergic to procaine .	ALLERGIES : HE IS ALLERGIC TO IODINE .
ABDOMEN : Soft with no tenderness .	Abdomen : Soft with no organomegaly .
He had an unknown syncopalepisode .	He underwent a third cardiopulmonary resuscitation .
There was no significant ST depression .	There was no distal pedal edema .
There was no associated mass shift .	There was no apparent air leak .
The sheath was removed from the sling material .	The patient was resuscitated in the emergency room .
The patient was intubated in the emergency room .	The patient was placed on a CPAP mask .

Appendix C: Example of Sentence Header and Similar Patterns

Header Sentence	Similar Sentence
The patient was admitted into the hospital under observation .	The patient was hospitalized for this in 04/12 .
Sodium is 131 , potassium is 3.9 , chloride is 104 , bicarbonate is 23 , glucose is 174 , BUN is 12 , and creatinine is 0.82 .	Total protein is 7.4 , albumin is 4.8 , total bili 0.3 , alkphos is 99 , AST is 53 , ALT is 112 , serum osmo is 271 .
LUNGS : Lung sounds reveal still scattered wheezes .	LUNGS : Lung reveals some scattered wheezes .
ALLERGIES : He is allergic to sulfa medications .	ALLERGIES : He has no allergies to medications .
Pleasant Caucasian gentleman in no acute distress.	She is in no apparent distress.
Left L5-S1 stenosis with associated left S1 radiculopathy.	Left hip impingement syndrome with probable labral tear.
Lab work today shows the following hemoglobin 11.7 , white cell count 9.8 , platelet count is 59.	Shows hemoglobin is stable , WBC count is stable , and platelet count is stable.

Part-of-speech Tagset and Corpus Development for Igbo, an African Language

Ikechukwu E. Onyenwe
Dept. of Computer Science,
University of Sheffield
Sheffield S1 4DP, UK
i.onyenwe@shef.ac.uk

Dr. Chinedu Uchechukwu
Dept. of Linguistics
Nnamdi Azikiwe University
Anambra State, Nigeria
neduchi@yahoo.com

Dr. Mark Hepple
Dept. of Computer Science,
University of Sheffield
Sheffield S1 4DP, UK
m.r.hepple@shef.ac.uk

Abstract

This project aims to develop linguistic resources to support computational NLP research on the Igbo language. The starting point for this project is the development of a new part-of-speech tagging scheme based on the EAGLES tagset guidelines, adapted to incorporate additional language internal features. The tags are currently being used in a part-of-speech annotation task for the development of POS tagged Igbo corpus. The proposed tagset has 59 tags.

1 Introduction

Supervised machine learning methods in NLP require an adequate amount of training data. The first crucial step for a part-of-speech (POS) tagging system for a language is a well designed, consistent, and complete tagset (Bamba Dione et al., 2010) which must be preceded by a detailed study and analysis of the language. Our tagset was developed from scratch through the study of linguistics and electronic texts in Igbo, using the EAGLES recommendations.

This initial manual annotation is important. Firstly, information dealing with challenging phenomena in a language is expressed in the tagging guideline; secondly, computational POS taggers require annotated text as training data. Even in unsupervised methods, some annotated texts are still required as a benchmark in evaluation. With this in mind, our tagset design follows three main goals: to determine the tagset size, since a smaller granularity provides higher accuracy and less ambiguity (de Pauwy et al., 2012); to use a sizeable scheme to capture the grammatical distinctions at a word level suited for further grammatical analysis, such as parsing; and to deliver good accuracy for automatic tagging, using the manually tagged data. We discuss the development of the tagset and corpus for Igbo. This work is, to the best of our knowledge, the first published work attempting to develop statistical NLP resources for Igbo.

2 Some Grammatical Features of the Igbo Language

2.1 Language family and speakers

The Igbo language has been classified as a Benue-Congo language of the Kwa sub-group of the Niger-Congo family[1] and is one of the three major languages in Nigeria, spoken in the eastern part of Nigeria, with about 36 million speakers[2]. Nigeria is a multilingual country having around 510 living languages[1], but English serves as the official language.

2.2 Phonology

Standard Igbo has eight vowels and thirty consonants. The 8 vowels are divided into two harmony groups that are distinguished on the basis of the Advanced Tongue Root (ATR) phenomenon. They are -ATR: ị [ɪ], ụ [ʊ], a [ɑ], ọ [ɔ] and +ATR: i [i], u [u], e [e], o [o] (Uchechukwu, 2008). Many Igbo words select their vowels from the same harmony group. Also, Igbo is a tonal language. There are three distinct tones

[1]http://nigerianwiki.com/wiki/Languages
[2]http://en.wikipedia.org/wiki/Igbo_people

LAW VIII - The 8th Linguistic Annotation Workshop, pages 93–98,
Dublin, Ireland, August 23-24 2014.

recognized in the language viz; High, Low, and Downstep. The tones are represented as *High* [H] = [´], *Low* [L] = [`], *downstep* = [¯] (Emenanjo, 1978; Ikekeonwu, 1999) and are placed above the tone bearing units (TBU) of the language.

There are two tone marking systems, either: all high tones are left unmarked and all low tones and downsteps are marked (Green and Igwe, 1963; Emenanjo, 1978), or only contrastive tones are marked (Welmers and Welmers, 1968; Nwachukwu, 1995). We used the first system to illustrate the importance of tonal feature in the language's lexical or grammatical structure. For example, at the lexical level the word *akwa* without a tone mark can be given the equivalent of 'bed/bridge', 'cry', 'cloth', or 'egg'. But these equivalents can be properly distinguished when tone marked, as follows: akwa "cry", akwà "cloth", àkwà "bed or brigde", àkwa "egg". At the grammatical level, an interrogative sentence can be distinguished from a declarative sentence through a change in tone of the person pronouns from a high tone (e.g. *Ọ nà-àbịa* "He is coming") to a low tone (e.g. *Ọ̀ nà-àbịa* "Is he coming?"). Also, there are syllabic nasal consonants, which are tone bearing units in the language. The nasal consonants always occur before a consonant. For example: ǹdo 'Sorry' or explicitly tone marked as ǹdó.

2.3 Writing System

The Igbo orthography is based on the Standard Igbo by the Ọnwụ Committee (Ọnwụ Committee, 1961). There are 28 consonants: *b gb ch d f g gh gw h j k kw kp l m n nw ny ṅ p r s sh t v w y z*, and 8 vowels (see phonology section). Nine of the consonants are digraphs: *ch, gb, gh, gw, kp, kw, nw, ny, sh*.

Igbo is an agglutinative language in which its lexical categories undergo affixation, especially the verbs, to form a lexical unit. For example, the word form *ericharịrị* is a verbal structure with four morphemes: verbal vowel prefix *e-*, verb root *-ri-*, extensional suffix *-cha-*, and a second extensional suffix *-rịrị*. Its occurrence in the sentence "*Obi must eat up that food*" is *Obi ga-ericharịrị nri ahụ*, that is, *Obi aux-eat.completely.must food DET*. Igbo word order is Subject-Verb-Object (SVO), with a complement to the right of the head.

2.4 Grammatical Classes

Generally, Emenanjo (1978) identified the following broad word classes for Igbo: verbal, nominal, nominal modifier, conjunction, preposition, suffixes, and enclitics. The verbal is made up of verbs, auxiliaries and participles, while the nominal is made up of nouns, numerals, pronouns and interrogatives. Nouns are further classified into five lexical classes, viz; proper, common, qualificative, adverbial and ideophones. However, we identified extra five in the tagset design phase (see the appendix). Nominal modifiers occur in a noun phrase. Its four classes are adjectives, demonstratives, quantifiers and pronominal modifiers. Conjunctions link words or sentences together, while prepositions are found preceding nominals and verbals and cannot be found in isolation. Suffixes and enclitics are the only bound elements in the language. Suffixes are primarily affixed to verbals only, while enclitics are used with both verbals and other word classes. Suffixes are found in verb phrase slots and enclitics can be found in both verb phrase and noun phrase slots. The language does not have a grammatical gender system.

3 Language Resources

The development of NLP resources for any language is based on the linguistics resources available for the language. This includes appropriate fonts and text processing software as well as the available electronic texts for the work. The font and software problems of the language have been addressed through the Unicode development (Uchechukwu, 2005; Uchechukwu, 2006). The next is the availability of Igbo texts.

Any effort towards the Igbo corpus development is a non-trivial task. There are basic issues connected with the nature of the language. The first major surprise is that Igbo texts 'by native speakers' written 'for native speakers' vary in forms due to dialectal difference and are usually not tone-marked. Indeed, the tone marking used in the sections above are usually found in academic articles. It would be strange to find an Igbo text (literary work) that is fully tone marked and no effort has been made to undertake a tone marking of existing Igbo texts. Such an effort looks impossible as more Igbo texts are written and published. Such is the situation that confronts any effort to develop an Igbo corpus. Hence, developing NLP resources for the language has to start with the available resources; otherwise, such an endeavour would have to first take a backward step of tone marking all the texts to be added to its corpus and normalizing the dialectal differences. This is a no mean task.

It is for this reason that we chose the New World Translation (NWT) Bible version for Igbo corpus with its English parallel text[3]. The NWT Bible does not adopt a particular tone marking system, neither is there a consistent use of tone marks for all the sentences in the Bible. Instead, there is narrow use of tone marks in specific and restricted circumstances throughout the book. An example is when there is a need to disambiguate a particular word. For instance, *ihe* without tone mark could mean 'thing' or 'light'. These two are always tone marked in the Bible to avoid confusion; hence *ìhè* 'light' and *íhé* 'thing'. The same applies to many other lexical items. Another instance is the placement of a low tone on the person pronouns to indicate the onset of an interrogative sentence, which otherwise would be read as a declarative sentence. This particular example has already been cited as one of the uses of tone mark in the language. Apart from such instances, the sentences in the Bible are not tone marked. As such, one cannot rely on such restricted use of tone marks for any major conclusions on the grammar of the language. With regard to corpus work in general, the Bible has been described as consistent in its orthography, most easily accessible, carefully translated (most translators believe it is the word of God), and well structured (books, chapters, verses), etc. (Resnik et al., 1999; Kanungo and Resnik, 1999; Chew et al., 2006). The NWT Bible is generally written in standard Igbo.

4 Tokenization

We outline here the method we used in the tokenization of the text. For the sake of a start-up, we tokenized based on the whitespace. The Igbo language uses whitespace to represent lexical boundaries; we used the following regex:

Separate characters if the string matches:

- "ga-" or "n'" or "N'" or "na-" or "Na-" or "ana-" or "ịna-"; for example, the following samples *n'elu, na–erugharị, ịna-akwa, ana-egbu* in the Bible will be separated into *n', elu, na–, erugharị, ịna-, akwa, ana-, egbu* tokens.
- Any non-zero length sequence consisting of a–z, A–Z, 0–9, combining grave accent (̀), combining acute accent (́), combining dot below (̣); for example, these words *ìhè, ahụ́, ájá* in the corpus will be separated as tokens with their diacritics.
- Any single character from: left double-quotation mark ("), right double-quotation mark ("), comma (,), colon (:), semicolon (;), exclamation (!), question (?), dot (.).
- Any single non-whitespace character.

In place of sentence splitting, we use verses since all 66 books of the Bible is written in verse level. Our major aim is to use this Igbo corpus to implement our new tagset, which will capture all the inflected and non-inflected tokens in the corpus. For lack of space, issues with tokenization with respect to morphemes, manual annotation implemetations and platform used will not be discussed in this paper.

5 Tagset Design

We adopt the (Leech, 1997) definition of a POS tagset as a set of word categories to be applied to the tokens of a text. We designed our tagset following the standard EAGLES guidelines, diverging where necessary (e.g. EAGLES, which favours European languages, specifies *articles* at the obligatory level, but this category does not apply for Igbo). A crucial question in tagset design is the extent of fine-grained distinctions to encode within the tagset. A too coarsely grained tagset may fail to capture distinctions that would be valuable for subsequent analysis, e.g. syntactic parsing; too fine-grained may make automatic (and manual) POS tagging difficult, resulting in errors that lead to different problems for later processing. In what follows, we introduce a sizeable tagset granularity with the intention of providing a basis for practical POS tagging.

[3]Obtained from `jw.org`.

NNM	Number marking nouns	NNT	Instrumental nouns
NNQ	Qualificative nouns	VrV	$-rV$ implies suffix
NND	Adverbial nouns	VCJ	Conjunctional verbs
NNH	Inherent complement nouns	α_XS	any POS tag with affixes
NNA	Agentive nouns		

Table 1: Selected distinctive tags from the tagset scheme

The tagset is intended to strike an appropriate balance for practical purposes regarding granularity, capturing what we believe will be the key lexico-grammatical distinctions of value for subsequent processing, such as parsing. Further subcategorization of the grammatical classes, as described in section 2.4, results in 59 tags which apply to whole tokens (produced by the tokenisation stage described above). An important challenge comes from the complex morphological behaviour of Igbo. Thus, a verb such as *bịa*, which we assign the tag VSI (a verb in its simple or base form), can combine with extensional suffixes, such as *ghị* and *kwa*, to produce variants such as *bịaghị*, *bịakwa* and *bịaghịkwa*, which exhibit similar grammatical behaviour to the base form. As such, we might have assigned these variants the VSI tag also, but have instead chosen to assign VSI_XS, which serves to indicate both the core grammatical behaviour and the presence of extensional suffixes. In *abịakwa*, we find the same base form *bịa*, plus a verbal vowel prefix *a*, resulting in the verb being a participle, which we assign the tag VPP_XS. For the benefit of cross-lingual training and other NLP tasks, a smaller tagset that captures only the grammatical distinctions between major classes is required. The present 59 tags can easily be simplified to a coarse-grained tagset of 15 tags, which will principally preserve just the core distinctions between word classes, such as nouns, verb, adjective, etc.

Athough Emenanjo (1978) classified **ideophones** as a form of noun, we have assigned them a separate tag **IDEO**, as these items can be found performing many grammatical functions. For instance, the **ideophone** *kọị*, "to say that someone walks *kọị kọị*" has no nominal meaning, rather its function here is adverbial. A full enumeration of this scheme is given in the appendix.

5.1 The developement of an POS tagged Igbo Corpus

Here we analyse the manual POS tagging process that is ongoing based on the tagset scheme. The Bible books were allocated randomly to six groups, producing six corpora portions of approximately 45,000 tokens each. Our plan was for each human annotator to tag at least 1000 tokens per day, resulting in complete POS tagging in 45 days. The overall corpus size allocated is 264,795 tokens of the new testament Bible. There are six human annotators, who are students of the Department of Linguistics at Nnamdi Azikiwe University, Awka, supervised by a senior lecturer in the same department; giving an effective total of seven human annotators. Additionally, a common portion of the corpus (38,093 tokens) was given to all the annotators, as a basis for calculating inter-annotator agreement.

6 Conclusions

We have outlined our current progress in the development of a POS tagging scheme for Igbo from scratch. Our project aims to build linguistic computational resources to support research in natural language processing (NLP) for Igbo. It is important to note that these tags are applicable on unmarked, not fully marked, and fully tone marked Igbo texts, since the fully tone marked tokens play the same grammatical roles as in the none tone marked texts, written by native speakers for fellow native speakers.

Our method of tagset design could be used for other African or under-resourced languages. African languages are morphologically rich, and of around 2000 languages in the continent, only a small number have featured in NLP research.

Acknowledgements

We acknowledge the support of Tertiary Education Trust Fund (TETFund) in Nigeria, and would like to thank Mark Tice for his useful comments and help in preparing this paper.

References

Cheikh M. Bamba Dione, Jonas Kuhn, and Sina Zarrieß. 2010. Design and Development of Part-of-Speech-Tagging Resources for Wolof (Niger-Congo, spoken in Senegal). In *Proceedings of the Seventh International Conference on Language Resources and Evaluation (LREC'10)*. ELRA).

Peter A. Chew, Steve J. Verzi, Travis L. Bauer, and Jonathan T. McClain. 2006. Evaluation of the Bible as a Resource for Cross-Language Information Retrieval. In *Proceedings of the Workshop on Multilingual Language Resources and Interoperability*. Association for Computational Linguistics.

E. Nọlue Emenanjo. 1978. *Elements of Modern Igbo Grammar: A Descriptive Approach*. Ibadan Ox. Uni. Press.

Margaret M. Green and G. Egemba Igwe. 1963. *A descriptive grammar of Igbo*. London: Oxford University Press and Berlin: Akademie-Verlag.

Clara Ikekeonwu. 1999. *"Igbo", Handbook of the International Phonetic Association*. C. U. Press.

Tapas Kanungo and Philip Resnik. 1999. The Bible, Truth, and Multilingual OCR Evaluation. In *Proceedings of SPIE Conf. on Document Recognition and Retrieval*, pages 86–96.

Geoffrey Leech. 1997. *Introducing Corpus Annotation*. Longman, London.

P. Akujuoobi Nwachukwu. 1995. Tone in Igbo Syntax. Technical report, Nsukka: Igbo Language Association.

Guy de Pauwy, Gilles-Maurice de Schryverz, and Janneke van de Loo. 2012. Resource-Light Bantu Part-of-Speech Tagging. In *Proceedings of the Workshop on Language Technology for Normalisation of Less-Resourced Languages*, pages 85–92.

Philip Resnik, Mari Broman Olsen, and Mona Diab. 1999. The Bible as a Parallel Corpus: Annotating the 'Book of 2000 Tongues'. *Computers and the Humanities*, 33.

Chinedu Uchechukwu. 2005. The Representation of Igbo with the Appropriate Keyboard. In Clara Ikekeonwu and Inno Nwadike, editors, *Igbo Lang. Dev.: The Metalanguage Perspective*, pages 26–38. CIDJAP Enugu.

Chinedu Uchechukwu. 2006. Igbo Language and Computer Linguistics: Problems and Prospects. In *Proceedings of the Lesser Used Languages and Computer Linguistics Conference*. European Academy (EURAC).

Chinedu Uchechukwu. 2008. African Language Data Processing: The Example of the Igbo Language. In *10th International pragmatics conference, Data processing in African languages*.

Beatrice F. Welmers and William E. Welmers. 1968. Igbo: A Learner's Manual. Published by authors.

Ọnwụ Committee. 1961. The Official Igbo Orthography.

A A Tagset Design for the Igbo Language

Noun Class	
Tag	Description/Example
NNP	**Noun Proper**. *Chineke* 'God', Onyeka, Okonkwo, Osita.
NNC	**Noun Common**. *Ọkụ* 'fire', *ụwa* 'earth', *osisi* 'tree, stick', *ala* 'ground', *eluigwe* 'sky, heaven'
NNM	**Number Marking Noun**. *Ndị* 'people', *nwa* 'child', *ụmụ* 'children'. *ndị* is classified as a common noun with an attached phrase of "thing/person associated with" (Emenanjo, 1978). *ndị* preceding a noun marks plurality of that noun, *nwa* marks it singular (e.g. *nwa agbọghọ* 'a maiden'), and *ụmụ* also indicate plurality (e.g. *ụmụ agbọghọ* 'maidens').
NNQ	**Qualificative noun**. Nouns that are inherently semantically descriptive. E.g. *ogologo* [height, long, tall]
NND	**Adverbial noun**. This lexical class function to modify verbals, e.g. *O ji* ***nwayọọ*** *eri nri ya*
NNH	**Inherent Complement**. Igbo verb has a [verb + NP/PP] structure. NP/PP are the verb complement. They cooccur with the verb, at times quite distant from the verb, e.g. (1) *ịgụ egwu* 'to sing' , (2) *iti ịgba* 'to drum', (3) *igwu ji* 'harvest yam'.
NNA	**Agentive Noun**. Nouns are formed through verbs nominalization. Compare (1) with *ọgọ egwu* 'singer' and (2) with *oti ịgba* 'drummer'. For links *NNAV . . . NNAC*.
NNT	**Instrumental Noun**. Refer to instruments and are formed via nominalization. Compare (3) with *ngwu ji* 'digger'. For links *NNTV . . . NNTC*.
NOTE: We introduced link indicators in NNA and NNT, V and C, Where V and C stand for verbal and Complementary respectively. So, NNAV indicates derivation from the verbal component of the inherent complement verb and NNAC is the inherent complement of the whole verbal complex. E.g., *ọgụ/NNAV egwu/NNAC*. Also, NNTV and NNTC, where NNTV is derived from the verbal component of the inherent complement verb and NNTC is the inherent complement of the whole verbal complex. E.g. , *ngwu/NNTV ji/NNTC*	

	Verb Class
VIF	**Infinitive**. Marked through the addition of the vowel [i] or [ị] to the verb root.
VSI	**Simple verb**. Has only one verb root.
VCO	**Compound Verb**. Involves a combination of two verb roots.
VIC	**Inherent Complement Verb (ICV)**. Involves the combination of a simple or compound verb with a noun phrase or a prepositional phrase. It gives rise to the structures (1) V + NP, or (2) V + PP
VMO	**Modal Verb**. Its formed by inherent complement verbs and simple verbs. [See the section on suffixes]
VAX	**Auxiliary Verb**. ga [Future marking], na [progressive]
VPP	**Participle**. Always occurs after the auxiliary, and prefixed e/a to the verb root using vowel harmony.
VCJ	**Conjunctional Verb**. A verb that has a conjuntional meaning, especially in narratives: *wee*
VBC (BVC)	**Bound Verb Complment or Bound Cognate Noun**. Its formed by harmonizing prefix *a/e* to the verb root. It looks like the participle but occurs after the participle in same sentence as the verb. It can be formed from every verb.
VGD	**Gerund**. Reduplication of the verb root plus harmonizing vowel o/ọ. Also, internal vowel changes can occur. E.g. *ba* 'enter' [ọ + bụ + ba]=*ọbụba* 'the entering'
	Inflectional Class
VrV	$-rV$ (e.g. *-ra*). If attached to an active verb, it means simple past; but a stative meaning with a stative verb.
VPERF	**Perfect** (e.g. *-la/-le*, *-go*). Describes the 'perfect tense'. *-la/-le* obeys vowel harmony and the variant *-go* does not.
	Other part-of-speech tags
ADJ	**Adjective**. The traditional part of speech 'adjective' that qualifies a noun. Igbo has very few of them.
PRN	**Pronoun**. The 3 persons are 1st (sing + pl), 2nd (sing + pl), and 3rd (sing + pl) person Pronouns.
PRNREF	**Reflexive Pronoun**. Formed by combination of the personal pronouns with the noun *onwe* 'self'.
PRNEMP	**Emphatic pronoun**. This involves the structure [pronoun+onwe+pronoun].
ADV	**Adverb**. Changes or simplifies the meaning of a verb. They are few in Igbo.
CJN	**Conjunction**. There are complex and simple conjunctions distinguish based on grammatical functions viz; co-rodinators, sub-ordinators and correlatives. Link indicators *CJN1...CJN2* are for "correlative CJN". E.g. *ma/CJN1...ma/CJN2*.
PREP	**Preposition**. The preposition *na* is realised as *n'* if the modified word begins with a vowel.
WH	**Interrogative**. Questions that return useful data through explanation. *Ònye, gịnị, olee, ...*
PRNYNQ	**Pronoun question**. Questions that return YES or NO answer. E.g. *m̀, à, hà, ò, `ọ, ...*
IDEO	**Ideophone**. This is used for sound-symbolic realization of various lexico-grammatical function. E.g. *nịganịga, mụrịị, kọị, etc.*
QTF	**Quantifier**. This can be found after their nominals in the NP structure. E.g. *dum, naabọ, nille*.
DEM	**Demonstrative**. This is made up of only two deictics and always used after their nominals. E.g. *a, ahụ*.
INTJ	**Interjection**.*Ee*
FW	**Borrowed word**. *amen*.
SYM	**Punctuation**. It includes all symbols.
CD	**Number**. This includes all digits 1,2,3, ... and *otu, mbụ, abụa, atọ, ...*
DIGR	**Digraph**. All combined graphemes that represent a character in Igbo, which occur in the text. *gb, gw, kp, nw, ...*
TTL	**Title** . Includes foreign and Igbo titles. E.g. *Maazị*.
CURN	**Currency**.
ABBR	**Abbreviation**.
	Any type of suffixes
α_XS	**any POS tag with affixes**. for $\alpha \in$ {VIF, VSI, VCO, VPP, VGD, VAX, CJN, WH, VPERF, VrV, PREP, DEM, QTF, ADJ,ADV}. See verb, other POS, inflectional classes.
NOTE: Tags with affixes identify inflected token forms in the corpus for use in further analysis, e.g. morphology. For practical POS tagging, such tags may be simplified, i.e. $\alpha\_XS \Rightarrow \alpha$.	
	Any type of Enclitics
ENC	**Collective**. *cha, sị nụ, kọ* – means all, totality forming a whole or aggregate. **Negative Interrogative**. *dị, rị, dụ* – indicates scorn or disrespect and are mainly used in Rhetorical Interrogatives. **Adverbial 'Immediate present and past'**. *fọ/hụ* – it indicates action that is just/has just taking/taken place. *rịị* – indicates that an action/event has long taken place **Adverbial 'Additive'**. *kwa (kwọ), kwu* – mean 'also', 'in addition to', 'denoting', 'repetition or emphasis'. **Adverbial 'Confirmative'**. *nọọ (nọọ; nnọọ)* – this means really or quite.

B The Major Classes of the Tagset

ADJ	adjective	FW	foreign word	QTF	quantifier	ADV	adverb	NNC	common noun		
INTJ	interjection	SYM	symbol	CJN	conjunction	NNP	proper noun	PREP	preposition		
WH	interrogative	PRN	pronoun	V	verb	CD	number	DEM	demonstration		
There is no **article** in the language.											

Annotating descriptively incomplete language phenomena

Fabian Barteld, **Sarah Ihden**, **Ingrid Schröder**, and **Heike Zinsmeister**
Institut für Germanistik
Universität Hamburg
Von-Melle-Park 6
20146 Hamburg, Germany
`{ fabian.barteld, sarah.ihden, ingrid.schroeder, heike.zinsmeister }`
`@uni-hamburg.de`

Abstract

When annotating non-standard languages, descriptively incomplete language phenomena (EAGLES, 1996) are often encountered. In this paper, we present examples of ambiguous forms taken from a historical corpus and offer a classification of such descriptively incomplete language phenomena and its rationale. We then discuss various approaches to the annotation of these phenomena, arguing that multiple annotations provide the most appropriate encoding strategy for the annotator. Finally, we show how multiple annotations can be encoded in existing standards such as PAULA and GrAF.

1 Introduction

In grammatical annotations, a lack of ambiguity is of great benefit: The more distinctive the relationship between a token and its morphological and syntactic attributes, the more successful and reliable the annotation. However, especially in corpora of non-standard language varieties annotators are confronted with a significant number of cases of doubt and ambiguity. This problem has been more relevant in semantic and syntactic analyses than in PoS tagging and morphological annotation, and consequently has already been addressed in the former processes (Kountz et al., 2008; Bunt, 2007; Spranger and Kountz, 2007; Regneri et al., 2008) and incorporated into tools such as SALTO (Burchardt et al., 2006). With respect to corpora of non-standard languages, ambiguous forms must be taken into consideration in morphosyntactic tagging as well. This has been confirmed by current corpus projects of historical varieties of German – for example, the "MERCURIUS Corpus of Early New High German" (ENHG[1]) (Pauly et al., 2012) and the "Historical Tagset" (HiTS) (Dipper et al., 2013), which provide different options for dealing with ambiguities at the level of part of speech. Below we will discuss examples of ambiguities at the morphological level.

Within the extensive field of non-standard language annotations, we have concentrated on historical linguistics, showcasing the kinds of ambiguities that historical corpus linguists must confront and how they can be managed. Historical corpus linguistics based on annotation necessarily faces the challenge of avoiding circular argumentation. The description of a historic language must be based on the annotated texts of the corpus, since they are the only sources of linguistic material in historical grammatography. However, no annotation of the material can be accomplished without a basic knowledge of the language and its structure. Thus, an annotator confronted with a dubious case cannot know whether it is actually a case of ambiguity in the language system or whether the grammatical categories adopted for the annotation do not fit the grammatical system of the non-standard language. Transferring the annotation standards developed for a standardized language such as written New High German (NHG) to a historical corpus might at first seem tempting, but this process would conceal the actual grammatical characteristics of the language to be described.

[1] All language abbreviations in this article correspond to ISO 639.

LAW VIII - The 8th Linguistic Annotation Workshop, pages 99–104,
Dublin, Ireland, August 23-24 2014.

		Masc	Neut	Fem
Sg	**Nom**	hê, hî	it, et	sê, sî, sû̂
	Gen	is, es, sîn, sîner	is, es	ere, er erer, örer
	Dat	***en***, eme, öme	***en***, em, eme, öm, öme	
	Acc	***en***, ene, ön, öne	it, et	sê, sî, sû̂
Pl	**Nom**	sê, sî		
	Gen	ere, er, erer, örer		
	Dat	***en***, em, öm, jüm		
	Acc	sê, sî		

Table 1
GML pronouns - 3rd person; freely based on Lasch (1974)

Type of phenomenon	**True analysis**	**Annotator**	**Token**
Uncertainty	Dat	Dat?Acc?	*en*
Underspecification	Obj	Dat?Acc?	*en*
Ambiguity	{Dat,Acc}	Dat?Acc?	*en*

Table 2
Types of descriptively incomplete language phenomena

2 Cases of descriptively incomplete phenomena

The project "Reference Corpus Middle Low German/ Low Rhenish (1200–1650)"[2] transliterates and grammatically annotates the Middle Low German (GML) texts from which we take our examples. Because GML is a non-standardized language that is not well described, ambiguous forms occur frequently, and accurately interpreting them is a matter of high priority for any annotation. First, with regard to nouns and pronouns, GML's case syncretism[3] should be mentioned. For personal pronouns, in particular the syncretism of the dative and accusative forms in the first- and second-person singular and plural leads to problems in annotation. However, in this section, we concentrate on the third person.

Table 1 illustrates the many identical forms of third person personal pronouns that are used for several morphological feature values. Moreover, it reveals the distribution of case syncretism across the three different genders of the third-person singular.[4] While the neuter paradigm shows syncretism in the nominative and accusative forms, for the feminine pronouns there are ambiguous forms not only for nominative and accusative but also for genitive and dative. The masculine paradigm includes a partial syncretism of dative and accusative for the pronoun *en* ('him').

In addition, there is syncretism in the dative forms of the third-person singular masculine and neuter and in the third-person plural. Hence, in example (1),[5] the word *en* could be either masculine or neuter if there is no context providing reliable information on the gender of the referent, or it could even be plural (where there is syncretism between the three genders). If *en* is plural or neuter, it can only be a dative form, but if it is masculine, it could be either dative or accusative.

(1) vppe dat god-es sone ge-ere-t werd-e dor en
upon that god-M.GEN.PL son-M.NOM.SG PTCP-honour-PTCP will-3SG.PRS.SBJV through EN
'so that god's son would be honoured through EN'
(BuxtehEv, Joh 11,4)

Even where the context provides additional information, often not all ambiguities can be resolved. In example (1), the antecedent of *en* provides information on gender (masculine) and number (singular), but the ambiguity with respect to case can only be resolved in a local context – here, the prepositional phrase. The problem is that in GML the preposition *dor* ('through') can govern different cases. Consequently, the case ambiguity in (1) cannot be resolved.

There are many other examples of ambiguous forms, for instance, the gender of nouns or the inflection paradigm of verbs. For all these cases of ambiguity the annotation should provide as much grammatical information on a given form as possible.

[2]The "Referenzkorpus Mittelniederdeutsch/ Niederrheinisch (1200–1650)" ("Reference Corpus Middle Low German/ Low Rhenish", or "ReN"), supported by the German Research Foundation (DFG)) and in development since February/ March 2013 at the universities of Hamburg and Münster, is part of the "Corpus of Historical German Texts", together with the corpora "Altdeutsch" (Old German), "Mittelhochdeutsch" (Middle High German), and "Frühneuhochdeutsch" (Early New High German). More information on the structure of ReN can be found in Nagel and Peters (In print) and on the website `www.referenzkorpus-mnd-nrh.de`. For information on the annotation used in ReN and possible grammatical analyses, see Schröder (In print).

[3]Baerman (2006) asserts that "syncretism refers to the situation when a single inflectional form corresponds to multiple morphosyntactic feature values" (363). With respect to the feature case, this means that identical forms are used for different cases, e.g., for dative and accusative.

[4]The order of the pronouns was chosen for presentational reasons. The example *en* that we refer to in this paper is shown in bold italics.

[5]This glossing is based on the Leipzig Glossing Rules (`http://www.eva.mpg.de/lingua/pdf/LGR08.02.05.pdf`).

3 Types of descriptively incomplete language phenomena

In cases of descriptively incomplete language phenomena such as those described above, the annotator (which could be a tool or a human) is unable to unambiguously assign an analysis to the language data. This inability can have various causes. Consequently, EAGLES (1996) distinguishes between two types of "descriptively incomplete phenomena": *underspecification* and *ambiguity*. In the first case, the inability arises because "the distinction between the different values of an attribute is not relevant". The second case is characterized as "the phenomenon of lack of information, where there is uncertainty between two or more alternative descriptions". For both of these types, EAGLES provides subtypes; however, in the case of ambiguity, these subtypes also differ with respect to the reason for the uncertainty. In one subtype, the apparent ambiguity could be resolved given more information. In the other, the uncertainty results from a real ambiguity in the language or the given text and therefore cannot be resolved. Consequently, we propose a differentiation between three types of descriptively incomplete language phenomena that can occur during annotation: (i) **uncertainty**, i.e., incomplete information due to infrequent occurrence in the training material (automatic annotation), incomplete treatment in annotation guidelines, or an incomplete understanding of the language system (manual annotation); (ii) **underspecification**, i.e., incomplete information due to an undistinguished feature of the language system; and (iii) **ambiguity**, i.e., incomplete information due to an ambiguity in the language data.

Returning to example (1), further analyses could provide evidence that the preposition *dor* ('through') unambiguously takes the accusative case, such that this would represent a case of *uncertainty*. In English personal pronouns, there is no distinction made between dative and accusative, both of which are represented by the objective case (Obj) (Quirk et al., 1985). If this were also true for GML, the example would be a case of *underspecification*. However, it could also represent a true case of *ambiguity*. As long as this categorization is unclear, the types cannot be distinguished.

Table 2 summarizes the distinction between these three types. Although all of them result in the same situation for the annotator (machine or human), they differ with respect to the *true analysis*, which is unknown to the annotator; it is therefore impossible for him or her to definitively assign a tag to the token, as exemplified in Table 2. In situations of *uncertainty* or *underspecification*, an unambiguous, true analysis exists. In the case of uncertainty, it is a matter of redefining the annotation guidelines to help the annotating system to find this true analysis. In the case of underspecification, the tagset is too fine-grained to provide the true analysis. Only by adjusting the tagset would the annotator be able to determine the true analysis. Adjustments to the annotation guidelines and the tagset during the process of annotation can be accomplished through the use of an annotation development cycle such as the MATTER methodology (Pustejovsky and Stubbs, 2012, 23–32). In the case of *ambiguity*, however, both analyses are true. They should be retrievable for further interpretation and thus should both be assigned to the token.

Optimally, the different types of incomplete information "should be distinguishable by different markup" (EAGLES, 1996). But as we have argued, when annotating historical languages (or less-studied languages in general), it is not always possible to decide at the time of annotation whether there is an ambiguity, an underspecification, or an uncertainty, as all three result in the same problem for the annotator. Thus, in many cases, the annotator can only distinguish between the three types (if at all) after the annotation has been completed and the quantitative results based on the annotated data have become available. The three types must therefore be dealt with similarly during the annotation process, and the possible interpretations should be retrievable from the annotations. Consequently, the annotator should have the possibility to assign any number of annotations to every possible feature. This would require special tools to create and retrieve these annotations, but existing standards to encode annotations are already flexible enough to allow annotations. Some examples are shown in the next section.

4 Encoding multiple annotations in markup standards

This section presents three formats for encoding multiple annotations of descriptively incomplete structures in XML markup. We return to the ambiguous GML pronoun *en* 'him/ it' introduced in example (1) in Section 2.

Our first option is TüPP-D/Z DTD (Ule, 2004), an *inline-XML specification* that was designed to represent a ranked list of multiple competing tagger outputs resulting from ensemble tagging. Using the same kind of structure, all possible interpretations of the pronoun *en* could be encoded and made available for further analysis and disambiguation.

The other two options are generic *XML-standoff* formats that represent annotations as directed acyclic graphs: PAULA (Dipper, 2005; Chiarcos et al., 2008), derived from early drafts of the Linguistic Annotation Framework (LAF) (Ide and Romary, 2004), and GrAF (Ide and Suderman, 2007), a more recent specification of the LAF. Each level of annotation is represented separately, such that features are related to annotation objects ("markables") only by links. Markables themselves are defined on the basis of text tokens or other markables. Multiple markables can be related to the same token, as each markable is uniquely identified by its ID. These options also allow us to encode all interpretations of *en*.[6]

In certain cases, there are dependencies between multiple ambiguous features. Concerning 'en', if the gender is *Neut*, the case is not ambiguous, but if the gender is *Masc*, the case could be either *Dat* or *Acc* (cf. Table 1). The above strategies do not allow us to encode these dependencies. However, the generic LAF-derived standoff formats can be employed to do this because they also allow us to define labels for edges, such that they can be annotated and typed. Kountz et al. (2008) propose an extension to GrAF in which such dependencies are explicitly modeled. As depicted in Figure 1, we make use of this property to combine a choice structure with a collect structure. In this way, each token correlates with one MorphSet object that can be instantiated by a set of MorphInst objects, thereby explicitly encoding the dependencies between the multiple ambiguous features of gender and case.

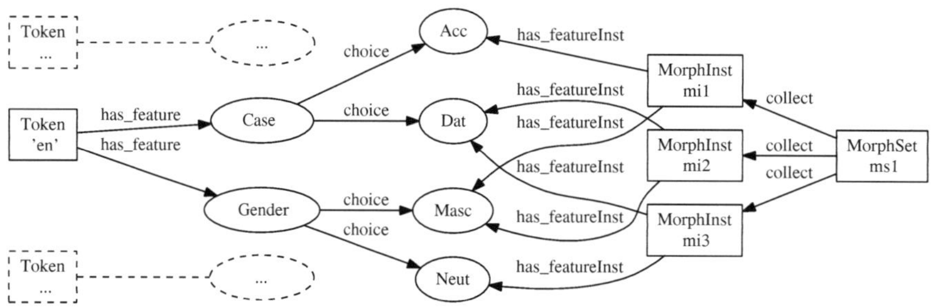

Figure 1: Representation of an encoding of the ambiguous GML pronoun *en* 'him/it' with typed edges

5 Conclusion and Outlook

In order to avoid circular argumentation and to reveal the actual grammatical characteristics of the language under investigation, historical corpus linguistics must go beyond simply adapting the rules of a standardized language, both by disambiguating ambiguous forms but also by encoding ambiguities. By means of data taken from the "ReN" corpus, we have demonstrated that in historical language corpora, annotators must deal with descriptively incomplete language phenomena. Furthermore, they need to decide what type of phenomena these are, i.e., real ambiguities, underspecifications or uncertainties. Often this decision is impossible at the time of the annotation, since all three types result in the same problem for the annotator, as discussed in Section 3. In Section 4, we have shown that in markup formats such PAULA or GrAF, the straightforward encoding of multiple annotations and their dependencies is possible. Nevertheless, linguists still lack sufficient tools to create, query, and visualize the multiple annotations represented in the underlying data structure. For these reasons, corpus projects such as "ReN" are currently unable to use multiple annotations, even though this is the most appropriate encoding strategy for the grammatical annotation of historical languages.

[6]In addition, PAULA offers a *multiFeat* structure (Zeldes et al., 2013, 14f.) for linking sets of fully-specified features to one markable. However, each piece of information must be unambiguous.

Acknowledgements

We would like to thank Kerstin Eckart for very helpful discussion and suggestions, and also Claire Bacher for improving our English. All remaining errors are ours. Figure 1 was created with GraphvizFiddle (`https://stamm-wilbrandt.de/GraphvizFiddle/`) an online editor for Graphviz (`http://www.graphviz.org/`). Part of this work was funded by the German Research Foundation (DFG).

Sources of Attested Examples

BuxtehEv Qvator Evangeliorum versio Saxonica. A GML handwritten gospel from the fifteenth century. Transliterated by the DFG-funded project "ReN". For further information, see Pettke and Schröder (1992).

References

Matthew Baerman. 2006. Syncretism. In Keith Brown, editor, *Encyclopedia of Language and Linguistics.*, volume 12, pages 363–366. Elsevier, Amsterdam [a.o.], 2nd edition.

Harry Bunt. 2007. Semantic underspecification: Which technique for what purpose? In Harry Bunt and Reinhard Muskens, editors, *Computing Meaning*, volume 83 of *Studies in Linguistics and Philosophy*, pages 55–85. Springer.

Aljoscha Burchardt, Katrin Erk, Anette Frank, Andrea Kowalski, and Sebastian Pado. 2006. SALTO: A versatile multi-level annotation tool. In *Proceedings of LREC 2006*, pages 517–520.

Christian Chiarcos, Stefanie Dipper, Michael Götze, Ulf Leser, Anke Lüdeling, Julia Ritz, and Manfred Stede. 2008. A flexible framework for integrating annotations from different tools and tagsets. *Traitement Automatique des Langues*, 49(2):271–293.

Stefanie Dipper, Karin Donhauser, Thomas Klein, Sonja Linde, Stefan Müller, and Klaus-Peter Wegera. 2013. HiTS: ein Tagset für historische Sprachstufen des Deutschen. [HiTS: A tagset for historical varieties of German]. *JLCL*, 28(1):1–53.

Stefanie Dipper. 2005. XML-based stand-off representation and exploitation of multi-level linguistic annotation schema. In *Proceedings of Berliner XML Tage 2005 (BXML 2005)*, pages 39–50, Berlin.

EAGLES. 1996. Recommendations for the morphosyntactic annotation of corpora. EAGLES document EAG-TCWG-MAC/R. Technical report.

Nancy Ide and Laurent Romary. 2004. International standard for a linguistic annotation framework. *Journal of Natural Language Engineering*, 10(3-4):211–225.

Nancy Ide and Keith Suderman. 2007. GrAF: A graph-based format for linguistic annotation. In *Proceedings of the Linguistic Annotation Workshop (LAW)*, pages 1–8, Prague, Czech Republic. Association for Computational Linguistics.

Manuel Kountz, Ulrich Heid, and Kerstin Eckart. 2008. A LAF/GrAF-based encoding scheme for underspecified representations of dependency structures. In *Proceedings of LREC-2008, Linguistic Resources and Evaluation Conference*, Marrakesh.

Agathe Lasch. 1974. *Mittelniederdeutsche Grammatik. [Middle Low German Grammar].* Sammlung kurzer Grammatiken germanischer Dialekte. A. Hauptreihe, 9. Niemeyer, Tübingen, 2nd edition.

Norbert Nagel and Robert Peters. In print. Das digitale "Referenzkorpus Mittelniederdeutsch/ Niederrheinisch (ReN)". [The digital Reference Corpus of Middle Low German/ Low Rhenish (ReN)]. In *Jahrbuch für germanistische Sprachgeschichte 5*. De Gruyter.

Dennis Pauly, Ulyana Senyuk, and Ulrike Demske. 2012. Strukturelle Mehrdeutigkeit in frühneuhochdeutschen Texten. [Structural ambiguities in Early New High German texts]. *JLCL*, 27(2):65–82.

Sabine Pettke and Ingrid Schröder. 1992. Eine Buxtehuder Evangelienhandschrift. Die vier Evangelien in einer mittelniederdeutschen Übersetzung des 15. Jahrhunderts aus dem Alten Kloster. [A Buxtehude handwritten gospel. A GML translation of the four gospels from the fifteenth century]. In Bernd Utermöhlen, editor, *Qvatuor Evangeliorum versio Saxonica. Eine mittelniederdeutsche Evangelienhandschrift aus dem 15. Jahrhundert. Textedition*, Buxtehuder Notizen Nr. 5, pages 99–266. Stadt Buxtehude, Buxtehude.

James Pustejovsky and Amber Stubbs. 2012. *Natural language annotation for machine learning*. O'Reilly, Beijing [a.o.].

Randolph Quirk, Sidney Greenbaum, Geoffrey Leech, and Jan Svartvik. 1985. *A Comprehensive Grammar of the English Language*. Longman, London.

Michaela Regneri, Markus Egg, and Alexander Koller. 2008. Efficient processing of underspecified discourse representations. In *Proceedings of the 46th Annual Meeting of the Association for Computational Linguistics on Human Language Technologies: Short Papers*, pages 245–248. Association for Computational Linguistics.

Ingrid Schröder. In print. Das Referenzkorpus: Neue Perspektiven für die mittelniederdeutsche Grammatikographie. [The reference corpus: New perspectives for GML grammatography]. In *Jahrbuch für germanistische Sprachgeschichte 5*. De Gruyter.

Kristina Spranger and Manuel Kountz. 2007. Efficient ambiguity-handling using underspecified representations. In Georg Rehm, Andreas Witt, and Lothar Lemnitzer, editors, *Data Structures for Linguistic Resources and Applications*. Gunter Narr Verlag, Tübingen.

Tylman Ule. 2004. Markup manual for the Tübingen Partially Parsed Corpus of Written German (TüPP-D/Z). Technical report, University of Tübingen.

Amir Zeldes, Florian Zipser, and Arne Neumann. 2013. PAULA XML Documentation: Format version 1.1. Technical Report Version: P1.1.2013.1.21a, Humboldt-Universität zu Berlin, Berlin.

Annotating Discourse Connectives in Spoken Turkish

Işın Demirşahin
Middle East Technical University
Informatics Institute
Department of Cognitive Science
e128500@metu.edu.tr

Deniz Zeyrek
Middle East Technical University
Informatics Institute
Department of Cognitive Science
dezeyrek@metu.edu.tr

Abstract

In an attempt to extend Penn Discourse Tree Bank (PDTB) / Turkish Discourse Bank (TDB) style annotations to spoken Turkish, this paper presents the first attempt at annotating the explicit discourse connectives in the Spoken Turkish Corpus (STC) demo version. We present the data and the method for the annotation. Then we reflect on the issues and challenges of transitioning from written to spoken language. We present the preliminary findings suggesting that the distribution of the search tokens and their use as discourse connectives are similar in the TDB and the STC demo.

1 Introduction

Turkish Discourse Bank (TDB) is the first discourse-annotated corpus of Turkish, which follows the principles of Penn Discourse Tree Bank (PDTB) (Prasad *et al.*, 2008) and includes annotations for discourse connectives, their arguments, modifiers and supplements of the arguments. The TDB is built on a ~ 400,000-word sub-corpus of METU Turkish Corpus (MTC) (Say *et al.*, 2002), a 2 million-word multi-genre corpus of post-1990 written Turkish[1].

In both PDTB and TDB, the discourse connectives link two text spans that can be interpreted as, or can be anaphorically resolved to abstract objects (Asher, 2003). The PDTB includes annotations for both explicit and implicit connectives, whereas TDB has covered only explicit connectives so far.

The explicit discourse connectives annotated in TDB come from a variety of syntactic classes, namely coordinating conjunctions (*ve* 'and'), subordinating conjunctions (*için* 'for/since') and discourse adverbials (*ancak* 'however'). It also annotates phrasal expressions (Zeyrek *et al*, 2013).

The coordinating and subordinating conjunctions are 'structural' discourse connectives that take their arguments syntactically, whereas discourse adverbials only take one argument syntactically, and the other one anaphorically (Forbes-Riley *et al.* 2006). For all syntactic types, the argument that syntactically accommodates the discourse connective is called the second argument (Arg2). The other argument is called the first argument (Arg1). In TDB, phrasal expressions consist of an anaphoric element and a subordinating conjunction. In PTDB, similar expressions are annotated as AltLex, a subtype of implicit connectives (Prasad *et al.* 2008). For example, *onun için* 'because of that' in (1) is annotated as a discourse connective with its two argument spans. In the rest of the paper, the connective is underlined, the Arg2 is in bold face, and Arg1 is shown in italics. Supplementary materials and modifiers are shown in square brackets labelled with subscripts when necessary.

---

[1] The MTC and the TDB are freely available to researches at http://ii.metu.edu.tr/corpus and http://medid.ii.metu.edu.tr, respectively.

LAW VIII - The 8th Linguistic Annotation Workshop, pages 105–109,
Dublin, Ireland, August 23-24 2014.

(1) O ses dinleme cihazı. *Ödev var da.* Onun için **sizi dinliyorum şu anda.**
"That is a recording device. *I have homework.* Because of that **I'm recording you right now.**"

The TDB has chosen to annotate these expressions as discourse connectives because they are highly frequent and have limited compositional productivity. Furthermore, some phrasal expressions such as *bunun aksine* 'contrary to this', *aksi takdirde* 'however' are so frequent that the native speakers perceive them as single lexical entries.

In an attempt to extend the PDTB/TDB style discourse annotation to spoken Turkish, we have annotated the search tokens in TDB on the Spoken Turkish Corpus (STC) (Ruhi *et al.*2009; 2010) demo version[2]. Following the TDB conventions, we annotated the phrasal expressions such as *onun için* 'because of that' and *ondan sonra* 'after that'. The annotation of 77 search tokens identified in TDB yielded a total of 416 relations in the STC demo.

In this paper we first present the data from the STC demo release, the method we used for annotations, and issues and challenges we have met. Then we present our preliminary findings. Finally, we discuss the methods and the findings of the study and draw a road map for future work.

2 Annotating Spoken Turkish

2.1 The Data

The Spoken Turkish Corpus demo version is a ~20,000-word resource of spoken Turkish. The demo version contains 23 recordings amounting to 2 hours 27 minutes. Twenty of the recordings include casual conversations and encounters, comprising 2 hours 1 minutes of the total, the 3 remaining recordings are broadcasts lasting a total of 26 minutes. The casual conversations include a variety of situations such as conversations among families, relatives and friends, and service encounters. The broadcasts are news commentaries. The topics of conversation range from daily activities such as infant care and naming babies to biology e.g. the endocrine system, to politics such as European Union membership process or the clearing of the mine fields on Syrian border. Such wide range of topics provide for a wide coverage of possible uses of discourse connectives even in such a relatively small corpus.

2.2 Annotation Method

Since our main aim was to follow the PDTB/TDB style, we chose to use the Discourse Annotation Tool for Turkish (DATT) (Aktaş et al., 2010). We used the transcription texts included in the STC demo version as the DATT input and provided the annotators with separate audio files.

This approach was a trade-off: the annotators could not make use of the rich features of the time-aligned annotation of the STC; but by importing text transcripts directly into an existing specialized annotation tool we did not have to go through any software development and/or integration stage. The annotators reported only slight discomfort in matching the text and the audio file during annotation, but stated that it was manageable as none of the files are long enough to get lost between the two environments.

2.3 Issues and Challenges

Some of the challenges of annotating discourse connectives we have already observed in written language transfer to the spoken modality. For example, in written discourse it is possible for an expression to be ambiguous between a discourse and non-discourse use, as the anaphoric elements can refer to both abstract objects and non-abstract entities. This applies to spoken language as well.

(2) SER000062: Şey Glomerulus o yuvarlak topun adı mıydı (bu)? Ordan şey oluyor…
AFI000061: hı-hı hı-hı
AFI000061: Süzülme ondan sonra oluyor ama. Şu Henle kulpu falan var ya. Şöyle geri.

[2] The STC demo version is freely available to researches at http://std.metu.edu.tr

"SER000062: Um Glomerulus was (this) the name of that round ball? Stuff happens there ...
AFI000061: Yes, yes.
AFI000061: Filtration occurs after that, though. That Loop of Henle and such. Reverse like this."

In (2) *ondan sonra* 'after that' could be interpreted as resolving to the clause 'Stuff happens there', which is an abstract object although a vague one. The pronoun can also refer to the glomerulus, which is an NP. This was exactly the case during the annotation of this specific example: one annotator interpreted it as a temporal discourse connective that indicates the order of two sub-processes of kidney function, whereas the other annotator interpreted that *o* 'that' refers to the NP and did not annotate this instance of *ondan sonra*. As a TDB principle, if an expression has at least one discourse connective meaning, it is annotated. As a result, this example was annotated as per the first annotator's annotation.

In spoken language, particularly spontaneous casual dialogues, phrasal expressions can take their first arguments from anywhere in the previous discourse. This is very much like discourse adverbials. For example, *için* in (3) displays an unattested use in TDB, as it appears distant from *both* its arguments, allowing the participant to question the discourse relation between two previous text spans. Given the supplemental material "thyroxin increases the metabolism" in line (a) by speaker AFI, speaker SER provides two propositions, "thyroxin is secreted by the thyroid gland" in line (b) and "people with overactive thyroids tend to be hyperactive" in line (e). In line (h), AFI offers a discourse connective "because" in order to show her understanding of the preceding discourse, i.e., something like '(so they tend to be very active) because of that?', where the material in parentheses are elided. One can argue that this connective builds a new discourse relation with one anaphoric and one elliptic argument. Nevertheless, we kept the annotations as shown in the example, because (a) it was the most intuitive annotation according to the annotators and (b) the DATT does not allow annotation of ellipsis as arguments for now.

(3) (a) AFI000061: [$_{\text{SUPP1}}$Tiroksin. Ha bak. Metabolizma hızını arttırıyor.]
[...]
(b) SER000062: *Tiroit bezinden tiroksin salgılanıyor.*
(c) AFI000061: Hmm salgılanıyor dedin sen. Tamam. Doğru.
(d) SER000062: Tamam.
(e) SER000062: Hatta tiroit şey olan... Emm **tiroidinde sorun olanlar çok ee şey olur ya aktif olur ya.**
(f) AFI000061: Hmm?
(g) SER000062: Çok hareketli olurlar. Evet.
(h) AFI000061: **Onun için** [$_{\text{MOD}}$mi]?

"(a) AFI000061: [$_{\text{SUPP1}}$Thyroxin. Oh look. It speeds up the metabolism.]
[...]
(b) SER000062: *Thyroxin is secreted by the thyroid gland.*
(c) AFI000061: Hmm you said secreted. Ok. Right.
(d) SER000062: Ok.
(e) SER000062: Actually thyroid is the one that... Emm **you know, those who have problems with thyroid are ee they tend to be very active.**
(f) AFI000061: Hmm?
(g) SER000062: They tend to be very energetic. Yes.
(h) AFI000061: [$_{\text{MOD}}$ Is (it)] **because of that**?"

Another problem with spoken corpus is that some elements may be missing. There are many examples that could not be annotated as discourse connectives, because the speakers were interrupted before they could complete, or at times even start, the latter argument of a possible discourse relation. In other examples, the argument may be there but not recorded clearly, or may be completely inaudible even though they were uttered because of background noise or overlapping arguments.

3 Preliminary Findings

In this section we present some of our preliminary findings and compare them to the TDB to the extent possible. Because of the large difference in size between the two corpora, we converted the raw numbers to frequencies. We used number/1000 words as the frequency unit in Table 1.

The top five most frequent connectives in the TDB in descending order are *ve* 'and', *için* 'for', *ama* 'but', *sonra* 'later' and *ancak* 'however' and the top five most frequent connectives in the STC are *ama* 'but', *ve* 'and', *mesela* 'for example', *sonra* 'later' and *için* 'for'. Here we compare the four most frequent connectives, namely, *ve, için, ama* and *sonra*, which make up 4951 (58.3%) of the total 8484 annotations in TDB and 217 (52.2%) of the total 416 relations annotated in the STC.

	TDB						**STC demo**					
	Discourse connectives			**Total instances**			**Discourse connectives**			**Total instances**		
Conn	#	*f*	%	#	*f*	%	#	*f*	%	#	*f*	%
ve 'and'	2112	5.31	28.2	7501	18.86	100	50	2.40	48.1	104	5.00	100
için 'because'	1102	2.77	50.9	2165	5.44	100	32	1.54	61.5	52	2.50	100
ama 'but'	1024	2.57	90.6	1130	2.84	100	96	4.61	80.7	119	5.72	100
sonra 'later'	713	1.79	56.7	1257	3.16	100	39	1.87	72.2	54	2.60	100

Table 1 - Written and spoken uses of *ve, için, ama,* and *sonra.*

Although both the frequency of the total occurrences of the connectives and their discourse uses seem to be lower in the spoken corpus, chi square tests show that the differences are not statically significant ($p>0.5$). The percentage of the use of tokens as discourse connectives across modalities is not significant either ($p>0.5$). The preliminary results indicate that the distribution of these five connectives and their uses as discourse connective are similar in written and spoken language.

The similarity is expected, as the MTC and the subcorpus that the TDB is built on are multi-genre corpora. Specifically, the TDB includes novels and stories, which in turn include dialogues. Also, there are interviews in news excerpts, which are basically transcriptions of spoken language. As a result, the TDB texts reflect some aspects of spoken language. In addition, 3 of the 23 files of the STC demo are news broadcasts and interviews, which are probably scripted and/or prepared. Thus they may not necessarily reflect all aspects of spontaneous spoken language.

4 Discussion and Conclusion

In this paper we presented a preliminary attempt at annotating Turkish Spoken Language in PDTB/TDB style. We used the transcripts and audio files of STC demo as our source, and used DATT of TDB to annotate the discourse relations. As future work, we intend to integrate the discourse annotation to the time-aligned annotation of the STC, thus allowing the users to benefit from the features of both annotation schemes.

During the annotation process, we encountered the use of discourse connectives unattested in TDB, specifically *için* 'since/for' in a predicative/interrogative position, where the connective occurs with its deictic Arg1. We assume that the question in which this connective is used has a rhetorical role, possibly expressing the speaker's understanding of the discourse relation in the previous discourse. Apart from this newly attested use, the distribution of the search tokens and their use as discourse connectives remain largely similar to that of the TDB. We conclude that this similarity results from the fact that the TDB includes some features of the spoken language just as the STC demo may include scripted recording. Yet, we suspect that the occurrence of discourse connectives with a deictic Arg1 is quite frequent in spoken language. We leave the investigation of such occurrences, and other issues such as the genre breakdown of the frequency of discourse connectives in STC for further study.

Our goal for the near future is to complete at least a second set of double-blind annotations and the agreement statics on the STC, so that the discourse-level annotation of spoken Turkish can be compared to those of the TDB.

Reference

Aktaş, B., Bozsahin, C., & Zeyrek, D. 2010. Discourse relation configurations in Turkish and an annotation environment. *Proceedings of the Fourth Linguistic Annotation Workshop*, pp. 202-206.

Asher, N. 1993. *Reference to Abstract Objects in Discourse.* Kluwer Academic Publishers.

Demirşahin, I., Sevdik-Çallı, A., Ögel Balaban, H., Çakıcı, R. & Zeyrek, D. 2012. Turkish Discourse Bank: Ongoing Developments. *Proceedings of LREC 2012 The First Turkic Languages Workshop.*

Forbes-Riley, K., Webber, B., & Joshi, A. 2006. Computing discourse semantics: The predicate-argument semantics of discourse connectives in D-LTAG. Journal of Semantics, 23(1), 55–106.

Prasad, R., Dinesh, N., Lee, A., Miltsakaki, E., Robaldo, L., Joshi, A., and Webber, B. 2008. The Penn Discourse Treebank 2.0. In *Proceedings of the Sixth International Conference on Language Resources and Evaluation.* (LREC'08).

Ruhi, Şükriye, Çokal Karadaş, Derya. 2009. Features for an internet accessible corpus of spoken Turkish discourse. *Working Papers in Corpus-based Linguistics and Language Education* 3, 311-320.

Ruhi, Şükriye, Eröz Tuğa, Betil, Hatipoğlu, Çiler, Işık-Güler, Hale, Can, Hümeyra, Karakaş, Özlem, Acar, Güneş, Eryılmaz, Kerem (2010). Türkçe için genel amaçlı sözlü derlem oluşturmada veribilgisi, çeviriyazı ölçünleştirmesi ve derlem yönetimi. *XXIV. Dilbilim Kurultayı*, 17-18 Mayıs, 2010, Yuvarlak Masa Toplantısı.

Say, B., Zeyrek, D., Oflazer, K., and Özge, U. 2002. Development of a Corpus and a Treebank for Present-day Written Turkish. In *Proceedings of the Eleventh International Conference on Turkish Linguistics* (ICTL 2002).

Zeyrek, D., and Webber, B. (2008). A Discourse Resource for Turkish: Annotating Discourse Connectives in the METU Turkish Corpus. In *Proceedings of the 6thWorkshop on Asian Language Resources, The Third International Joint Conference on Natural Language Processing (IJNLP).*

Zeyrek, D., Demirşahin, I., Sevdik-Çallı, A. B., Çakıcı, Ruket. 2013. Turkish Discourse Bank: Porting a discourse annotation style to a morphologically rich language. *Discourse and Dialogue* 4 (3), 174-184.

Exploiting the human computational effort dedicated to message reply formatting for training discursive email segmenters

Nicolas Hernandez **Soufian Salim**
LINA UMR 6241 Laboratory
University of Nantes (France)
firstname.lastname@univ-nantes.fr

Abstract

In the context of multi-domain and multimodal online asynchronous discussion analysis, we propose an innovative strategy for manual annotation of dialog act (DA) segments. The process aims at supporting the analysis of messages in terms of DA. Our objective is to train a sequence labelling system to detect the segment boundaries. The originality of the proposed approach is to avoid manually annotating the training data and instead exploit the human computational efforts dedicated to message reply formatting when the writer replies to a message by inserting his response just after the quoted text appropriate to his intervention. We describe the approach, propose a new electronic mail corpus and report the evaluation of segmentation models we built.

1 Introduction

Automatic processing of online conversations (forum, emails) is a highly important issue for the industrial and the scientific communities which care to improve existing question/answering systems, identify emotions or intentions in customer requests or reviews, detect messages containing requests for action or unsolved severe problems...

In most works, conversation interactions between the participants are modelled in terms of dialogue acts (DA) (Austin, 1962). The DAs describe the communicative function conveyed by each text utterance (e.g. question, answer, greeting,...). In this paper, we address the problem of rhetorically segmenting the new content parts of messages in online asynchronous discussions. The process aims at supporting the analysis of messages in terms of DA. We pay special attention to the processing of electronic mails.

The main trend in automatic DA recognition consists in using supervised learning algorithms to predict the DA conveyed by a sentence or a message (Tavafi et al., 2013). The hypothesized message segmentation results from the global analysis of these individual predictions over each sentence. A first remark on this paradigm is that it is not realistic to use in the context of multi-domain and multimodal processing because it requires the building of training data which is a very substantial and time-consuming task. A second remark is that the model does not have a fine-grained representation of the message structure or the relations between messages. Considering such characteristics could drastically improve the systems to allow to focus on specific text parts or to filter out less relevant ones. Indeed, apart from the closing formula, a message may for example be made of several distinct information requests, the description of an unsuccessful procedure, the quote of third-party messages...

So far, few works address the problem of message segmentation. (Lampert et al., 2009a) propose to segment emails in prototypical zones such as the author's contribution, quotes of original messages, the signature, the opening and closing formulas. In comparison, we focus on the segmentation of the author's contribution (what we call the new content part). (Joty et al., 2013) identifies clusters of topically related sentences through the multiple messages of a thread, without distinguishing email and forum messages. Apart from the topical aspect, our problem differs because we are only interested in the cohesion between sentences in nearby fragments and not on distant sentences.

LAW VIII - The 8th Linguistic Annotation Workshop, pages 110–119,
Dublin, Ireland, August 23-24 2014.

[Hi!]^{S1}

[I got my ubuntu cds today and i'm really impressed.]^{S2} [My friends like them and my teachers too (i'm a student).]^{S3}

[It's really funny to see, how people like ubuntu and start feeling geek and blaming microsoft when they use it.]^{S4}

[Unfortunately everyone wants an ubuntu cd, so can i download the cd covers anywhere or an 'official document' which i can attach to self-burned cds?]^{S5}

[I searched the entire web site but found nothing.]^{S6} [Thanks in advance.]^{S7}

[John]^{S8}

(a) Original message.

[On Sun, 04 Dec 2005, John Doe <john@doe.com> wrote:]^{R1}

> [I got my ubuntu cds today and i'm really impressed.]^{R2} [My
> friends like them and my teachers too (i'm a student).]^{R3}
> [It's really funny to see, how people like ubuntu and start feeling geek
> and blaming microsoft when they use it.]^{R4}

[Rock!]^{R5}

> [Unfortunately everyone wants an ubuntu cd, so can i download the cd
> covers anywhere or an 'official document' which i can attach to
> self-burned cds?]^{R6}

[We don't have any for the warty release, but we will have them for hoary, because quite a few people have asked. :-)]^{R7}

[Bob.]^{R8}

(b) Reply message.

Figure 1: An original message and its reply (*ubuntu-users* email archive). Sentences have been tagged to facilitate the discussion.

Original	Reply	Label
S1		
	R1	
S2	> *R2*	`Start`
S3	> *R3*	`Inside`
S4	> *R4*	`End`
	R5	
S5	> *R6*	`Start&End`
	R7	
	[...]	
S6		
[...]		

Figure 2: Alignment of the sentences from the original and reply messages shown in Figure 1 and labels inferred from the re-use of the original message text. Labels are associated to the original sentences.

Despite the drawbacks mentioned above, a supervised approach remains the most efficient and reliable method to solve classification problems in Natural Language Processing. Our aim is to train a system to detect the segment boundaries, i.e. to determine, through a classification approach, if a given sentence starts, ends or continues a segment.

The originality of the proposed approach is to avoid manually annotating the training data and instead to exploit the human computational efforts dedicated to a similar task in a different context of production (von Ahn, 2006). As recommended by the *Netiquette*[1], when replying to a message (email or forum post), the writer should "summarize the original message at the top of its reply, or include (or "quote") just enough text of the original to give a context, in order to make sure readers understand when they start to read the response[2]." As a corollary, the writer should "edit out all the irrelevant material." Our idea is to use this effort, in particular when the writer replies to a message by inserting his response or comment just after the quoted text appropriate to his intervention. This posting style is called *interleaved* or *inline replying*. The so built segmentation model should be usable for any posting styles by applying it only on new content parts. Figure 1a shows an example of an *original* message and, Figure 1b, one of its *reply*. We can see that the reply message re-uses only four selected sentences from the original message; namely $S2$, $S3$, $S4$ and $S5$ which respectively correspond to sentences $R2$, $R3$, $R4$ and $R6$ in the reply message. The author of the reply message deliberately discarded the remaining of the original message. The segment build up by sentences $S2$, $S3$, $S4$ and the one by the single sentence $S5$ can respectively be associated with two acts : a comment and a question.

In Section 2, we explain our approach for building an annotated corpus of segmented online messages at no cost. In Section 3, we describe the system and the features we use to model the segmentation. After

[1] Set of guidelines for Network Etiquette (*Netiquette*) when using network communication or information services RFC1855.

[2] It is true that some email software clients do not conform to the recommendations of Netiquette and that some online participants are less sensitive to arguments about posting style (many writers reply above the original message). We assume that there are enough messages with inline replying available to build our training data.

presenting our experimental framework in Section 4, we report some evaluations for the segmentation task in Section 5. Finally, we discuss our approach in comparison to other works in Section 6.

2 Building annotated corpora of segmented online discussions at no cost

We present the assumptions and the detailed steps of our approach.

2.1 Annotation scheme

The basic idea is to interpret the operation performed by a discussion participant on the message he replies as an annotation operation. Assumptions about the kind of annotations depend on the operation that has been performed. Deletion or re-use of the original text material can give hints about the relevance of the content: discarded material is probably less relevant than re-used one.

We assume that by replying inside a message and by only including some specific parts, the participant performs some cognitive operations to identify homogeneous self-contained text segments. Consequently, we make some assumptions about the role played by the sentences in the original message information structure. A sentence in a segment plays one of the following roles: `starting and ending` (*SE*) a segment when there is only one sentence in the segment, `starting` (*S*) a segment if there are at least two sentences in the segment and it is the first one, `ending` (*E*) a segment if there are at least two sentences in the segment and it is the last one, `inside` (*I*) a segment in any other cases.

Figure 2 illustrates the scheme by showing how sentences from Figure 1 can be aligned and the labels inferred from it. It is similar to the *BIO* scheme except it is not at the token level but at the sentence level (Ratinov and Roth, 2009).

2.2 Annotation generation procedure

Before being able to predict labels of the original message sentences, it is necessary to identify those that are re-used in a reply message. Identification of the quoted lines in a reply message is not sufficient for various reasons. First, the segmenter is intended to work on non-noisy data (i.e. the new content parts in the messages) while a quoted message is an altered version of the original one. Indeed, some email software clients involved in the discussion are not always standards-compliant and totally compatible[3]. In particular, the quoted parts can be wrongly re-encoded at each exchange step due to the absence of dedicated header information. In addition, the client programs can integrate their own mechanisms for quoting the previous messages when including them as well as for wrapping too long lines[4]. Second, accessing the original message may allow taking some contextual features into consideration (like the visual layout for example). Third, to go further, the original context of the extracted text also conveys some segmentation information. For instance, a sentence from the original message, not present in the reply, but following an aligned sentence, can be considered as starting a segment.

So in addition to identifying the quoted lines, we deploy an alignment procedure to get the original version of the quoted text. In this paper, we do not consider the contextual features from the original message and focus only on sentences that have been aligned.

The generation procedure is intended to "automatically" annotate sentences from the original messages with segmentation information. The procedure follows the following steps:

1. Messages posted in the interleaved replying style are identified
2. For each pair of original and reply messages:
    (a) Both messages are tokenized at sentence and at word levels
    (b) Quoted lines in the reply message are identified
    (c) Sentences which are part of the quoted text in the reply message are identified

[3]The *Request for Comments* (RFC) are guidelines and protocols proposed by working groups involved in the Internet Standardization `https://tools.ietf.org/html`, the message contents suffer from encoding and decoding problems. Some of the RFC are dedicated to email format and encoding specifications (See RFC 2822 and 5335 as starting points). There have been several propositions with updates and consequently obsoleted versions which may explain some alteration issues.

[4]Feature for making the text readable without any horizontal scrolling by splitting lines into pieces of about 80 characters.

(d) Sentences in the original message are aligned with quoted text in the reply message [5]

(e) Aligned original sentences are labelled in terms of position in segment

(f) The sequence of labelled sentences is added to the training data

Messages with *inline replying* are recognized thanks to the presence of at least two consecutive quoted lines separated by new content lines. Pairs of original and reply messages are constituted based on the `in-reply-to` field present in the email headers. As declared in the RFC 3676[6], we consider as *quoted lines*, the lines beginning with the ">" (greater than) sign. Lines which are not quoted lines are considered to be *new content* lines. The word tokens are used to index the quoted lines and the sentences.

Labelling of aligned sentence (sentence from the original message re-used in the reply message) uses this simple rule-based algorithm:

For each aligned original sentence:
    if the sentence is surrounded by new content in the reply message, the label is `Start&End`
    else if the sentence is preceded by a new content, the label is `Start`
    else if the sentence is followed by a new content, the label is `End`
    else, the label is `Inside`

2.3 Alignment module

For finding alignments between two given text messages, we use a *dynamic programming (DP) string alignment algorithm* (Sankoff and Kruskal, 1983). In the context of speech recognition, the algorithm is also known as the *NIST align/scoring algorithm*. Indeed, it is widely used to evaluate the output of speech recognition systems by comparing the hypothesized text output by the speech recognizer to the correct, or reference text. The algorithm works by "performing a global minimization of a Levenshtein distance function which weights the cost of correct words, insertions, deletions and substitutions as 0, 75, 75 and 100 respectively. The computational complexity of DP is $O(MN)$."

The Carnegie Mellon University provides an implementation of the algorithm in its speech recognition toolkit[7]. We use an adaptation of it which allows working on lists of strings[8] rather than directly on strings (as sequences of characters).

3 Building the segmenter

Each email is processed as a sequence of sentences. We choose to define the segmentation problem as a sequence labelling task whose aim is to assign the globally best set of labels for the entire sequence at once. The underlying idea is that the choice of the optimal label for a given sentence is dependent on the choices of nearby sentences. Our email segmenter is built around a linear-chain Conditional Random Field (CRF), as implemented in the sequence labelling toolkit Wapiti (Lavergne et al., 2010).

Training the classifier to recognize the different labels of the previously defined annotation scheme can be problematic. It has indeed some disadvantages that can undermine the effectiveness of the classifier. In particular, sentences annotated *SE* will, by definition, share important characteristics with sentences bearing the annotation *S* and *E*. So we chose to transform these annotations into a binary scheme and merely differentiate sentences that starts a new segment (*True*), or "boundary sentences", from those that do not (*False*). The conversion process is trivial, and can easily be reversed[9].

We distinguish four sets of features: n-gram features, information structure based features, thematic features and miscellaneous features. All the features are domain-independent. Almost all features are language-independent as well, save for a few that can be easily translated. For our experiments, the CRF window size is set at 5, i.e. the classification algorithm takes into account features of the next and previous two sentences as well as the current one.

[5] Section 2.3 details how alignment is performed.

[6] `http://www.ietf.org/rfc/rfc3676.txt`

[7] Sphinx 4 `edu.cmu.sphinx.util.NISTAlign` `http://cmusphinx.sourceforge.net`

[8] `https://github.com/romanows/WordSequenceAligner`

[9] Sentences labelled with *SE* or *S* are turned into *True*, the other ones into *False*. To reverse the process, a *True* is turned into *SE* if the next sentence is also a boundary (i.e. a True) and into *S* otherwise. While a *False* is turned into *E* if the next sentence is a boundary (i.e. a True) and into *I* otherwise.

n-gram features We select the case-insensitive word bi-grams and tri-grams with the highest document frequency in the training data (empirically we select the top 1,000 n-grams), and check for their presence in each sentence. Since the probability of having multiple occurrences of the same n-gram in one sentence are extremely low, we do not record the number of occurrences but merely a boolean value.

Information structure based features This feature set is inspired by the information structure theory (Kruijff-Korbayová and Kruijff, 1996) which describes the information imparted by the sentence in terms of the way it is related to prior context. The theory relates these functions with particular syntactic constructions (e.g. topicalization) and word order constraints in the sentence.

We focus on the first and last three *significant* tokens in the sentence. A token is considered as significant if its occurrence frequency is higher than 1/2,000[10]. As features we use n-grams of the surface form, lemma and part-of-speech tag of each triplet (36 features).

Thematic feature The only feature we use to account for thematic shift recognition is the output of the TextTiling algorithm (Hearst, 1997). TextTiling is one of the most commonly used algorithms for automatic text segmentation. If the algorithm detects a rupture in the lexical cohesion of the text (between two consecutive blocks), it will place a boundary to indicate a thematic change. Due to the short size of the messages, we define a block size to equate the sum of three times the sentence average size in our corpus. We set the step-size (overlap size of the rolling window) to the average size of a sentence.

Miscellaneous features This feature set includes stylistic and semantic features. 24 features, several of them borrowed from related work in speech act classification (Qadir and Riloff, 2011) and email segmentation (Lampert et al., 2009b), are in the set: *Stylistic features* capture information about the visual structure and composition of the message: the position of the sentence in the email, the average length of a token, the total number of tokens and characters, the proportion of upper-case, alphabetic and numeric characters, the number of greater-than signs (">"); whether the sentence ends with or contains a question mark, a colon or a semicolon; whether the sentence contains any punctuation within the first three tokens (this is meant to recognize greetings (Qadir and Riloff, 2011)).

Semantic features check for meaningful words and phrases: whether the sentence begins with or contains a "wh*" question word or a phrase suggesting an incoming interrogation (e.g. *"is it"*, *"are there"*); whether the sentence contains a modal; whether any plan phrases (e.g. *"i will"*, *"we are going to"*) are present; whether the sentence contains first person (e.g. *"we"*, *"my"*) second person or third person words; the first personal pronoun found in the sentence; the first verbal form found.

4 Experimental framework

We describe the data, the preprocessing and the evaluation protocol we use for our experiments.

4.1 Corpus

The current work takes place in a project dealing with multilingual and multimodal discussion processing, mainly in interrogative technical domains. For these reasons we did not consider the Enron Corpus (30,000 threads) (Klimt and Yang, 2004) (which is from a corporate environment), neither the W3C Corpus (despite its technical consistence) or its subset, the British Columbia Conversation Corpus (BC3) (Ulrich et al., 2008).

We rather use the *ubuntu-users* email archive[11] as our primary corpus. It offers a number of advantages. It is free, and distributed under an unrestrictive license. It increases continuously, and therefore is representative of modern emailing in both content and formatting. Additionally, many alternatives archives are available, in a number of different languages, including some very resource-poor languages. Ubuntu also offers a forum and a FAQ which are interesting in the context of multimodal studies.

We use a copy of December 2013. The corpus contains a total of 272,380 messages (47,044 threads). 33,915 of them are posted in the inline replying style that we are interested in. These messages are made

[10]This value was set up empirically on our data. More experimentation needs to be done to generalize it.

[11]Ubuntu mailing lists archives (See *ubuntu-users*): `https://lists.ubuntu.com/archives/`

of 418,858 sentences, themselves constituted of 76,326 unique tokens (5,139,123 total). 87,950 of these lines (21%) are automatically labelled by our system as the start of a new segment (either *SE* or *S*).

4.2 Evaluation protocol

In order to evaluate the efficiency of the segmenter, we perform a 10-fold cross-validation on the Ubuntu corpus, and compare its performance to two different baselines. The first one, the "regular" baseline, is computed by segmenting the test set into regular segments of the same length as the average training set segment length, rounded up. The second one is the TextTiling algorithm we described in section 3. While it is used as a feature in the proposed approach in the previous section, the direct output of the TextTiling algorithm is used for the baseline.

The results are measured with a panel of metrics used in text segmentation and Information Retrieval (IR). Precision (P) and Recall (R) are provided for all results. P is the percentage of boundaries identified by the classifier that are indeed true boundaries. R is the percentage of true boundaries that are identified by the classifier. We also provide the harmonic mean of precision and recall: $F_1 = 2 \cdot \frac{P \cdot R}{P+R}$

However, automatic evaluation of speech segmentation through these metrics is problematic as predicted segment boundaries seldom align precisely. Therefore, we also provide an array of metrics relevant to the field of text segmentation : P_k, *WindowDiff* and the *Generalized Hamming Distance (GHD)*. The P_k metric is a probabilistically motivated error metric for the assessment of segmentation algorithms (Beeferman et al., 1999). *WindowDiff* compares the number of segment boundaries found within a fixed-sized window to the number of boundaries found in the same window of text for the reference segmentation (Pevzner and Hearst, 2002). The *GHD* is an extension of the Hamming distance[12] that gives partial credit for near misses (Bookstein et al., 2002).

4.3 Preprocessing

To reduce noise in the corpus we filter out undesirable emails based on several criteria, the first of which is encoding. Messages that are not UTF-8 encoded are removed from the selection. The second criterion is MIME type: we keep single-part plain text messages only, and remove those with HTML or other special contents. In addition, we choose to consider only replies to thread starters. This choice is based on the assumption that the alignment module would have more difficulty in recognizing properly sentences that were repeatedly transformed in successive replies. Indeed, these replies - that would contain quoted text from other messages - would be more likely to be poorly labelled through automatic annotation. The last criterion is length. The dataset being built from a mailing list that can cover very technical discussions, users sometimes send very lengthy messages containing many lines of copied-and-pasted code, software logs, bash command outputs, etc. The number of these messages is marginal, but their lengths being disproportionately high, they can have a negative impact on the segmenter's performance. We therefore exclude messages longer than the average message length plus the standard length deviation. After filtering, the dataset is left with 6,821 messages out of 33,915 (20%).

For building the segmenter features, we use the Stanford Part-Of-Speech Tagger for morpho-syntactic tagging (Toutanova et al., 2003), and the WordNet lexical database for lemmatization (Miller, 1995).

5 Experiments

Table 1 shows the summary of all obtained results. On the left side are shown results about segmentation metrics, on the right side results about information retrieval metrics. First, we examine baseline scores, and display them in the top section. Second, in the middle section, we show results for segmenters based on individual feature sets (with A standing for n-grams, B for information structure, C for TextTiling and D for miscellaneous features). Finally, in the lower section, we show results based on feature sets combinations.

[12]Wikipedia article on the Hamming distance: `http://en.wikipedia.org/wiki/Hamming_distance`

	Segmentation metrics			Information Retrieval metrics		
	WD	P_k	GHD	P	R	F_1
regular baseline	.59	.25	.60	.31	.49	.38
TextTiling baseline	.41	.07	.38	.75	.44	.56
$\phi(A)$ with A = n-grams	.38	**.05**	.39	**1**	.39	.56
$\phi(B)$ with B = info. structure	.43	.11	.38	.60	.68	**.64**
$\phi(C)$ with C = TextTiling	.39	.05	.38	.94	.40	.56
$\phi(D)$ with D = misc. features	.41	.09	.38	.69	.49	.57
$\phi(A+B+C+D)$	.38	**.05**	.39	**1**	.39	.56
$\phi(\phi(A)+\phi(B)+\phi(C)+\phi(D))$	.38	.06	.36	.81	.47	.59
$\phi(A) \cup \phi(B+C+D)$	.45	.12	.40	.58	**.69**	.63
$\phi(A) \cup \delta(\phi(B+C+D))$	**.36**	.06	**.34**	.80	.53	**.64**

Table 1: Comparative results between baselines and tested segmenters. All displayed results show *WindowDiff* (*WD*), P_k and *GHD* as error rates, therefore a lower score is desirable for these metrics. This contrasts with the three IR scores, for which a low value denotes poor performance. Best scores are shown in bold.

5.1 Baseline segmenters

The first section of Table 1 shows the results obtained by both of our baselines. Unsurprisingly, TextTiling performs much better than the basic regular segmentation algorithm across all metrics save recall.

5.2 Segmenters based on individual feature sets

The second section of Table 1 shows the results for four different classifiers, each trained with a distinct subset of the feature set. The ϕ function is the classification function, its parameters are features, and its output a prediction. While all classifiers easily beat the regular baseline, and match the TextTiling baseline when it comes to IR metrics, only the thematic and the n-grams segmenters manage to surpass TextTiling when performance is measured by segmentation metrics. In terms of IR scores, the n-grams classifier in particular stands out as it manages to achieve an outstanding 100% precision, although this result is mitigated by a meager 39% recall. It is also interesting to see that the thematic classifier, based only on contextual information about TextTiling output, performs better than the TextTiling baseline.

5.3 Segmenters based on feature sets combinations

The last section of Table 1 shows the results of four different segmenters. The first one, $\phi(A+B+C+D)$, is a simple classifier that takes all available features into account. Its results are exactly identical to that of the n-grams classifier, most certainly due to the fact that other features are filtered out due to the sheer number of lexical features. The second one, $\phi(\phi(A) + \phi(B) + \phi(C) + \phi(D))$, uses as features the outputs of the four classifiers trained on each individual feature set. Results show this approach isn't significantly better. The third one, $\phi(A) \cup \phi(B + C + D)$, segments according to the union of the boundaries detected by a classifier trained on n-grams features and those identified by a classifier trained on all other features. This idea is motivated by the fact that we know all boundaries found by the n-grams classifier to be accurate ($P = 1$). Doing this allows the segmenter to obtain the best possible recall ($R = .69$), but at the expense of precision ($P = .58$). The last one, $\phi(A) \cup \delta(\phi(B + C + D))$, attempts to increase the n-grams classifier's recall without sacrificing too much precision by being more selective about boundaries. The δ function is the "cherry picking" function, which filters out boundaries predicted without sufficient confidence. Only those identified by the n-grams classifier and those classified as boundaries with a confidence score of at least .99 by a classifier trained on the other feature sets are considered. This system outperforms all others both in terms of segmentation scores and F_1, however it is still relatively conservative and the segmentation ratio (the number of guessed boundaries divided by the number of true boundaries) remains significantly lower than expected, at 0.67. Tuning the minimum confidence score (c) allows to adjust P from .58 ($c = 0$) to 1 ($c = 1$) and R from .39 ($c = 1$) to .69 ($c = 0$).

6 Related work

Three research areas are directly related to our study: a) collaborative approaches for acquiring annotated corpora, b) detection of email structure, and c) sentence alignment. In the (Wang et al., 2013)'s taxonomy of the collaborative approaches for acquiring annotated corpora, our approach could be related to the *Wisdom of the Crowds* (WotC) genre where motivators are altruism or prestige to collaborate for the building of a public resource. As a major difference, we did not initiate the annotation process and consequently we did not define annotation guidelines, design tasks or develop tools for annotating which are always problematic questions. We have just rerouted *a posteriori* the result of an existing task which was performed in a distinct context. In our case the burning issue is to determine the adequacy of our segmentation task. Our work is motivated by the need to identify important snippets of information in messages for applications such as being able to determine whether all the aspects of a customer request were fully considered. We argue that even if it is not always obvious to tag topically or rhetorically a segment, the fact that it was a human who actually segmented the message ensures its quality. We think that our approach can also be used for determining the relevance of the segments, however it has some limits, and we do not know how labelling segments with dialogue acts may help us do so.

Detecting the structure of a thread is a hot topic. As mentioned in Section 1, very little works have been done on email segmentation. We are aware of recent works in linear text segmentation such as (Kazantseva and Szpakowicz, 2011) who addresses the problem by modelling the text as a graph of sentences and by performing clustering and/or cut methods. Due to the size of the messages (and consequently the available lexical material), it is not always possible to exploit this kind of method. However, our results tend to indicate that we should investigate in this direction nonetheless. By detecting sub-units of information within the message, our work may complement the works of (Wang et al., 2011; Kim et al., 2010) who propose solutions for detecting links between messages. We may extend these approaches by considering the possibility of pointing from/to multiple message sources/targets.

Concerning the alignment process, our task can be compared to the detection of monolingual text derivation (otherwise called plagiarism, near–duplication, revision). (Poulard et al., 2011) compare, for instance, the use of n–grams overlap with the use of text hapax. In contrast, we already know that a text (the reply message) derives from another (the original message). Sentence alignment has also been a very active field of research in statistical machine translation for building parallel corpora. Some methods are based on sentence length comparison (Gale and Church, 1991), some methods rely on the overlap of rare words (cognates and named entities) (Enright and Kondrak, 2007). In comparison, in our task, despite some noise, the compared text includes large parts of material identical to the original text. The kinds of edit operation in presence (no inversion[13] only deletion, insertion and substitution) lead us to consider the Levenshtein distance as a serious option.

7 Future work

The main contribution of this work is to exploit the human effort dedicated to reply formatting for training discursive email segmenters. We have implemented and tested various segmenter models. There is still room for improvement, but our results indicate that the approach merits more thorough examination. Our segmentation approach remains relatively simple and can be easily extended. One way would be to consider contextual features in order to characterize the sentences in the original message structure. As future works, we plan to complete our current experiments with two new approaches for evaluation. The first one will consists in comparing the automatic segmentation with those performed by human annotators. This task remains tedious since it will then be necessary to define an annotation protocol, write guidelines and build other resources. The second evaluation we plan to perform is an extrinsic evaluation. The idea will be to measure the contribution of the segmentation in the process of detecting the dialogue acts, i.e. to check if existing sentence-level classification systems would perform better with such contextual information.

[13]When computing the Levenshtein distance, the inversion edit operation is the most costly operation.

References

John L. Austin. 1962. *How to do Things with Words: The William James Lectures delivered at Harvard University in 1955*. Oxford: Clarendon Press.

Doug Beeferman, Adam Berger, and John Lafferty. 1999. Statistical models for text segmentation. *Machine learning*, 34(1-3):177–210.

Abraham Bookstein, Vladimir A Kulyukin, and Timo Raita. 2002. Generalized hamming distance. *Information Retrieval*, 5(4):353–375.

Jessica Enright and Grzegorz Kondrak. 2007. A fast method for parallel document identification. In *Human Language Technologies 2007: The Conference of the North American Chapter of the Association for Computational Linguistics; Companion Volume, Short Papers*, pages 29–32, Rochester, New York, April. Association for Computational Linguistics.

William A. Gale and Kenneth Ward Church. 1991. A program for aligning sentences in bilingual corpora. In *Proceedings of the 29th Annual Meeting of the Association of Computational Linguistics (ACL)*.

Marti A Hearst. 1997. Texttiling: Segmenting text into multi-paragraph subtopic passages. *Computational linguistics*, 23(1):33–64.

Shafiq Joty, Giuseppe Carenini, and Raymond Ng. 2013. Topic segmentation and labeling in asynchronous conversations. *Journal of AI Research (JAIR)*, 47:521–573.

Anna Kazantseva and Stan Szpakowicz. 2011. Linear text segmentation using affinity propagation. In *Proceedings of the Conference on Empirical Methods in Natural Language Processing*, EMNLP '11, pages 284–293, Stroudsburg, PA, USA. Association for Computational Linguistics.

Su Nam Kim, Li Wang, and Timothy Baldwin. 2010. Tagging and linking web forum posts. In *Proceedings of the Fourteenth Conference on Computational Natural Language Learning*, CoNLL '10, pages 192–202, Stroudsburg, PA, USA. Association for Computational Linguistics.

Bryan Klimt and Yiming Yang. 2004. The enron corpus: A new dataset for email classification research. In Jean-François Boulicaut, Floriana Esposito, Fosca Giannotti, and Dino Pedreschi, editors, *ECML*, volume 3201 of *Lecture Notes in Computer Science*, pages 217–226. Springer.

Ivana Kruijff-Korbayová and Geert-Jan M. Kruijff. 1996. Identification of topic-focus chains. In S. Botley, J. Glass, T. McEnery, and A. Wilson, editors, *Approaches to Discourse Anaphora: Proceedings of the Discourse Anaphora and Anaphora Resolution Colloquium (DAARC96)*, volume 8, pages 165–179. University Centre for Computer Corpus Research on Language, University of Lancaster, UK, July 17-18.

Andrew Lampert, Robert Dale, and Cécile Paris. 2009a. Segmenting email message text into zones. In *Proceedings of the 2009 Conference on Empirical Methods in Natural Language Processing: Volume 2 - Volume 2*, EMNLP '09, pages 919–928, Stroudsburg, PA, USA. Association for Computational Linguistics.

Andrew Lampert, Robert Dale, and Cécile Paris. 2009b. Segmenting email message text into zones. In *Proceedings of the 2009 Conference on Empirical Methods in Natural Language Processing: Volume 2-Volume 2*, pages 919–928. Association for Computational Linguistics.

Thomas Lavergne, Olivier Cappé, and François Yvon. 2010. Practical very large scale CRFs. In *Proceedings the 48th Annual Meeting of the Association for Computational Linguistics (ACL)*, pages 504–513. Association for Computational Linguistics, July.

George A Miller. 1995. Wordnet: a lexical database for english. *Communications of the ACM*, 38(11):39–41.

Lev Pevzner and Marti A Hearst. 2002. A critique and improvement of an evaluation metric for text segmentation. *Computational Linguistics*, 28(1):19–36.

Fabien Poulard, Nicolas Hernandez, and Béatrice Daille. 2011. Detecting derivatives using specific and invariant descriptors. *Polibits*, (43):7–13.

Ashequl Qadir and Ellen Riloff. 2011. Classifying sentences as speech acts in message board posts. In *Proceedings of the Conference on Empirical Methods in Natural Language Processing*, pages 748–758. Association for Computational Linguistics.

L. Ratinov and D. Roth. 2009. Design challenges and misconceptions in named entity recognition. In *CoNLL*, 6.

D Sankoff and J B Kruskal. 1983. *Time Warps, String Edits, and Macromolecules: The Theory and Practice of Sequence Comparison*. Addison-Wesley Publishing Company, Inc., Reading, Massachusetts. ISBN 0-201-07809-0.

Maryam Tavafi, Yashar Mehdad, Shafiq Joty, Giuseppe Carenini, and Raymond Ng. 2013. Dialogue act recognition in synchronous and asynchronous conversations. In *Proceedings of the 14th Annual Meeting of the Special Interest Group on Discourse and Dialogue (SIGDIAL 2013)*, SIGDIAL'13.

Kristina Toutanova, Dan Klein, Christopher D Manning, and Yoram Singer. 2003. Feature-rich part-of-speech tagging with a cyclic dependency network. In *Proceedings of the 2003 Conference of the North American Chapter of the Association for Computational Linguistics on Human Language Technology-Volume 1*, pages 173–180. Association for Computational Linguistics.

J. Ulrich, G. Murray, and G. Carenini. 2008. A publicly available annotated corpus for supervised email summarization. In *AAAI08 EMAIL Workshop*, Chicago, USA. AAAI.

L. von Ahn. 2006. Games with a purpose. *Computer*, 39(6):92–94.

Li Wang, Diana Mccarthy, and Timothy Baldwin. 2011. Predicting thread linking structure by lexical chaining. In *Proceedings of the Australasian Language Technology Association Workshop 2011*, pages 76–85, Canberra, Australia, December.

Aobo Wang, CongDuyVu Hoang, and Min-Yen Kan. 2013. Perspectives on crowdsourcing annotations for natural language processing. *Language Resources and Evaluation*, 47(1):9–31.

Annotating Multiparty Discourse: Challenges for Agreement Metrics

Nina Wacholder* Smaranda Muresan† Debanjan Ghosh* Mark Aakhus*
*School of Communication and Information, Rutgers University
†Center for Computational Learning Systems, Columbia University
ninwac|debanjan.ghosh|aakhus@rutgers.edu, smara@ccls.columbia.edu

Abstract

To computationally model discourse phenomena such as argumentation we need corpora with reliable annotation of the phenomena under study. Annotating complex discourse phenomena poses two challenges: fuzziness of unit boundaries and the need for multiple annotators. We show that current metrics for inter-annotator agreement (IAA) such as P/R/F1 and Krippendorff's α provide inconsistent results for the same text. In addition, IAA metrics do not tell us what parts of a text are easier or harder for human judges to annotate and so do not provide sufficiently specific information for evaluating systems that automatically identify discourse units. We propose a hierarchical clustering approach that aggregates overlapping text segments of text identified by multiple annotators; the more annotators who identify a text segment, the easier we assume that the text segment is to annotate. The clusters make it possible to quantify the extent of agreement judges show about text segments; this information can be used to assess the output of systems that automatically identify discourse units.

1 Introduction

Annotation of discourse typically involves three subtasks: segmentation (identification of discourse units, including their boundaries), segment classification (labeling the role of discourse units) and relation identification (indicating the link between the discourse units) (Peldszus and Stede, 2013a). The difficulty of achieving an Inter-Annotator Agreement (IAA) of .80, which is generally accepted as good agreement, is compounded in studies of discourse annotations since annotators must unitize, i.e. identify the boundaries of discourse units (Artstein and Poesio, 2008). The inconsistent assignment of boundaries in annotation of discourse has been noted at least since Grosz and Sidner (1986) who observed that although annotators tended to identify essentially the same units, the boundaries differed slightly. The need for annotators to identify the boundaries of text segments makes measurement of IAA more difficult because standard coefficients such as κ assume that the units to be coded have been identified before the coding begins (Artstein and Poesio, 2008). A second challenge for measuring IAA for discourse annotation is associated with larger numbers of annotators. Because of the many ways that ideas are expressed in human language, using multiple annotators to study discourse phenomena is important. Such an approach capitalizes on the aggregated intuitions of multiple coders to overcome the potential biases of any one coder and helps identify limitations in the coding scheme, thus adding to the reliability and validity of the annotation study. The more annotators, however, the harder it is to achieve an IAA of .80 (Bayerl and Paul, 2011). What to annotate also depends, among other characteristics, on the phenomenon of interest, the text being annotated, the quality of the annotation scheme and the effectiveness of training. But even if these are excellent, there is natural variability in human judgment for a task that involves subtle distinctions about which competent coders disagree. An accurate computational model should reflect this variability (Aakhus et al., 2013).

LAW VIII - The 8th Linguistic Annotation Workshop, pages 120–128,
Dublin, Ireland, August 23-24 2014.

# Type	Statement
Target	I'm going to quit the iphone and switch to an android phone because I can no long (sic) put up with the AT&T service contract
Callout	I am going to switch too
Callout	There is no point quitting the iphone because of the service package, just jail break it and use the provider you want

Table 1: Examples of Callouts and Targets

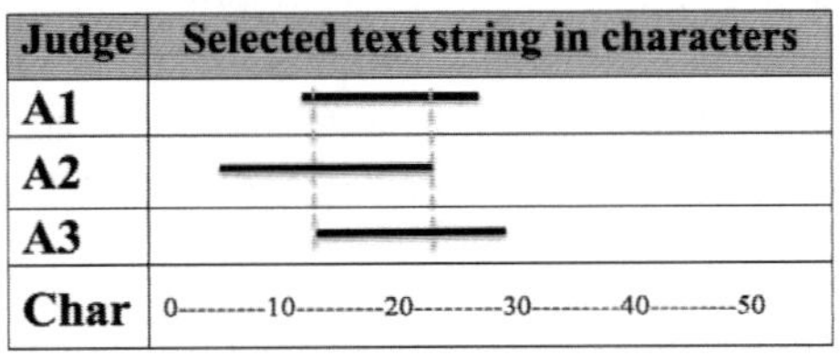

Figure 1: Cluster where 3 judges identify a core

We propose an approach for overcoming these challenges based on evidence from an annotation study of arguments in online interactions. Our scheme for argumentation is based on Pragmatic Argumentation Theory (PAT) (Van Eemeren et al., 1993; Hutchby, 2013; Maynard, 1985). PAT states that argument can arise at any point when two or more actors engage in calling out and making problematic some aspect of another actor's prior contribution for what it (could have) said or meant (Van Eemeren et al., 1993). The argumentative relationships among contributions to a discussion are indicated through links between what is targeted and how it is called out. Table 1 shows two Callouts that refer back to the same Target.

Callouts and Targets are Argumentative Discourse Units (ADUs) in the sense of Peldszus and Stede (2013a), "minimal units of analysis ... inspired ... by a ... relation-based discourse theory" (p.20). In our case the theory is PAT. Callouts are related to Targets by a relationship that we may refer to as Response, though we do not discuss the Response relationship in this paper.

The hierarchical clustering technique that we propose systematically identifies clusters of ADUs; each cluster contains a core of overlapping text that two or more judges have identified. Figure 1 shows a schematic example of a cluster with a core identified by three judges. The variation in boundaries represents the individual judges' differing intuitions; these differences reflect natural variation of human judgments about discourse units. We interpret differences in the number (or percentage) of judges that identify a core as evidence of how hard or easy a discourse unit is to recognize.

The contributions of this paper are two-fold. First, we show that methods for assessing IAA, such as the information retrieval inspired (P/R/F1) approach (Wiebe et al., 2005) and Krippendorff's α (Krippendorff, 1995; Krippendorff, 2004b), which was developed for content analysis in the social sciences, provide inconsistent results when applied to segmentations involving fuzzy boundaries and multiple coders.

In addition, these metrics do not tell us which parts of a text are easier or harder to annotate, or help choose a reliable gold standard. Our second contribution is a new method for assessing IAA using hierarchical clustering to find parts of text that are easier or harder to annotate. These clusters could serve as the basis for assessing the performance of systems that automatically identify ADUs - the system would be rewarded for identifying ADUs that are easier for people to recognize and penalized for identifying ADUs that are relatively hard for people to recognize.

2 Annotation Study of Argumentative Discourse Units: Callouts and Targets

In this section, we describe the annotation study we conducted to determine whether trained human judges can reliably identify Callouts and Targets. The main annotation task was to find Callouts and the Targets to which they are linked and unitize them, i.e., assign boundaries to each ADU. As mentioned above, these are the steps for argument mining delineated in Peldszus and Stede (2013a). The design of the study was consistent with the conditions for generating reliable annotations set forth in Krippendorff (2004a, p. 217).

We selected five blog postings from a corpus crawled from Technorati (technorati.com) between 2008-2010; the comments contain many disputes. We used the first 100 comments on each blog as our corpus, along with the original posting. We refer to each blog and the associated comments as a thread.

The complexity of the phenomenon required the perspective of multiple independent annotators, despite the known difficulty in achieving reliable IAA with more than two annotators. For our initial study, in which our goal was to obtain naturally occurring examples of Callouts and Targets and assess the challenges of reliably identifying them, we engaged five graduate students with a strong humanities background. The coding was performed with the open-source Knowtator software (Ogren, 2006). All five judges annotated all 100 comments in all five threads. While the annotation process was under way, annotators were instructed not to communicate with each other about the study.

The annotators' task was to find each instance of a Callout, determine the boundaries, link the Callout to the most recent Target and determine the boundaries of the Target. We prepared and tested a set of guidelines with definitions and examples of key concepts. The following is an adapted excerpt from the guidelines:

- **Callout:** A Callout is (a part of) a subsequent action that selects (a part of) a prior action and marks and comments on it in some way. In Table 1, Statements 2 and 3 are both Callouts, i.e., they perform the action of calling out on Statement 1. Statement 2 calls out the first part of Statement 1 dealing with switching phones. Statement 3 calls out all of Statement 1 – both what's proposed and the rationale for the disagreement.

- **Target:** A Target is a part of a prior action that has been called out by a subsequent action. Statement 1 is a Target of Statements 2 and 3. But Statements 2 and 3 link to different parts of Statement 1, as described above.

- **Response:** A link between Callout and Target that occurs when a subsequent action refers back to (is a response to) a prior action.

Annotators were instructed to mark any text segment (from words to entire comments) that satisfied the definitions above. A single text segment could be a Target and a Callout. To save effort on a difficult task, judges were asked only to annotate the most recent plausible Target. We plan to study chains of responses in future work.

Prior to the formal study, each annotator spent approximately eight hours in training, spread over about two weeks, under the supervision of a PhD student who had helped to develop the guidelines. Training materials included the guidelines and postings and comments from Technorati that were not used in the formal study. Judges were reminded that our research goal was to find naturally occurring examples of Callouts and Targets and that the research team did not know in advance what were the right answers – the subjects' job was to identify Callouts and Targets that satisfied the definitions in the guidelines. In response to the judges' questions, the guidelines were iteratively updated: definitions were reviewed, additional examples were added, and a list of FAQs was developed[1].

Table 2 shows the wide range of results among the annotators for Callouts that illustrates a problem to be addressed when assessing reliability for multiple annotators.

Averaged over all five threads, A1 identified the fewest Callouts (66.8) while A4 and A5 identified the most (107 and 109, respectively). Furthermore, the number of annotations assigned by A4 and A5 to each corpus is consistently higher than those of the other annotators, while the number of annotations A1 assigned to each thread is consistently lower than that of all of the other annotators. Although these differences could be due to issues with training, we interpret the consistent variation among coders as potential evidence of two distinct types of behavior: some judges are 'lumpers' who consider a text string as a single unit; others are 'splitters' who treat the same text string as two (or more) distinct units. The high degree of variability among coders is consistent with the observations of Peldszus and Stede

[1]The corpus, annotations and guidelines are available at <http://wp.comminfo.rutgers.edu/salts/projects/opposition/>.

Thread	A1	A2	A3	A4	A5
Android	73	99	97	118	110
Ban	46	73	66	86	83
iPad	68	86	85	109	118
Layoffs	71	83	74	109	117
Twitter	76	102	70	113	119
Avg.	66.8	88.6	78.4	107	109.4

Table 2: Callouts per annotator per thread

(2013b). These differences could be due to issues with training and individual differences among coders, but even so, the variability highlights an important challenge for calculating IAA with multiple coders and fuzzy unit boundaries.

3 Some Problems of Unitization Reliability with Existing IAA Metrics

In this section we discuss two state-of-the-art metrics frequently used for measuring IAA for discourse annotation and we show that these methods offer limited informativeness when text boundaries are fuzzy and there are multiple judges. These methods are the information retrieval inspired precision-recall (P/R/F1) metrics used in Wiebe and her collaborators' important work on sentiment analysis (Wiebe et al., 2005; Somasundaran et al., 2008) and Krippendorff's α, a variant of the α family of IAA coefficients specifically designed to handle fuzzy boundaries and multiple annotators (Krippendorff, 1995; Krippendorff, 2004b). Krippendorff's α determines IAA based on observed disagreement relative to expected agreement and calculates differences in annotators' judgments. Although it is possible to use number of words or even clauses to measure IAA, we use length in characters both for consistency with Wiebe's approach and because Krippendorff (2004b, pp.790-791) recommends using "... the smallest distinguishable length, for example the characters in text..." to measure IAA. We next show the results of using P/R/F and Krippendorff's α to measure IAA for our annotation study and provide examples of some challenges that need to be addressed.

3.1 Precision, Recall and F measures

Implementing P/R/F1 requires a gold standard annotation against which the other annotations can be compared. P/R/F1 is calculated here, following (Wiebe et al., 2005), as follows: the units selected by one annotator are taken as the gold standard and the remaining annotators are calculated against the selected gold standard. To determine whether annotators selected the same text span, two different types of matches were considered, as in Somasundaran et al. (2008): exact matches and overlap matches (variation of their lenient match):

- **Exact Matches (EM):** Text spans that vary at the start or end point by five characters or less are considered an exact match. This minor relaxation of exact matching (Somasundaran et al., 2008) compensates for minor inconsistencies such as whether a judge included a sentence ending punctuation mark in the unit.

- **Overlap Matches (OM):** Any overlap between text spans of more than 10% of the total number of characters is considered a match. OM is weaker than EM but still an indicator of shared judgments by annotators.

Tables 3 and 5 and Tables 4 and 6 show the P/R/F1-based IAA using EM and OM respectively. The results are averaged across all five threads. Besides average P/R/F1 we also show Max F1 and Min F1, which represent the maximum and minimum F1 relative to a particular annotator used as gold standard.

These tables show that the results vary greatly. Among the reasons for the variation are the following:

- Results are sensitive to which annotator is selected as the gold standard. In Table 4, pairing A4 with the judge who agrees maximally produces an F measure of 90.2 while pairing A4 with the annotator who agrees minimally produces an F measure of 73.3. In Tables 3 and 4, if we select A4 as the gold standard we get the most variation; selecting A3 produces the least.

Ann	Avg P	Avg R	Avg F1	MaxF1	Min F1
A1	40.7	57.7	47.8	60	36.7
A2	51.7	51.2	51.4	58.3	43
A3	54.2	57.8	55.9	61.4	47.9
A4	59.7	49.1	53.9	61.4	47.3
A5	55	45.6	49.9	58.3	36.7

Table 3: Callouts: EM P/R/F1 over 5 threads

Ann	Avg P	Avg R	Avg F1	MaxF1	Min F1
A1	67.4	95.7	79.1	86.8	73.3
A2	85	83.7	84.3	88.7	76.1
A3	82.7	88	85.2	88.7	80.9
A4	92.7	76.8	84	90.2	73.3
A5	91.4	75.1	82.4	89.6	74

Table 4: Callouts: OM P/R/F1 over 5 threads

Ann	Avg P	Avg R	Avg F1	MaxF1	Min F1
A1	24.1	34.6	28.4	34.5	18.7
A2	26.9	24.7	25.7	37.6	18.7
A3	35.2	35.1	35.1	48.4	19.4
A4	37.3	34.5	35.8	50.4	22.1
A5	36.9	31.4	33.9	50.4	19.9

Table 5: Targets: EM P/R/F1 over 5 threads

Ann	Avg P	Avg R	Avg F1	MaxF1	Min F1
A1	60.1	86.5	70.9	76.1	64.2
A2	74.5	69.4	71.9	79.6	62.9
A3	75.9	74.5	75.1	80.1	67.7
A4	78.1	71.5	74.6	84.2	64
A5	83.8	70.3	76.4	83.8	67.2

Table 6: Targets: OM P/R/F1 over 5 threads

- The type of matching matters. As expected, OM, which is less strict than EM, produces substantially higher F1 scores both for Callouts (Tables 3 and 4) and Targets (Tables 5 and 6).
- Different phenomena are associated with different levels of difficulty of annotation. The F1 scores for Targets are considerably lower than the F1 scores for Callouts. We suspect that Callouts are easier to recognize since they are often introduced with standard expressions that signal agreement or disagreement such as 'yes', 'no', 'I agree', or 'I disagree'. Targets, on the other hand, generally lack such distinguishing lexical features.

We also observe differences across threads. For example, the Ban thread seems harder to annotate than the other threads. Figure 2 and 3 show IAA results for OM for Callout and Target annotations for annotators A1 and A5 respectively, across the five threads. We chose A1 and A5 because in general A1 annotated the fewest Callouts and A5 annotated the most Callouts in the corpus. These figures show different annotator behavior. For instance, for both Callout and Target annotations, A1 has higher average R than P, while A5 has higher P but lower R. Figures 2 and 3 hint that the Ban thread is harder to annotate than the others.

The examples in this section show two downsides to the P/R/F1 metric. First, the scores do not reflect the extent to which two annotations match. This is crucial information for fuzzy boundary matching, because the agreement between two annotations can be over only a few characters or over the full length of the selected text. Second, the variation across multiple judges demonstrates the disadvantage of arbitrary selection of a gold standard set of annotations against which to measure IAA.

3.2 Krippendorff's α

Krippendorff's α calculates IAA based on the observed and expected disagreement between annotators. We use the version of Kripendorff's α discussed in Krippendorff (2004b) which takes into account multiple annotators and fuzzy boundaries. Detailed proof and an explanation of the calculation can be found in (Krippendorff, 2004b; Krippendorff, 1995).

Thread	F1	Krippendorff's α
Android	87.8	0.64
Ban	85.3	0.75
iPad	86.0	0.73
Layoffs	87.5	0.87
Twitter	88.5	0.82

Table 7: F1 and α for all 5 threads

Thread Rank by IAA (Descending)	
F1	K's α
Twitter	Layoffs
Android	Twitter
Layoffs	Ban
iPad	iPad
Ban	Android

Table 8: Threads ranked by IAA in descending order

Comparison of α and P/R/F1 metrics shows that they generate inconsistent results that are difficult to interpret. For example, in Table 7, the F1 measure for Callouts indicates lower agreement on the Ban thread in comparison to Android while α suggests higher agreement on the Ban subcorpus relative to the

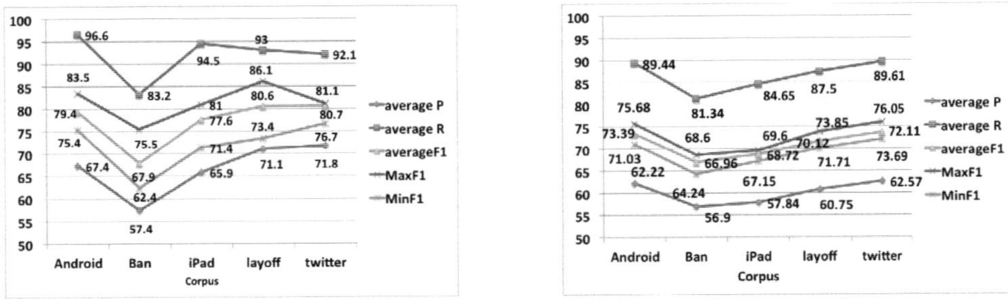

Figure 2: IAA metrics per thread when A1 is gold standard (Left: Callout. Right: Target.)

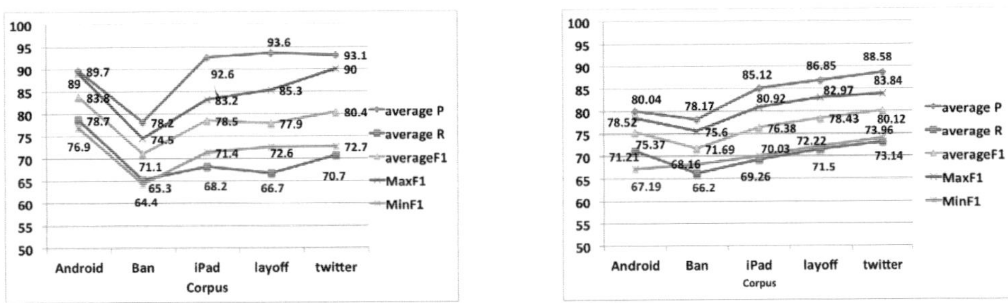

Figure 3: IAA metrics per thread when A5 is gold standard (Left: Callout. Right: Target.)

Android subcorpus. The inconsistencies are also apparent in Table 8, which ranks threads in descending order of IAA. For example, the Android corpus receives the highest IAA using F1 but the lowest using α.

We do not show the results for Krippendorff's α for Targets for the following reason. Relevant units from a continuous text string are assigned to categories by individual annotators. But identification of Targets is dependent on (temporally secondary to) identification of Callouts. In multiple instances we observe that an annotator links multiple Callouts to two or more overlapping Targets. Depending on the Callout, the same unit (i.e., text segment) can represent an annotation (a Target) or a gap between two Targets. Computation of α is based on the overlapping characters of the annotations and the gaps between the annotations. Naturally, if a single text string is assigned different labels (i.e. annotation or a gap between annotations) in different annotations, α does not produce meaningful results. The inapplicability of Krippendorff's α to Targets is a significant limitation for its use in discourse annotation (To save space we only show results for Callouts in subsequent tables.)

The examples in Section 3 show a fundamental limitation of both P/R/F1 and Krippendorff's α: They do not pinpoint the location in a document where the extent of variation can be observed. This limits the usefulness of these measures for studying the discourse phenomenon of interest and for analyzing the impact of factors such as text difficulty, corpus and judges on IAA. The impact of these factors on IAA also makes it hard to pick gold standard examples on a principled basis.

4 Hierarchical Clustering of Discourse Units

In this section we introduce a clustering approach that aggregates overlapping annotations, thereby making it possible to quantify agreement among annotators within a cluster. Then we show examples of clusters from our annotation study in which the extent of annotator support for a core reflects how hard or easy an ADU is for human judges to identify. The hierarchical clustering technique (Hastie et al., 2009) assumes that overlapping annotations by two or more judges constitutes evidence of the approximate location of an instance of the phenomenon of interest. In our case, this is the annotation of ADUs that contain overlapping text. Each ADU starts in its own cluster. The start and end points of each ADU are utilized to identify overlapping characters in pairs of ADUs. Then, using a bottom-up clustering

# Annots	Text selected
A1, A2, A3, A4, A5	I remember Apple telling people give the UI and the keyboard a month and you'll get used to it. Plus all the commercials showing the interface. So, no, you didn't just pick up the iPhone and know how to use it. It was pounded into to you.

Table 9: A cluster in which all five judges agreement on the boundaries of the ADU

# Annots	Text selected
A1	*I'm going to agree that my experience required a bit of getting used to* ...
A2, A3, A4	*I'm going to agree that my experience required a bit of getting used to* ... I had arrived to the newly minted 2G Gmail and browsing
A5	*I'm going to agree that my experience required a bit of getting used to* ... I had arrived to the newly minted 2G Gmail and browsing. Great browser on the iPhone but ... Opera Mini can work wonders

Table 10: A cluster in which all 5 annotators agree on the core but disagree on the closing boundary of the ADU

technique, pairs of clusters (e.g. pairs of Callout ADUs) with overlapping text strings are merged as they move up in the hierarchy. An ADU that does not overlap with ADUs identified by any other judge will remain in its own cluster.

Aggregating overlapping annotations makes it possible to quantify agreement among the annotators within a cluster. Table 9 shows an example of a cluster that contains five annotations; all five annotators assign identical unit boundaries, which means that there is a single core, with no variation in the extent of the ADU. Table 9 thus shows an optimal case – there is complete agreement among the five annotators. We take this as strong evidence that the text string in Table 9 is an instance of a Callout that is relatively easy to identify.

But of course, natural language does not make optimal annotation easy (even if coders were perfect). Table 10 shows a cluster in which all five annotators agree on the core (shown in italics) but do not agree about the boundaries of the ADU. A1 picked the shortest text segment. A2, A3 and A4 picked the same text segment as A1 but they also included the rest of the sentence, up to the word 'browsing'. In A5's judgment, the ADU is still longer - it also includes the sentence 'Great browser ... work wonders.' Although not as clear-cut as the examples in Table 9, the fact that in Table 10 all annotators chose overlapping text is evidence that the core has special status in the context of in an annotation task where it is known that even expert annotators disagree about borders. Examples like those in Table 10 can be used to study the reasons for variation in the judges' assignment of boundaries. Besides ease of recognition of an ADU and differing human intuitions, the instructions in the guidelines or characteristics of the Callouts may be also having an effect.

Table 11 shows a more complex annotation pattern in a cluster. Annotators A1 and A2 agree on the boundaries of the ADU, but their annotation does not overlap with A4 at all. A3's boundaries subsume all other annotations. But because A4's boundaries do not overlap with those of A1 and A2, technically this cluster has no core (a text segment included in all ADUs in a cluster). 5% or less of the clusters have this problem. To handle the absence of a core in this type of cluster, we split the clusters that fit this pattern into multiple 'overlapping' clusters, that is, we put A1, A2, and A3 into one cluster and we put A3 and A4 into another cluster. Using this splitting technique, we get two cores, each selected by two judges: i) "actually the only ... app's developer" from the cluster containing A1, A2, and A3 (shown in italics) and ii) "I think it hilarious ... another device" from the cluster containing A3 and A4 (shown in bold). The disagreement of the judges in identifying the Callout suggests that judges have quite different judgments about boundaries of the Callouts.

Table 12 and 13 respectively show the number of clusters with overlapping annotations for Callouts for each thread before and after splitting. The splitting process has only a small impact on results. The number of clusters with five and four annotators shows that in each corpus there are Callouts that are evidently easier to identify. On the other hand, clusters selected by only two or three judges are harder to

# Annots	Text selected
A1, A2	*Actually the only one responsible for the YouTube and Twitter multitasking is the app's developer*
A3	*Actually the . . . app's developer.* The Facebook app allows you to watch videos posted by . . . **I think it hilarious that people complain about features that arent even available on another device**
A4	**I think it hilarious that people complain about features that arent even available on another device**

Table 11: A cluster with 2 cores, each selected by 2 judges

identify. The clusters containing a text string picked by only one annotator are hardest to identify. This may be an indication that this text string is not a good example of a Callout, though it also could be an indication that the judge is particularly good at recognizing subtly expressed Callouts. The clustering technique thus scaffolds deeper examination of annotation behavior and annotation/concept refinement. Table 13 also shows that overall, the number of clusters with five or four annotators is well over 50% for each thread except Ban, even when we exclude the clusters with an ADU identified by only one judge. This is another hint that the IAA in this thread should be much lower than in the other threads. (See also Figures 2 and 3).

Thread	# of Clusters	Annots in each cluster				
		5	4	3	2	1
Android	91	52	16	11	7	5
Ban	89	25	18	12	20	14
Ipad	88	41	17	7	13	10
Layoffs	86	41	18	11	6	10
Twitter	84	44	17	14	4	5

Table 12: Callouts: Clusters before splitting process

Thread	# of Clusters	Annots in each cluster				
		5	4	3	2	1
Android	93	51	15	14	8	5
Ban	91	25	19	12	21	14
iPad	89	41	16	9	13	10
Layoffs	89	40	17	14	8	10
Twitter	87	43	15	20	4	5

Table 13: Callouts: Clusters after splitting process

The clusters with cores supported by four or five annotators show strong annotator agreement and are very strong candidates for a gold standard, regardless of the IAA for the entire thread. Clusters with an ADU selected by only one annotator are presumably harder to annotate and are more likely than other clusters not to be actual instances of the ADU. This information can be used to assess the output of systems that automatically identify discourse units. For example a system could be penalized more for missing to identifying ADUs on which all five annotators agree on the boundaries, as in Table 9; the penalty would be decreased for not identifying ADUs on which fewer annotators agree. Qualitative analysis may help discover the reason for the variation in strength of clusters, thereby supporting our ability to interpret IAA and to create accurate computational models of human judgments about discourse units. As a related research, PAT and the clustering technique discussed in this paper allow the development of a finer-grained annotation scheme to analyze the type of links between Target-Callout (e.g., Agree/Disagree/Other), and the nature of Callouts (e.g., Stance/Rationale) (Ghosh et al., 2014).

5 Conclusion and Future Work

Reliability of annotation studies is important both as part of the demonstration of the validity of the phenomena being studied and also to support accurate computational modeling of discourse phenomena. The nature of ADUs, with their fuzzy boundaries, makes it hard to achieve IAA of .80 or higher. Furthermore, the use of a single figure for IAA is a little like relying on an average to convey the range of variation of a set of numbers. The contributions of this paper are i) to provide concrete examples of the difficulties of using state of the art metrics like P/R/F1 and Krippendorff's α to assess IAA for ADUs and ii) to open up a new approach to studying IAA that can help us understand how factors like coder variability and text difficulty affect IAA. Our approach supports reliable identification of discourse units independent of the overall IAA of the document.

References

Mark Aakhus, Smaranda Muresan, and Nina Wacholder. 2013. Integrating natural language processing and pragmatic argumentation theories for argumentation support. pages 1–12.

Ron Artstein and Massimo Poesio. 2008. Inter-coder agreement for computational linguistics. *Computational Linguistics*, 34(4):555–596.

Petra Saskia Bayerl and Karsten Ingmar Paul. 2011. What determines inter-coder agreement in manual annotations? a meta-analytic investigation. *Computational Linguistics*, 37(4):699–725.

Debanjan Ghosh, Smaranda Muresan, Nina Wacholder, Mark Aakhus, and Matthew Mitsui. 2014. Analyzing argumentative discourse units in online interactions. In *Proceedings of the First Workshop on Argumentation Mining*, pages 39–48, Baltimore, Maryland, June. Association for Computational Linguistics.

Barbara J Grosz and Candace L Sidner. 1986. Attention, intentions, and the structure of discourse. *Computational linguistics*, 12(3):175–204.

Trevor Hastie, Robert Tibshirani, Jerome Friedman, T Hastie, J Friedman, and R Tibshirani. 2009. *The elements of statistical learning*, volume 2. Springer.

Ian Hutchby. 2013. *Confrontation talk: Arguments, asymmetries, and power on talk radio*. Routledge.

Klaus Krippendorff. 1995. On the reliability of unitizing continuous data. *Sociological Methodology*, pages 47–76.

Klaus Krippendorff. 2004a. *Content analysis: An introduction to its methodology*. Sage.

Klaus Krippendorff. 2004b. Measuring the reliability of qualitative text analysis data. *Quality & quantity*, 38:787–800.

Douglas W Maynard. 1985. How children start arguments. *Language in society*, 14(01):1–29.

Philip V Ogren. 2006. Knowtator: a protégé plug-in for annotated corpus construction. In *Proceedings of the 2006 Conference of the North American Chapter of the Association for Computational Linguistics on Human Language Technology: companion volume: demonstrations*, pages 273–275. Association for Computational Linguistics.

Andreas Peldszus and Manfred Stede. 2013a. From argument diagrams to argumentation mining in texts: A survey. *International Journal of Cognitive Informatics and Natural Intelligence (IJCINI)*, 7(1):1–31.

Andreas Peldszus and Manfred Stede. 2013b. Ranking the annotators: An agreement study on argumentation structure. In *Proceedings of the 7th linguistic annotation workshop and interoperability with discourse*, pages 196–204.

Swapna Somasundaran, Josef Ruppenhofer, and Janyce Wiebe. 2008. Discourse level opinion relations: An annotation study. In *Proceedings of the 9th SIGdial Workshop on Discourse and Dialogue*, pages 129–137. Association for Computational Linguistics.

Frans H Van Eemeren, Rob Grootendorst, Sally Jackson, and Scott Jacobs. 1993. *Reconstructing argumentative discourse*. University of Alabama Press.

Janyce Wiebe, Theresa Wilson, and Claire Cardie. 2005. Annotating expressions of opinions and emotions in language. *Language resources and evaluation*, 39(2-3):165–210.

Towards Automatic Annotation of Clinical Decision-Making Style

Limor Hochberg[1] **Cecilia O. Alm**[1] **Esa M. Rantanen**[1]
Qi Yu[2] **Caroline M. DeLong**[1] **Anne Haake**[2]
1 College of Liberal Arts 2 College of Computing & Information Sciences
Rochester Institute of Technology
lxh6513|coagla|emrgsh|qi.yu|cmdgsh|anne.haake@rit.edu

Abstract

Clinical decision-making has high-stakes outcomes for both physicians and patients, yet little research has attempted to model and automatically annotate such decision-making. The dual process model (Evans, 2008) posits two types of decision-making, which may be ordered on a continuum from *intuitive* to *analytical* (Hammond, 1981). Training clinicians to recognize decision-making style and select the most appropriate mode of reasoning for a particular context may help reduce diagnostic error (Norman, 2009). This study makes preliminary steps towards detection of decision style, based on an annotated dataset of image-based clinical reasoning in which speech data were collected from physicians as they inspected images of dermatological cases and moved towards diagnosis (Hochberg et al., 2014). A classifier was developed based on lexical, speech, disfluency, physician demographic, cognitive, and diagnostic difficulty features. Using random forests for binary classification of intuitive vs. analytical decision style in physicians' diagnostic descriptions, the model improved on the baseline by over 30%. The introduced computational model provides construct validity for decision styles, as well as insights into the linguistic expression of decision-making. Eventually, such modeling may be incorporated into instructional systems that teach clinicians to become more effective decision makers.

1 Introduction

Diagnostic accuracy is critical for both physicians and patients, but there is insufficient training on clinical decision-making strategy in medical schools, towards avoiding diagnostic error (Graber et al., 2012; Croskerry & Norman, 2008). Berner and Graber (2008) estimate that diagnostic error in medicine occurs at a rate of 5-15%, and that two-thirds of diagnostic errors involve cognitive root causes.

The dual process model distinguishes between *intuitive* and *analytic* modes of reasoning (Kahneman & Frederick, 2002; Evans, 1989). Use of the intuitive system, while efficient, may lead to cognitive errors based on heuristics and biases (Graber, 2009). Croskerry (2003) distinguished over 30 such biases and heuristics that underlie diagnostic error, including anchoring, base-rate neglect, and hindsight bias.

Hammond's (1981) *Cognitive Continuum Theory* proposes that decision-making lies on a continuum from intuitive to analytical reasoning. Intuitive reasoning is described as rapid, unconscious, moderately accurate, and employing simultaneous use of cues and pattern recognition (Hammond, 1981). Analytical decision-making is described as slow, conscious, task-specific, more accurate, making sequential use of cues, and applying logical rules (Hammond, 1996). Much reasoning is *quasirational*: between the two poles of purely intuitive and purely analytical decision-making (Hamm, 1988; Hammond, 1981).

Cader et al. (2005) suggested that cognitive continuum theory is appropriate for the evaluation of decision-making in medical contexts. The current study links to another work (Hochberg et al., 2014), where the cognitive continuum was applied to physician decision-making in dermatology. Decision style was manually assessed in physician verbalizations during medical image inspection. Figure 1 shows the 4-point annotation scheme, ranging from intuitive to analytical; the two intermediate points on the scale reflect the presence of both styles, with intuitive (*BI*) or analytical (*BA*) reasoning more prevalent.

LAW VIII - The 8th Linguistic Annotation Workshop, pages 129–138,
Dublin, Ireland, August 23-24 2014.

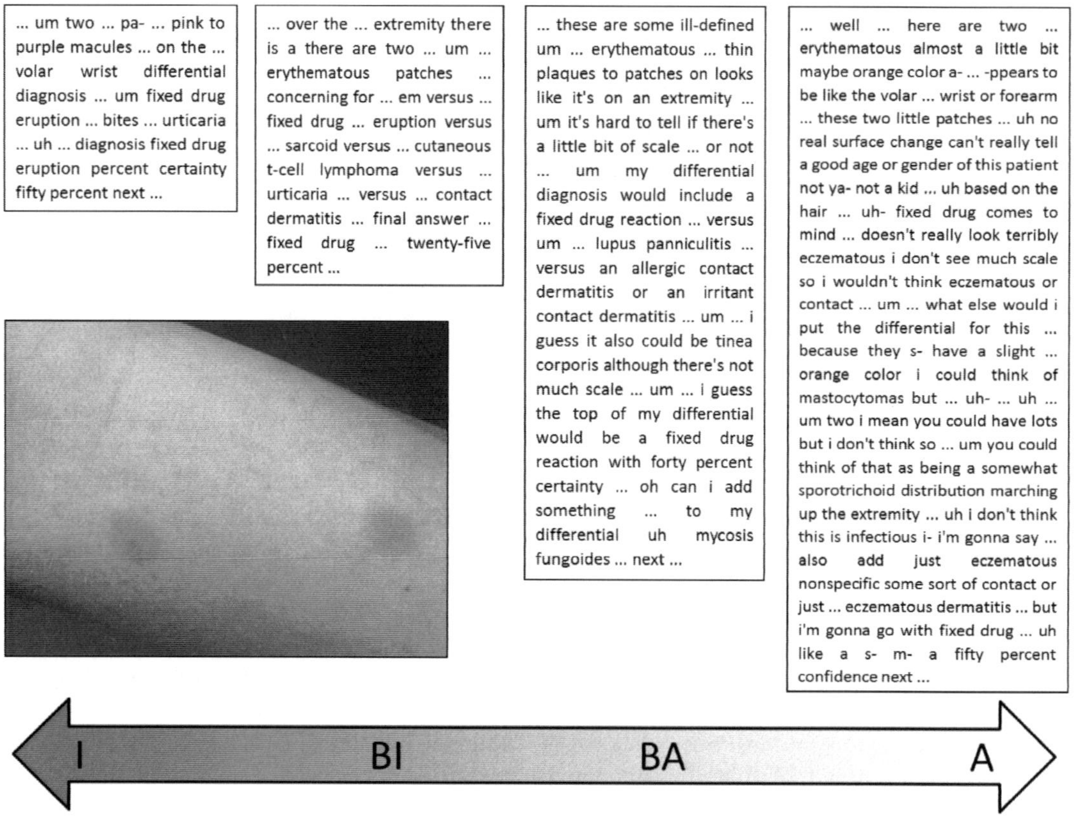

Figure 1: Four narratives along the intuitive-analytical decision-making continuum, for which annotators agreed on their labels, where *I=Intuitive, BI=Both-Intuitive, BA=Both-Analytical, A=Analytical.* The narratives were produced by different physicians for the same image case (left, used with permission from Logical Images, Inc.), and all four physicians were correct in their final diagnosis. (Confidence mentions were removed in narratives presented to annotators, to avoid any potential bias.)

This work describes computational modeling for automatic annotation of decision style using this annotated dataset, on the basis of linguistic, speaker, and image case features.

1.1 Contributions

To date, this appears to be the first study attempting to computationally predict physician decision style. Similar to the case of affect, automatic annotation of decision style can be characterized as a subjective natural language processing problem (Alm, 2011). This adds special challenges to the modeling process. Accordingly, this work details a thorough process for moving from manual to automatic annotation.

This study contributes to cognitive psychology, annotation methodology, and clinical computational linguistic analysis. Methodologically, the study details a careful process for selecting and labeling manually annotated data for modeling in the realm of subjective natural language phenomena, thus addressing the need for their characterization (Alm, 2011). Theoretically, acceptable annotator reliability on decision style, along with successful computational modeling, will lend construct validity to the dual process model. From a linguistic perspective, the identification of discriminative features for intuitive and analytical reasoning provides a springboard for further studying decision-making using language as a cognitive sensor.

Practically, prediction of decision style would also be useful for determining whether individuals are using the appropriate style for a particular task, based on analyses linking decision style to task performance. Importantly, detection of decision style from observable linguistic behaviors allows for objective measurement that avoids biases present in self-report surveys (Sjöberg, 2003; Allinson & Hayes, 1996).

2 Data and Manual Decision Style Annotation

The annotated corpus used in this study was introduced in Hochberg et al. (2014), which also discusses the manual annotation scheme and annotator strategies in greater detail. For clarity, the dataset and annotation scheme are described here briefly.

The dataset consisted of spoken narratives collected from 29 physicians as they examined 30 clinical images of dermatological cases, for a total of 867[1] narratives. Physicians described their reasoning process as they advanced towards a diagnosis, and they also estimated their confidence[2] in their final diagnosis. Narratives were assessed for correctness (based on final diagnoses) and image cases were evaluated for difficulty by a practicing dermatologist.[3]

For the manual annotation of decision style, anonymized text transcripts of the narratives were presented to two annotators with graduate training in cognitive psychology.[4] Analytical reasoning considers more alternatives in greater detail. Thus, it was expected to be associated with longer narratives, as Figure 1 illustrates. Therefore, annotators were asked not to use length as a proxy for decision style.

Narratives were randomized to ensure high-quality annotation, and 10% of narratives were duplicated to measure intra-annotator reliability. For analysis, primary ratings were used, and secondary ratings (on duplicated narratives) were used to measure intra-annotator consistency. The kappa scores and proportion agreement, detailed below, motivate the labeling and data selection process used for classification and modeling in this work.

Figure 2 shows the distribution of annotation labels for both annotators, respectively, for the whole dataset, on the original 4-point scale. In comparison, Figure 3 shows the annotators' distributions across a collapsed 2-point scale of intuitive vs. analytical, where, for each annotator, narratives labeled *BI* were assigned to *I* and those labeled *BA* assigned to *A*.

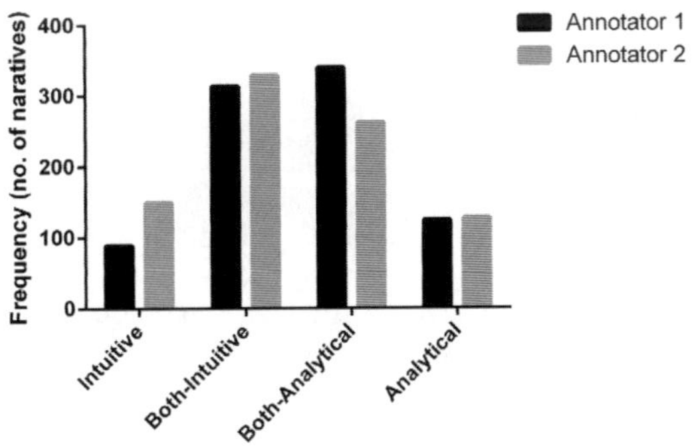

Figure 2: The distribution of ratings among the decision-making spectrum, on a 4-point scale.

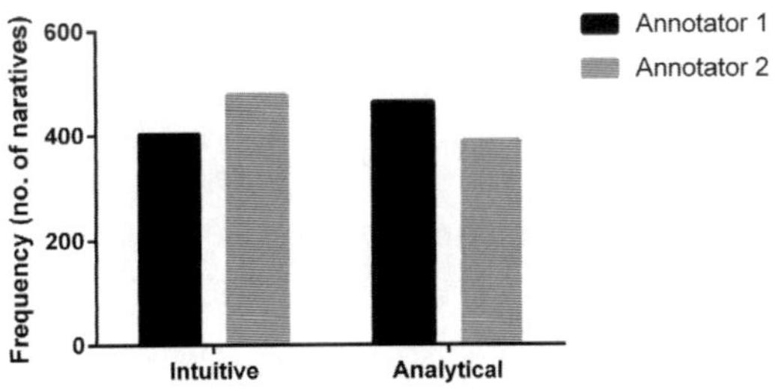

Figure 3: The distribution of ratings among the decision-making spectrum, on a 2-point scale.

Annotator agreement was well above chance for both the 4-point (Figure 4) and 2-point (Figure 5) scales. Notably, the annotators were in full agreement or agreed within one rating for over 90% of narratives on the original 4-point scale. This pattern of variation reveals both the fuzziness of the categories and also that the subjective perception of decision-making style is systematic.

Annotator agreement was also assessed via linear weighted kappa scores (Cohen, 1968). As shown in Figure 6, inter-annotator reliability was moderate, and intra-annotator reliability was moderate (Annotator 2) to good (Annotator 1); see Landis and Koch (1977) and Altman (1991).

Since both proportion agreement and kappa scores were slightly higher for the 2-point scale, the automatic annotation modeling discussed below used this binary scale. In addition, the distribution of

[1]One narrative was excluded due to extreme brevity, and two physicians each skipped an image during data collection.

[2]For consistency, this paper uses the term *confidence*, treated as interchangeable with *certainty* and similar synonymous expressions used by clinicians in the medical narratives, such as *sure*, *certain*, *confident*, just certainty percentages, etc.

[3]Some imperfections may occur in the data, e.g., in transcriptions, difficulty ratings, or annotations (or in extracted features).

[4]Annotator instructions included decision style definitions, a description of the 4-point scale and example narratives. Annotators were asked to focus on decision style as present in the text rather than speculate beyond it.

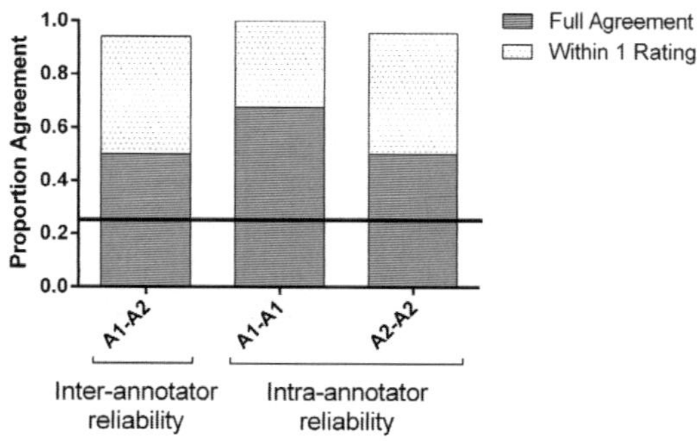

Figure 4: Inter- and intra-annotator reliability for the 4-point scheme, by proportion agreement. The reference line shows chance agreement (25%). *(A1=Annotator 1; A2=Annotator 2).*

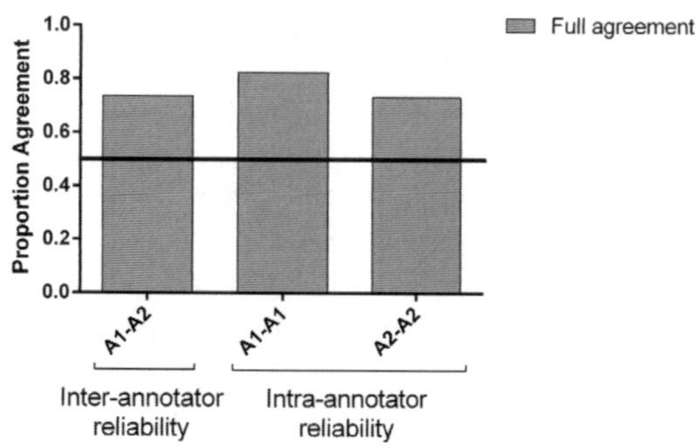

Figure 5: Inter- and intra-annotator reliability for the 2-point scheme, by proportion agreement. The reference line shows chance agreement (50%). *(A1=Annotator 1; A2=Annotator 2).*

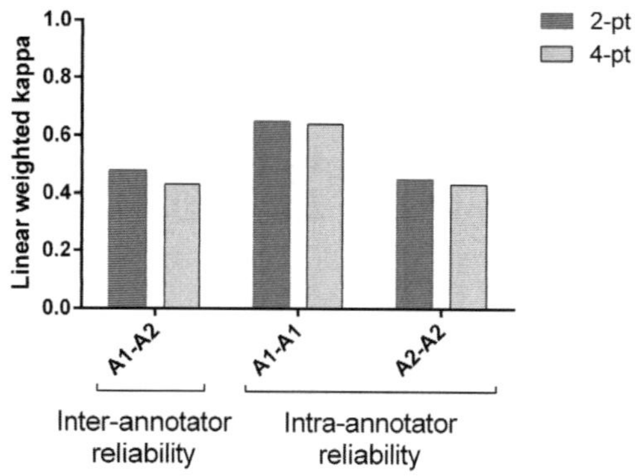

Figure 6: Annotator reliability, as measured by linear weighted kappa scores on the 2-pt and 4-pt scales.

data across binary classes was more balanced compared to the 4-point scale, as shown by the contrast between Figures 2 and 3, further making it a suitable starting point for computational modeling.

2.1 Data Selection and Labeling for Computational Modeling

This section details the systematic method used to select data for model development. The goal of the work was to develop a computational model that could automatically annotate narratives as intuitive or analytical, based on lexical, speech, disfluency, physician demographic, cognitive, and diagnostic difficulty features. The study employed a supervised learning approach, and since no real ground truth was available, it relied on manual annotation of each narrative for decision style. However, annotators did not always agree on the labels, as discussed above. Thus, strategies were developed to label narratives, including in the case of disagreement (Figure 7).

The dataset used for modeling consisted of 672 narratives.[5] Annotators were in full agreement for 614 ratings on the binary scale of intuitive vs. analytical (Figure 8).[6] Next, 49 narratives were assigned a binary label based on the center of gravity of both annotators' primary ratings (Figure 9). For example, if a narrative was rated as *Intuitive* and *Both-Analytical* by Annotators 1 and 2, respectively, the center of gravity was at *Both-Intuitive*, resulting in an *Intuitive* label. Finally, 9 narratives were labeled using the annotators' secondary ratings,[7] available for 10% of narratives, to resolve annotator disagreement.[8]

[5]Within a reasonable time frame, the text data are expected to be made publicly available.

[6]Excluding also narratives lacking confidence or correctness information.

[7]Collected to measure intra-annotator reliability.

[8]For example, if the primary ratings of Annotator 1 and Annotator 2 were *Both-Analytical* and *Both-Intuitive*, respectively, but both annotators' secondary ratings were intuitive (e.g., *Both-Intuitive* or *Intuitive*), the narrative was labeled *Intuitive*.

Narratives with disagreements that could not be resolved in these ways were excluded. As perception of decision-making style is subject to variation in human judgment, this work focused on an initial modeling of data which represent the clearer-cut cases of decision style (rather than the disagreement gray zone on this gradient perception continuum). From the perspective of dealing with a subjective problem, this approach enables an approximation of ground truth, as a validation concept.[9]

Figure 7: Narrative labeling pipeline. 614 narratives were labeled due to full binary agreement, and center-of-gravity and secondary rating strategies were used to label an additional 58 narratives for which annotators were not in agreement.

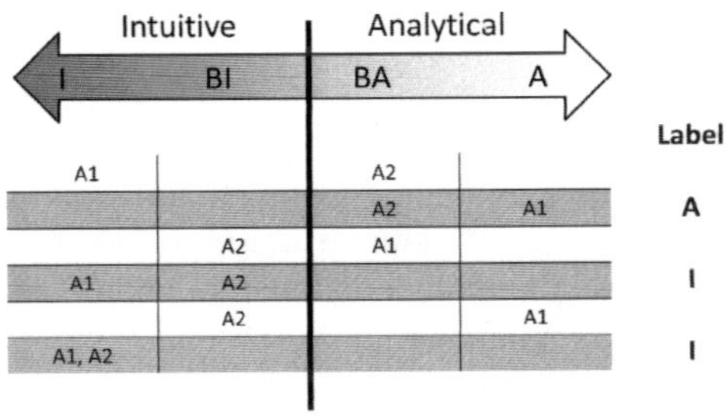

Figure 8: Demonstration of initial corpus labeling, in which 614 narratives were labeled on the basis of binary agreement.

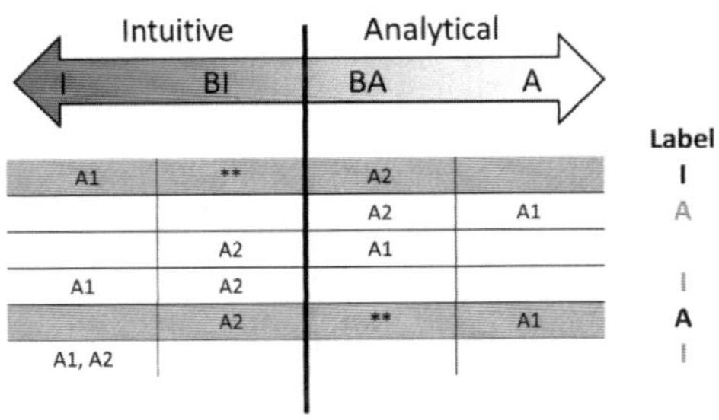

Figure 9: Demonstration of center-of-gravity strategy, used to label an additional 49 narratives.

2.2 Relationship Between Physicians' Diagnostic Correctness and Decision Style

Using the 672 narratives selected for modeling, Table 1 shows the relationship of physicians' diagnostic correctness by decision style (intuitive vs. analytical on a binary scale).

	Correct	**Incorrect**	**Total**
Intuitive	158	186	344
Analytical	106	222	328
Total	264	408	672

Table 1: Distribution of diagnostic correctness by decision style.

Overall, there was a slightly higher prevalence of intuitive reasoning, and there were more incorrect than correct diagnoses.[10] Table 1 also suggests a relationship between correctness and decision-making style, where for correct diagnoses, intuitive reasoning was more dominant. The opposite trend held for incorrect diagnoses: analytical reasoning was more frequent. Indeed, a chi-square test revealed a significant relationship between correctness and decision style, $\chi^2(1, N = 672) = 13.05, p < 0.01$.

This pattern is in line with claims that intuitive reasoning is linked to better performance when much information is to be processed; mechanisms of intuitive reasoning and pattern recognition allow individuals to overcome the limitations of their working memory (Evans, 2008). However, others have linked intuitive reasoning to decreased diagnostic accuracy, as intuitive reasoning may be prey to inappropriate

[9]Modeling of fuzzier, hard to label data, is left to future work. One possible approach is to learn the labels by using a k-nearest neighbor classifier, which identifies the most similar narratives and uses their labels to make the prediction.

[10]Contributing factors to the proportion of incorrect diagnoses might include case difficulty levels in the experimental scenario, and that physicians did not have access to additional information, such as patient history or follow-up tests.

heuristics and biases (Croskerry, 2003). Viewed from the perspective of cognitive continuum theory, the higher prevalence of incorrect diagnoses may be due to the use of decision styles that were not suited to the task demands of the particular case (Hammond, 1981). Finally, it might be the case that diagnostic difficulty was a moderating variable, where physicians preferred intuitive reasoning for less challenging cases, and analytical reasoning for more difficult cases.

3 Methods

A model was developed for the binary prediction case (intuitive vs. analytical), since the 2-point rating scheme had slightly higher annotator agreement (see Section 2). Model development and analysis were performed using the WEKA data mining software package (Hall et al., 2009). The dataset was split into 80% development and 20% final test sets (Table 2).[11] Parameter tuning was performed using 10-fold cross-validation on the best features in the development set.[12]

	80% Development Set	**20% Final Test Set**
Intuitive	276 (51%)	68 (51%)
Analytical	263 (49%)	65 (49%)
Total	539	133

Table 2: Class label statistics.

3.1 Features

Three feature types were derived from the spoken narratives to study the linguistic link to decision-making style: lexical (37), speech (13), and disfluency (3) features. Three other feature types relevant to decision-making were demographic (2), cognitive (2), and difficulty (2) features (Table 3).

Type	**Feature**	**Description / *Examples***
Lexical	exclusion	*but, without*
	inclusion	*both, with*
	insight	*think, know*
	tentative	*maybe, perhaps*
	cause	*because, therefore*
	cognitive process	*know, whether*
	. . .	
Speech	speech length	number of tokens
	pitch	min, max, mean, st. dev., time of min/max
	intensity	min, max, mean, st. dev., time of min/max
Disfluency	silent pauses	number of
	fillers	*like, blah*
	nonfluencies	*uh, um*
Demographic	gender	male, female
	status	resident, attending
Cognitive	confidence	percentage
	correctness	binary
Difficulty	expert rating	ordinal ranking
	% correctness/image	percentage

Table 3: Six feature types. The listed lexical features are a sub-sample of the total set.

Relevant *lexical* features were extracted with the Linguistic Inquiry and Word Count (LIWC) software, which calculates the relative frequency of syntactic and semantic classes in text samples based on val-

[11] This split rests on the assumption that physicians may share common styles. Thus, the testing data will represent different physicians, but the styles themselves have been captured by the training data so that they can be correctly classified; the same rationale can be applied to image cases. To further investigate the phenomenon and identify the degree of inter- and intra-individual variation in decision style, future work could experiment with holding out particular images and physicians.

[12] In Section 4.1, parameters were tuned for each case of feature combinations in a similar way.

idated, researched dictionaries (Tausczik & Pennebaker, 2010). *Disfluency* features were silent pauses, and the frequency of fillers and nonfluencies as computed by LIWC. *Speech* features are in Table 3.

Besides linguistic features, three additional groups of features were included, with an eye towards application. *Demographic* features were gender and professional status, while *cognitive* features were physician confidence in diagnosis and correctness of the final diagnosis. *Difficulty* features consisted of an expert-assigned rank of diagnostic case difficulty, and the percent of correct diagnoses given by physicians for each image, calculated on the development data only. In an instructional system, a trainee could input a demographic profile, and the system could also collect performance data over time, while also taking into account stored information on case difficulty when available. This information could then be used in modeling of decision style in spoken or written diagnostic narratives.

3.2 Feature Selection

WEKA's CfsSubsetEval, an attribute evaluator, was used for feature selection,[13] using 10-fold cross-validation on the development set only. Features selected by the evaluator in at least 5 of 10 folds were considered best features. The best features from the entire feature set were: *2nd person pronouns, conjunctions, cognitive process, insight, cause, bio*, and *time* words, plus *silent pauses, speech length, time of min. pitch, standard deviation of pitch, time of min. intensity*, and *difficulty: percent correctness/image*.

Feature selection, using the same attribute evaluator, was also performed on only the lexical features, which could be a starting point for analysis of decision-making style in text-only data. The best lexical features[14] included conjunctions, cause, cognitive process, inclusion, exclusion, and perception words. These lexical items seem associated with careful examination and reasoning, which might be more present in analytical decision-making and less present in intuitive decision-making. Some categories, especially inclusion (e.g., *with, and*), exclusion (e.g., *but, either, unless*), and cause words (e.g., *affect, cause, depend, therefore*), seem particularly good representatives of logical reasoning and justification, a key feature of analytical reasoning. But as shown in the next section, when available, speech and disfluency information is useful, and potentially more so than some lexical features.[15]

4 Results and Discussion

Table 4 lists the results for the Random Forest (Breiman, 2001) and Logistic Regression (Cox, 1972) classifiers on the best features (as selected from all features) on the final test set, after training on the development set. These results suggest that decision style can be quantified and classified on a binary scale; the percent error reduction (compared to baseline performance) for both classifiers is substantial.

Classifier	%Acc	%ER	Pr	Re
Random Forest	88	76	88	88
Logistic Regression	84	67	84	84
Majority Class Baseline	51	–	–	–

Table 4: Performance on final test set; reduction in error is calculated relative to majority class baseline. Precision and recall are macro-averages of the two classes.

4.1 Feature Combination Exploration

A study of feature combinations was performed on the final test set with Random Forest (Table 5) to explore the contribution of each feature type towards automatic annotation. The best performance was achieved after applying feature selection on all features. Lexical and disfluency features were useful for determining decision style, and the best linguistic features (chosen with feature selection) were slightly more useful. These latter feature types improve on the performance achieved when considering only

[13]With BestFirst search method.

[14]Best lexical features were: function words, singular pronouns, prepositions, conjunctions, quantifiers, and cognitive process, cause, discrepancy, tentative, inclusion, exclusion, perception, see, bio, motion, time, and assent words.

[15]Feature selection was also performed only on the linguistic (lexical, speech, and disfluency) features as a group. The best features of these types were: second personal pronouns, conjunctions, cognitive process, insight, cause, bio, and time words; silent pauses; and speech length, time of minimum pitch, standard deviation of pitch, and time of minimum intensity. They could represent a starting for point for analyzing speech data not enhanced by additional speaker and task information.

speech length and silent pauses, which were apparent characteristics to the human annotators and among the best features (see Section 3.2.).

Demographic features improved somewhat over the baseline, indicating an association between gender, professional status, and decision-making, and adding cognitive features increased performance. Importantly, overall these findings hint at linguistic markers as key indicators of decision style.

Features	Accuracy
All*	88
All	85
(Lexical + Speech + Disfluency)*	86
Lexical + Speech + Disfluency	84
Lexical + Disfluency	84
Only speech length and silent pauses	81
Disfluency	79
Lexical	77
Demographic + Cognitive	68
Demographic	64
Majority Class Baseline	51

Table 5: Performance on final test set. Star (*) indicates the use of feature selection (see Section 3.2.)

4.2 Limitations

In this study, doctors diagnosed solely on the basis of visual information (e.g., without tests or follow-up), so their speech may reflect only part of the clinical reasoning process. In addition, most decision style ratings on the 4-point scale were in the distribution center (Figure 2), so the binary labels used in the study only partially reflect purely intuitive or purely analytical reasoning. However, since clinician reasoning in the current dataset can be reliably measured by human and computational classification, linguistic features of decision style must be present. Finally, the LIWC software used for lexical features matches surface strings rather than senses; future work might operate on the sense rather than token level.

5 Related Work

Lauri et al. (2001) asked nurses in five countries to rate statements representative of intuitive or analytical decision-making on a 5-point scale. They found that reasoning varies with context and that styles in the middle of the cognitive continuum predominate. In this work, annotation ratings were prevalent in the middle of the spectrum. Thus, both studies endorse that most decision-making occurs in the central part of the continuum (Hamm, 1988; Hammond, 1981). Womack et al. (2012) proposed that silent pauses in physician narration may indicate cognitive processing. Here, silent pauses were also important, perhaps because analytical decision-making may recruit more cognitive resources than intuitive decision-making.

6 Conclusion

This work suggests that decision style is revealed in language use, in line with claims that linguistic data reflect speakers' cognitive processes (Pennebaker & King, 1999; Tausczik & Pennebaker, 2010). Theoretically, the study adds validity to the dual process and cognitive continuum theories. Methodologically, it articulates a method of transitioning from manual to automatic annotation of fuzzy semantic phenomena, including label adjudication and data selection for computational modeling. Future work may investigate modeling of the 4-point decision scale, as well as whether particular variables, such as difficulty or expertise, mediate the relationship between diagnostic correctness and decision style.

Practically, automatic detection of decision style is useful for both clinical educational systems and mission-critical environments. Clinical instructional systems can assess whether trainees are using the appropriate style for a particular task (Hammond, 1981), and they can help users determine and attend to their own decision styles, towards improving diagnostic skill (Norman, 2009). Finally, in mission-critical environments, linguistic markers of decision-making style may be used to determine the optimal modes of reasoning for a particular task in high-stakes human factors domains.

Acknowledgements

This work was supported by a COLA Faculty Development grant, Xerox award, and NIH award R21 LM01002901. Many thanks to the annotators and reviewers. This content is solely the responsibility of the authors and does not necessarily represent the official views of the National Institutes of Health.

References

Allinson, C. W., & Hayes, J. (1996). The cognitive style index: A measure of intuition-analysis for organizational research. *Journal of Management Studies, 33*(1), 119-135.

Alm, C. O. (2011, June). Subjective natural language problems: Motivations, applications, characterizations, and implications. *Proceedings of the 49th Annual Meeting of the Association for Computational Linguistics: Human Language Technologies: Short papers-Volume 2* (pp. 107-112). Association for Computational Linguistics.

Altman, D. (1991). *Practical statistics for medical research.* London: Chapman and Hall.

Berner, E. S., & Graber, M. L. (2008). Overconfidence as a cause of diagnostic error in medicine. *American Journal of Medicine, 121*, S2-S23.

Breiman, L. (2001). Random forests. *Machine Learning, 45*(1), 5-32.

Cader, R., Campbell, S., & Watson, D. (2005). Cognitive continuum theory in nursing decision-making. *Journal of Advanced Nursing, 49*(4), 397-405.

Cohen, J. (1968). Weighted kappa: Nominal scale agreement provision for scaled disagreement or partial credit. *Psychological Bulletin, 70*(4), 213-220.

Cox, D. R. (1972). Regression models and life tables. *Journal of the Royal Statistical Society, Series B, 34*(2), 187-220.

Croskerry, P. (2003). The importance of cognitive errors in diagnosis and strategies to minimize them. *Academic Medicine, 78*, 775-780.

Croskerry, P., & Norman, G. (2008). Overconfidence in clinical decision making. *The American Journal of Medicine, 121*(5), S24-S29.

Evans, J. (1989). *Bias in human reasoning: Causes and consequences.* Hillsdale, NJ: Erlbaum.

Evans, J. (2008). Dual-processing accounts of reasoning, judgment and social cognition. *Annual Review of Psychology, 59*, 255-278.

Graber, M. (2009). Educational strategies to reduce diagnostic error: Can you teach this stuff? *Advances in Health Sciences Education, 14*, 63-69.

Graber, M. L., Kissam, S., Payne, V. L., Meyer, A. N., Sorensen, A., Lenfestey, N., ... & Singh, H. (2012). Cognitive interventions to reduce diagnostic error: A narrative review. *BMJ Quality & Safety, 2*(7), 535-557.

Hall, M., Frank, E., Holmes, G., Pfahringer, B., Reutemann, P., & Witten, I. H. (2009). The WEKA data mining software: An update. *ACM SIGKDD Explorations Newsletter, 11*(1), 10-18.

Hamm, R. M. (1988). Clinical intuition and clinical analysis: Expertise and the cognitive continuum. In J. Dowie & A.S. Elstein (Eds.), *Professional judgment: A reader in clinical decision making* (pp. 78-105). Cambridge, England: Cambridge University Press.

Hammond, K. R. (1981). *Principles of organization in intuitive and analytical cognition (Report #231).* Boulder, CO: University of Colorado, Center for Research on Judgment & Policy.

Hammond, K. R. (1996). *Human judgement and social policy: Irreducible uncertainty, inevitable error, unavoidable injustice.* New York, NY: Oxford University Press.

Hochberg, L., Alm, C. O., Rantanen, E. M., DeLong, C.M., & Haake, A. (2014). Decision style in a clinical reasoning corpus. In *Proceedings of the BioNLP Workshop* (pp. 83-87). Baltimore, MD: Association for Computational Linguistics.

Kahneman, D., & Frederick, S. (2002). Representativeness revisited: Attribute substitution in intuitive judgment. In T. Gilovich, D. Griffin, & D. Kahneman (Eds.), *Heuristics of intuitive judgment: Extensions and applications* (pp. 49-81). New York, NY: Cambridge University Press.

Lauri, S., Salanterä, S., Chalmers, K., Ekman, S. L., Kim, H. S., Käppeli, S., & MacLeod, M. (2001). An exploratory study of clinical decision-making in five countries. *Journal of Nursing Scholarship, 33*(1), 83-90.

Landis, J. R., & Koch, G. G. (1977). The measurement of observer agreement for categorical data. *Biometrics, 33*(1), 159-174.

Norman, G. (2009). Dual processing and diagnostic errors. *Advances in Health Sciences Education, 14*(1), 37-49.

Pennebaker, J. W., & King, L. A. (1999). Linguistic styles: Language use as an individual difference. *Journal of Personality and Social Psychology, 77*(6), 1296-1312.

Sjöberg, L. (2003). Intuitive vs. analytical decision making: Which is preferred? *Scandinavian Journal of Management, 19*(1), 17-29.

Tausczik, Y. R., & Pennebaker, J. W. (2010). The psychological meaning of words: LIWC and computerized text analysis methods. *Journal of Language and Social Psychology, 29*(1), 24-54.

Womack, K., McCoy, W., Alm, C. O., Calvelli, C., Pelz, J. B., Shi, P., & Haake, A. (2012, July). Disfluencies as extra-propositional indicators of cognitive processing. *Proceedings of the Workshop on Extra-Propositional Aspects of Meaning in Computational Linguistics* (pp. 1-9). Association for Computational Linguistics.

Interactive Annotation for Event Modality in Modern Standard and Egyptian Arabic Tweets

Rania Al-Sabbagh[†], **Roxana Girju**[†], **Jana Diesner**[‡]
[†]Department of Linguistics and Beckman Institute
[‡]School of Library and Information Science
University of Illinois at Urbana-Champaign, USA
{alsabba1, girju, jdiesner} @illinois.edu

Abstract

We present an interactive procedure to annotate a large-scale corpus of Modern Standard and Egyptian Arabic tweets for event modality that comprises obligation, permission, commitment, ability, and volition. The procedure splits up the annotation process into a series of simplified questions, dispenses with the requirement of expert linguistic knowledge, and captures nested modality triggers and their attributes semi-automatically.

1 Introduction

Event modality, according to Palmer (2001), describes events that are not actualized but are merely potential. It comprises obligation, permission, commitment, ability, and volition. Both obligation and permission emanate from an external authority such as the law; whereas commitments are the obligations placed by speakers on themselves as in promises. Ability is the (in)capacity to do something. Volition is broadly defined as intensions, desires, wishes, and preferences. Event modality is used for several NLP tasks, including sales and marketing analysis (Ramanand et al. 2010, Carlos and Yalamanchi 2012), sentiment analysis (Chardon et al. 2013), the automatic detection of request emails (Lampert et al. 2010), and the classification of animacy and writers' emotions (Liao and Liao 2009, Bowman and Chopra 2012).

To-date, there are no large-scale Arabic corpora annotated for event modality compared to English (Baker et al. 2010, 2012; Rubinstein et al. 2013), Japanese (Matsuyoshi et al. 2010), Portuguese (Hendrickx et al. 2012), and Chinese (Cui and Chi 2013). One obstacle for the creation of modality-annotated corpora is the lack of consensus definitions of modality and its attributes to be rendered into annotation tasks and guidelines. Furthermore, most modality annotation schemes use sophisticated theoretical guidelines that need annotators with linguistic background; hence, annotation typically takes place in in-lab settings at small scales.

In this paper, we present an interactive annotation procedure to annotate event modality and its attributes of sense, polarity, intensification, tense, holders, and scopes in Modern Standard and Egyptian Arabic tweets. The procedure depicts the following ideas: first, it defines each annotation task as a series of questions displayed[1]/hidden based on prior answers; second, it avoids lengthy theoretically-sophisticated definitions and uses the questions instead as simplified self-explanatory annotation prompts; and third, based on the elicited answers it automatically determines nested triggers and their attributes. The fact that our procedure does not require special linguistic background and consists of easy-to-administer questions makes it eligible for large-scale crowdsourcing annotation.

Our corpus comprises 9949 unique tweets, annotated for 12134 tokens that map to 315 unique types of event modality triggers and their attributes of sense, polarity, intensification, tense, holders, and scopes. The reason to work on the genre of tweets is that our corpus is part of a larger project to incorporate linguistic features, such as modality, with network-based features to automatically identify the key players of political discourse on Twitter for countries with fast-changing politics such as Egypt. The fact that our corpus is harvested from the Arabic Egyptian Twitter entails that the corpus is diglossic for Modern Standard Arabic (MSA), the

LAW VIII - The 8th Linguistic Annotation Workshop, pages 139–148,
Dublin, Ireland, August 23-24 2014.

formal Arabic variety, and Egyptian Arabic (EA), the native Arabic dialect of Egypt. We evaluate the annotation results with Krippendorff's alpha (Krippendorff 2011). Results show high inter-annotator reliability rates, indicating that our annotation scheme and procedure are effective. The contribution of this paper, therefore, is twofold: first, we create a novel annotated resource for Arabic NLP that is larger than existing corpora even for languages other than Arabic; and second, we present an efficient and easy-to-administer annotation procedure with interactive crowdsourcing potentials.

The rest of this paper is organized as follows: Section 2 outlines the annotation scheme, guidelines and the interactive procedure; Section 3 gives examples for the final output representations; Section 4 describes corpus harvesting and sampling; Section 5 provides the annotation results and disagreement analysis; and Section 6 compares and contrasts our work with related work.

2 Annotation Scheme: Tasks and Guidelines

Our annotation scheme comprises six tasks to label sense, polarity, intensification, tense, holders, and scopes for each event modality. Prior to the beginning of the interactive procedure, we highlight all event modalities in each tweet using a string-match algorithm and the lexicons from Al-Sabbagh et al. (2013, 2014a). The algorithm finds all potential event modality triggers (i.e. words/phrases that convey event modality) within each tweet in our corpus and marks them as annotation units. A total of 12134 candidate triggers are highlighted in 9949 tweets.

2.1 Task 1: Sense

Sense annotation is to decide for each candidate trigger in context whether it actually conveys event modality given the tweet's context. The same present participle حابب *HAbb* in example 1 is a volition trigger meaning *I want/desire*; whereas in example 2 it is a non-modal present participle meaning *like/prefer/respect*.

1. طبعا أنا مش **حابب** [عمرو موسى يكسب][1]
   *TbEA >nA m$ **HAbb** [Emrw mwsY yksb]*
   Definitely, I do not **want** [Amr Moussa to win].
2. عمرو أديب: رسميا الكتاتني مش **حابب** أبو حامد #egypt #qalyoum
   *Emrw >dyb: rsmyA AlktAtny m$ **HAbb** >bw HAmd #egypt #qalyoum*
   Amr Adeeb: Alkatatny does not officially **like** Abu Hamed #egypt #qalyoum

We define sense annotation as a synonymy judgment task, following Al-Sabbagh et al. (2013, 2014b). Each event modality sense is represented by an exemplar set manually selected so that: (1) each exemplar is an unambiguous event modality trigger; (2) exemplars are in both MSA and EA; (3) exemplars comprise both simple words and multiword expressions; (4) exemplars are both affirmative and negative; and (5) exemplars are of different intensities. Presented with a pre-highlighted candidate trigger in context and the exemplar sets, annotations are to decide whether the candidate trigger is synonymous with any of the exemplar sets. If not, the trigger is then assumed as non-modal.

If an annotator decides that a given candidate trigger is a non-modal, no further questions about polarity, intensification, tense, holders, or scopes are displayed. In order to guarantee that annotators do not select the non-modal option as an easy escape, they are not allowed to move forward without giving at least one synonym of their own to the candidate trigger.

2.2 Task 2: Polarity

Task 2 uses as input the candidates labeled as valid event modality triggers in Task 1 and label each as either affirmative (AFF) or negative (NEG). To decide, annotators are instructed to consider the absence/presence of:

- **Negation particles** such as مش *m$* (not), لا *lA* (not), and غير *gyr* (not), among others.
- **Negation affixes**, especially in EA, like the circumfix *m...$* in مقدرش *mqdr$* (I cannot).

[1] Throughout the examples, modality triggers are marked in boldface, and scopes are in-between brackets.

- **Negative polarity items** like عمري *Emry* (never) and لم يعد *lm yEd* (no longer).
- **Negative auxiliaries** where negation is placed on the past tense auxiliary as in مكنتش عايز *mknt$ EAyz* (I did not want).
- **Inherently-negative triggers** that encode negation in their lexical meanings such as عاجز *EAjz* (incapable) and يمنع *ymnE* (prohibit).
- **Embedding** under negated epistemic modality triggers as in لا أعتقد أنه يجب *lA >Etqd >nh yjb* (I do not think it is necessary) which entails that the speaker is not actually setting an obligation.

Annotators are instructed that using multiple negation markers results in an affirmative sense. Thus, لم يعجز *lm yEjz* (he was not unable to) means that he was actually able to. Annotators are required to give the reason for negation if they decide that a given trigger is negative.

2.3 Task 3: Intensification

Event modality triggers have different lexical intensities (i.e. intensities encoded in the lexical meaning of the word/phrase regardless of the context). In obligation triggers, for instance, even without a context, Arabic speakers know that ضروري *Drwry* (necessary) expresses a higher necessity than المفروض *AlmfrwD* (should). When used in context, the trigger's lexical intensity can be maintained as is, or amplified/mitigated by such linguistic means as:

- **Modification:** adverbs like تماما *tmAmA* (absolutely) amplify lexical intensity; whereas mitigation is invoked by such adverbs as غالبا *gAlbA* (most probably).
- **Categorical negation** typically amplifies lexical intensity as in مش المفروض أبدا *m$ AlmfrwD >bdA* (it should never be).
- **Emphatic expressions** such as قد *qd* (indeed), والله *wAllh* (I swear), and من كل قلبي *mn kl qlby* (wholeheartedly), among others, lead to lexical intensity amplification.
- **Coordination** of two or more triggers typically results in intensity amplification as in لازم وضروري *lAzm wDrwry* (must and necessary).
- **Embedding** under epistemic modality triggers can affect the lexical intensities of event modality triggers. In أعتقد من الضروري أن *>Etqd mn AlDrwry >n* (I think it is necessary to) the strong obligation associated with الضروري *AlDrwry* (necessary) is mitigated by the moderate-intensity epistemic أعتقد *>Etqd* (I think), being embedded under it.

The annotators' task for intensification annotation is to decide for each candidate labeled as a valid event modality trigger in Task 1 whether its lexical intensity is amplified (AMP), mitigated (MTG) or maintained (AS IS). During interactive annotation, annotators are asked to provide the reason for their selection; that is, whether the lexical intensity is affected by modification, coordination, negation, embedding or any other reason whether listed above or not.

2.4 Task 4: Tense

In this version of our event modality corpus, we work on the present and past tenses only. Thus, Task 4 is to decide for each valid event modality trigger from Task 1 whether it is present (PRS) or past (PST). Annotators are required to give their reasons for selecting either PRS or PST.

2.5 Task 5: Holders

Holder annotation identifies the source of the obligation, permission, commitment, ability, or volition. In example 3, the source that sets the obligation that Egyptians have to learn the meaning of democracy is the Twitter user.

3. **لازم** [المصريين يتعلموا يعني إيه ديموقراطية الأول]
   lAzm *[AlmSryyn ytElmwA yEny <yh dymwqrATyp Al>wl]*
   [Egyptians **have** to learn what democracy is first]

The holder is not always the Twitter user, however. In example 4, the Twitter user quotes Kamal Alganzoury - a former Egyptian Prime Minster - stating that he does not want to continue as the Prime Minister. Therefore, the holder of the negated volition trigger ليس لدي رغبة *lys ldy rgbp* (not have a will) is Alganzoury not the Twitter user. This is an example of the nested holder notion first proposed by Wiebe et al. (2005) and Saurí and Pustejovsky (2009).

4. الدكتور كمال الجنزوري: ليس **لدي رغبة في** [الاستمرار] #SCAF #Tahrir #Egypt
   Aldktwr kmAl Aljnzwry: lys ***ldy rgbp fy*** *[AlAstmrAr] #SCAF #Tahrir #Egypt*
   Dr. Kamal Alganzoury: I do not **wish to** [continue] #SCAF #Tahrir #Egypt

Another example of nested holders is example 5. We know that the regime is incapable of maintaining security and protecting the people only because the Twitter user says so. Put differently, the best way to understand this tweet is that according to what the Twitter user holds as a true proposition, the regime is unable to maintain security and protect the people.

5. النظام غير **قادر على** [توفير الأمن أو حماية المواطنين]
   AlnZAm gyr ***qAdr ElY*** *[twfyr Al>mn >w HmAyp AlmwATnyn]*
   The regime is not **able to** [maintain security and protect the people]

We can have two or more nested holders. In example 4, the two holders are Alganzoury who expresses his unwillingness to continue as a Prime Minster and the Twitter user who is quoting Alganzoury. In example 5, the two holders are the regime that is incapable of marinating security and protecting its people and the Twitter user who holds this proposition as true. In example 6, we have three nested holders: the Iranians who are unwilling to confront the outside world, Obama who holds that as a true proposition about Iranians, and the Twitter user who is quoting Obama stating his proposition.

6. اوباما: الشعب الايراني لم يعد **يرغب في** [المواجهة مع العالم الخارجي]
   AwbAmA: Al$Eb AlAyrAny lm yEd ***yrgb fy*** *[AlmwAjhp mE AlEAlm AlxArjy]*
   Obama: the Iranians no longer **want to** [confront the other countries].

During the interactive procedure, annotators are first asked whether the holder is the same as the Twitter user. If not, more questions are displayed to determine (1) who the real holder is; (2) whether the tweet is a(n) (in)direct quote; or it conveys the Twitter user's assumptions.

When the holder is not the Twitter user, annotators are asked to mark the boundaries of the linguistic unit that corresponds to the holder in the tweet's text. Annotators are instructed to use the maximal length principle from Szarvas et al. (2008) so that they mark the largest possible meaningful linguistic unit. Thus, in example 4 the holder is الدكتور كمال الجنزوري *Aldktwr kmAl Aljnzwry* (Dr. Kamal Alganzoury) not only Kamal Alganzoury.

2.6 Task 6: Scopes

Scopes are the events modified by the trigger, syntactically realized as clauses, verb phrases, deverbal nouns or to-infinitives, according to Al-Sabbagh et al. (2013). We use the same maximal length principle from Task 5 so that the marked scope segment corresponds to the largest meaningful linguistic unit that describes the event. Typically, scope segments are delimited by: (1) punctuation markers and (2) subordinate conjunctions.

Annotators are instructed that: (1) a single trigger may have one or more scopes; (2) two or more triggers - especially conjoined by coordinating particles - can share the same scope; and (3) scopes are not necessarily adjacent to their triggers. Examples 7, 8 and 9 illustrate each of these guidelines, repecetively.

7. لو استبعد شفيق **يستطيع** [الطعن] و[العودة لسباق الرئاسة]
   lw AstbEd $fyq ***ystTyE*** *[AlTEn] w[AlEwdp lsbAq Alr}Asp]*
   If Shafiq is excluded, he **can** [appeal] and [run again for presidency].
8. ملايين المصريين اللي بره مصر **لازم** و**حتما** و**ضروري** **ويجب** [يبقى لهم حق التصويت]
   mlAyyn AlmSryyn Ally brh mSr ***lAzm*** *w**HtmA** w**Drwry** **wyjb** [ybqY lhm Hq AltSwyt]*
   It is necessary, **it is a must**, **it is a need** that [Egyptians abroad are given the right to vote].
9. **نفسي** والله بجد قبل ما اموت [اشوف #مصر احسن واحلى بلد فالدنيا]
   nfsy *wAllh bjd qbl mA Amwt [A$wf #mSr AHsn wAHlY bld fAldnyA]*
   I really **wish** before I die to [see #Egypt becoming one of the best countics in the world].

3 Final Output Representation

All elicited answers during annotation are organized into the representations illustrated in the following examples. The representation of example 10 reads as: the Twitter USER strongly did not want Shafiq to win the presidential elections. The trigger اتمنيت *Atmnyt* (wished) is tagged as synonymous with the volition exemplar set; therefore, it denotes a DESIRE. It is then labeled as a past tense (PST), negative (NEG) trigger. Furthermore, its lexical intensity is labeled as amplified (AMP) because of the categorical negation عمري ما *Emry mA* (never ever). Originally, اتمنيت *Atmnyt* (wished) is of moderate lexical intensity, being less intense than اشتهيت *A$thyt* (longed for) but more intense than أردت *>rdt* (wanted). Given the categorical negation, the lexical intensity of اتمنيت *Atmnyt* (wished) goes up the scale from moderate to strong (STRG).

10. عمري **ماتمنيت** ان [شفيق يكسب]. الحمد الله ربنا محرمنيش من حاجة #مرسي
*Emry m**Atmnyt** An [$fyq yksb]. AlHmd Allh rbnA mHrmny$ mn HAjp #mrsy*
I have never ever **wished** [Shafiq to win]. Thank God! #Morsi.
rep. USER, STRG PST NEG DESIRE (*$fyq yksb*)

Example 11 reads as: the Twitter USER reports Hegazy stating that he has the ability to become the Muslim's caliphate. The trigger أصلح *>SlH* (can) is labeled as synonymous with the ability exemplar set. It is also labeled as a present (PRS), affirmative (AFF) trigger whose lexical intensity is maintained (AS IS) in the context. Therefore, its lexical intensity is maintained to its original level which is moderate (MOD).

11. حجازي: أنا **أصلح** أن [أكون خليفةً للمسلمين] وسنكون سادة العالم #Ikhwan
HjAzy: >nA ***>SlH*** *>n [>kwn xlyfp llmslmyn] wsnkwn sAdp AlEAlm #Ikhwan*
Hegazy: I **can** [be the Muslims' caliphate] and we will become the world's masters. #Ikhwan
rep. USER, report, (*HjAzy*, MOD PRS AFF ABLE, (*>kwn xlyfp llmslmyn*))

Example 12 shows a Twitter user who holds as true that the only thing Egypt needed was a wise politician to avoid the bloodshed. The trigger تحتاج *tHtAj* (needs) is labeled as an obligation trigger synonymous with تتطلب *ttTlb* (requires). It is also labeled as past tense (PST) given the preceding past tense auxiliary تكن *tkn* (was). The assigned strong (STRG) lexical intensity label is attributed to the fact that the original moderate intensity of تحتاج *tHtAj* (needs) is amplified by the categorical negation structure لم ... إلا *lm ... <lA* (nothing but).

12. #مصر لم تكن **تحتاج** الا [رجل عاقل يخرج من الازمات بدون اراقة الدماء]
#mSr lm tkn ***tHtAj*** *AlA [rjl EAql yxrj mn AlAzmAt bdwn ArAqp AldmA']*
#Egypt **needed** nothing but [a rational politician who solves crises without bloodshed]
rep. USER, true, (*mSr* , STRG PST AFF REQUIRE (*rjl EAql yxrj mn AlAzmAt bdwn ArAqp AldmA'*))

Example 13 illustrates the representation of three-level nested holders. It reads as: the USER reports Obama's assumption as the latter holds as true that the Iranians do not want to confront other countries.

13. اوباما: الشعب الايراني لم يعد **يرغب في** [المواجهة مع العالم الخارجي]
AwbAmA: Al$Eb AlAyrAny lm yEd ***yrgb fy*** *[AlmwAjhp mE AlEAlm AlxArjy]*
Obama: the Iranians no longer **want to** [confront other countries].
rep. USER, report, (*AwbAmA*, true, (*Al$Eb AlAyrAny*, MOD PRS NEG DESIRE, (*AlmwAjhp mE AlEAlm AlxArjy*)))

Example 14 shows how two conjoined triggers (i.e. لازم *lAzm* (must) and ضروري *Drwry* (necessary)) that share the same holder and scope are merged into one representation, and the conjunction leads to amplifying the intensity of the obligation set by them both.

14. **لازم وضروري** [كلنا نكون قدام مقر المحاكمة ومعانا صورة الرئيس]
lAzm *w**Drwry** [klnA nkwn qdAm mqr AlmHAkmp wmEAnA Swrp Alr}ys]*
We **must** and **it is necessary** that [we go to the court with President's pictures].
rep. USER, STRG PRS AFF REQUIRE, (*klnA nkwn qdAm mqr AlmHAkmp wmEAnA Swrp Alr}ys*)

4 Corpus Harvesting

Tweets are harvested from the Arabic Egyptian Twitter provided that (1) each tweet has at least one trendy political English or Arabic hashtag; and (2) each tweet has at least one candidate event modality trigger from the Arabic modality lexicons (Al-Sabbagh et al. 2013, 2014a). We harvest tweets from a variety of users such as newspapers, TV stations, political and humanitarian campaigns, politicians, celebrities, and ordinary people. Thus, our corpus comprises both MSA, the formal Arabic variety, and EA, the native Arabic dialect of Egypt. The harvested corpus comprises 9949 unique tweets, with 12134 tokens of event modality triggers that map to 315 unique types.

5 Annotation Results

5.1 Evaluation Methodology and Metrics

Our annotation tasks are of two types: (1) Tasks 1-4 are label-based where there is a pre-defined set of labels from which annotators choose; and (2) Tasks 5-6 are segmentation-based where the output of the annotation is a text segment. For the segmentation-based tasks, we use an all-or-nothing method to measure inter-annotator reliability: for segments to be considered as agreement, they must share both the beginning and end boundaries. We use Krippendorff's alpha α (Krippendorff 2011) as our inter-annotator reliability measure, following the most recent work on modality annotation for other languages including English (Rubinstein et al. 2013) and Chinese (Cui and Chi 2013). For more details on Krippendorff's alpha and a, we refer the reader to Artstein and Poesio (2008).

5.2 Results

We use the surveygizmo survey services[2] to implement our interactive annotation procedure given that their survey structure is one that uses conditional branching and skip logic. We distribute the survey on Twitter and we have three annotators participating. According to the short qualifying quiz given at the beginning of the survey, all three participants are native Egyptian Arabic (EA) speakers who have at least two-year experience with Twitter. They are also university graduates who, therefore, master MSA. None of the participants has a linguistics background. Table 1 shows alpha rates for each annotation task.

	Sense	Polarity	Intensification	Tense	Holder	Scope
Obligation	0.890	0.893	0.892	0.978	0.829	0.744
Permission	0.864	0.905	0.821	0.983	0.800	0.739
Commitment	0.760	0.794	0.783	0.947	0.702	0.654
Ability	0.895	0.914	0.905	0.950	0.828	0.763
Volition	0.921	0.921	0.867	0.982	0.858	0.779
Averages	**0.866**	**0.885**	**0.854**	**0.968**	**0.803**	**0.736**

Table 1: Krippendorff's alpha rates for inter-annotator reliability

5.3 Discussion and Disagreement Analysis

Among the factors that lead to high inter-annotator reliability are that: (1) the vast majority of negation is explicitly marked by negation particles that are easy to detect by human annotators; (2) the vast majority of triggers are used without any amplification or mitigation markers; and (3) punctuation markers are surprisingly informative for marking scope boundaries and direct quotations; and hence, holders.

Sense-related disagreement is attributed to: (1) nominal triggers, (2) highly-polysemous triggers, and (3) different interpretations invoked by the −RATIONAL (i.e. non-human) holders.

Typically, event modality triggers are adjunct constituents that add an extra-layer of meaning and can be removed without disturbing the syntactic structure. Yet, in example 15, واجب *wAjb* (a must) and أوجب *>wjb* (a more important must) have main grammatical functions as the predicates of the phrases they modify. Most of the exemplars from Section 2.1 are adjuncts; and, thus, none can substitute واجب *wAjb* (a must) or أوجب *>wjb* (a more important must) in such a context.

15. [التحفظ من اختطاف الثورة] **واجب** لكن [التوحد خلف مشروع] **أوجب**
[AltHfZ mn AxtTAf Alvwrp] ***wAjb*** *lkn [AltwHd xlf m$rwE]* ***>wjb***
[Being cautious about manipulating the revolution] is a **must** but [getting united for one project] is a more important **must**.

Highly-polysemous triggers invoke disagreement because in many cases even the context is ambiguous. In example 16, أقسم *>qsm* (I swear) has two eligible interpretations: an epistemic trigger interpretation *I assure (you) that* and a commitment trigger interpretation *I promise (you)*

[2] http://www.surveygizmo.com/

that. Even the context is not enough to disambiguate the two interpretations and annotators go by the most common sense for the trigger according to their own opinions.

16. عمرو أديب: **أقسم** بالله [لن تسقط #مصر]، احنا شعب 90 مليون ومش إشارة هتسقط بلد
*Emrw >dyb: **>qsm** bAllh [ln tsqT #mSr], AHnA $Eb 90 mlywn wm$ <$Arp htsqT bld*
Amr Adeeb: I **promise/assure** (you) by God that [#Egypt will not collapse]. We are 90 million Egyptians and we will not be defeated by a sign.

Non-human or −RATIONAL holders invoke disagreement, especially for obligation versus volition triggers. The most common sense of such triggers as عايزة *EAyzp* (want) is volition. Yet, when the holder is −RATIONAL like الانتخابات *AlAntxAbAt* (the elections) in example 17, annotators disagree as to whether عايزة *EAyzp* means *want* (i.e. a volition trigger) or *need* (i.e. an obligation trigger).

17. الانتخابات **عايزة** [مرشحين] وحملات الأحزاب تيجي براحتها
*AlAntxAbAt **EAyzp** [mr$Hyn] wHmlAt Al>HzAb tyjy brAHthA*
Elections **want/need** [candidates] and later we can establish the political parties.

Intensity-related disagreement is attributed mostly to progressive verb aspect. Some annotators consider progressive verb aspect as indicated by the EA prefix *b* as a marker for lexical intensity amplification. Thus they tag the volition trigger بتمنى *btmnY* (I wish) in example 18 as amplified, especially it is modified by كل يوم *kl ywm* (everyday).

18. كل يوم **بتمنى** [سقوط حكم #مرسي]
*kl ywm **btmnY** [sqwT Hkm #mrsy]*
Every day, I **wish** for [#Morsi's regime to fall].

Polarity-related disagreement is mainly caused by (1) negated holders and (2) contextual negation. In مفيش حد يقدر *mfy$ Hd yqdr* (no one can), annotators disagree as to whether يقدر *yqdr* (can) should be labeled as affirmative or negative. By contextual negation we mean examples like من الصعب أن نتمنى أن *mn AlSEb >n ntmnY >n* (it is hard to wish to), which entails negation due to the adjective الصعب *AlSEb* (hard).

Holder-related disagreement is attributed mainly to generic nouns and impersonal pronouns like الشعب *Al$Eb* (the people) and الواحد *AlwAHd* (one), respectively. They are interpreted by some annotators as referring implicitly to the Twitter USER. Therefore, the annotators select the USER as the only holder with zero nesting. Other annotators interpret them as referring to people in general not necessarily the Twitter USER and thus they consider these as instances of nested holders.

Scope-related disagreement is attributed to (1) ambiguous subordinate conjunctions, (2) triggers' modifiers, and (3) absent punctuation markers.

Tense yields almost perfect inter-annotator reliability rates. Annotation disagreement does not show any particular pattern. Therefore, we attribute minor disagreement to random errors, resulting from fatigue.

5.4 Majority Statistics

Based on majority annotations, Table 2 gives the statistics for our corpus in terms of sense, polarity, intensification, and tense. As for holder annotations, approximately 60.5% of the triggers have zero-nested holders (i.e. the tweet's writer is the same as the holder).

	Sense		Polarity		Intensification			Tense	
	MD	NMD	AFF	NEG	AMP	MTG	ASIS	PRS	PST
Ability	1729	920	1047	682	348	308	1073	1175	554
Commitment	1048	495	599	449	221	220	607	639	409
Obligation	1786	848	1059	727	369	399	1018	1018	768
Permission	1699	980	1054	645	286	428	985	1053	646
Volition	1622	1007	974	648	341	292	989	1038	584
Totals	**7884**	**4250**	**4733**	**3151**	**1565**	**1647**	**4672**	**4923**	**2961**

Table 2: Token statistics for each annotation task per event modality sense where MD is modal, NMD is non-modal, AFF is affirmative, NEG is negative, AMP is amplified, MTG is mitigated, ASIS is as is, PRS is present, and PST is past

6 Related Work

Event modality is the focus of many annotation projects. Matsuyoshi et al. (2010) annotate a corpus of English and Japanese blog posts for a number of modality senses including volition, wishes, and permission. They annotate sense, tense, polarity, holders as well as other attributes that we have not covered in our scheme such as grammatical mood. They report macro kappa inter-annotator agreement rates of 0.69, 0.70, 0.66 and 0.72 for holders, tense, sense, and polarity, respectively.

Baker et al. (2010, 2012) simultaneously annotate modality and modality-based negation for Urdu-English machine translation systems. Among the modality senses they work on are requirement, permission, success, intention, ability, and desires. They report macro kappa inter-annotator agreement rates of 0.82 for sense annotation and 0.76 for scopes. They, however, do not annotate holders and do not consider nested modalities.

Hendrickx et al. (2012) annotate eleven modality senses in Portuguese, including necessity, capacity, permission, obligation, and volition, among others. They report a macro kappa inter-annotator rate of 0.85 for sense annotation.

Rubinstein et al. (2013) propose a linguistically-motivated annotation scheme for modalities in the MPQA English corpus. They annotate sense, polarity, holders, and scopes, among other annotation units. They work on obligation, ability, and volition among other modality senses. They attain macro alpha inter-annotator reliability rates of 0.89 and 0.65 for sense and scope, respectively.

Cui and Chi (2013) apply the same scheme of Rubinstein et al. (2013) to the Chinese Penn Treebank and get alpha inter-annotator reliability rates of 0.81 and 0.39 for sense and scope annotation, respectively.

Finally, Al-Sabbagh et al. (2013) annotate event modality in MSA and EA tweets. We attain kappa inter-annotator agreement rates of 0.90 and 0.93 for sense and scope annotation, respectively, for only 772 tokens of event modality triggers.

Our annotation results, therefore, are comparable to the results in the literature. Furthermore, our annotation scheme and its tasks are orthogonal to most of the aforementioned schemes. However, the key differences between our work and related work are:

- We use a standardized taxonomy of event modality - Palmer's (2001) - that has been proved valid for a variety of languages, including Arabic, according to Mitchell and Al-Hassan (1994), Brustad (2000), and Moshref (2012).
- We annotate nested holders unlike some of the aforementioned studies (e.g. Baker et al. 2010, 2012) and use a wider range of negation and intensification markers.
- We use crowdsourcing with simplified guidelines implemented interactively to annotate a larger-scale corpus of 12134 tokens for event modality and its attributes.

7 Conclusion and Outlook

We presented a large-scale corpus annotated for event modality in MSA and EA tweets. We use a simplified annotation procedure that defines each annotation task as a series of questions, implemented interactively. Our scheme covers a wide range of the most common annotation units mentioned in the literature, including modality sense, polarity, intensification, tense, holders, and scopes. We deal with nested holders - which are crucial in a highly interactive genre such as tweets where users frequently quote others and make assumptions about them. We also automatically merge triggers with shared holders and scopes based on elicited annotators' answers. The annotation procedure yields reliable results and creates a novel resources for Arabic NLP. The current version of our corpus does not, however, cover a number of issues including: the future tense, grammatical moods other than the declarative, and modality entailment. By modality entailment, we mean, for example, when a tweet's user criticizes the obligation of another quoted person, this entails that the user does not consider such an event as required. For a future version of the corpus, we plan to cover such points. Furthermore, we will use the corpus to train and test a machine learning system for the automatic processing of Arabic event modality.

References

Rania Al-Sabbagh, Jana Diesner and Roxana Girju. 2013. Using the Semantic-Syntactic Interface for Reliable Arabic Modality Annotation. In *Proceedings of IJCNLP'13*, pages 410-418, October 14-18, 2013, Nagoya, Japan.

Rania Al-Sabbagh, Roxana Girju and Jana Diesner. 2014a. Unsupervised Construction of a Lexicon and a Pattern Repository of Arabic Modal Multiword Expressions. In *Proceedings of the 10th Workshop of Multiword Expressions at EACL'14*, April 26-27, 2014, Gothenburg, Sweden.

Rania Al-Sabbagh, Roxana Girju and Jana Diesner. 2014b. *3arif*: A Corpus of Modern Standard and Egyptian Arabic Tweets Annotated for Epistemic Modality Using Interactive Crowdsourcing. In *Proceedings of the 25th International Conference on Computational Linguistics*, August 23-29, 2014, Dublin, Ireland.

Ron Artstein and Massimo Poesio. 2008. Inter-Coder Agreement for Computational Linguistics. *Computational Linguistics*, volume 34, issue 4, pages 555-596.

Kathrin Baker, Michael Bloodgood, Mona Diab, Bonnie Dorr, Nathaniel W. Filardo, Lori Levin and Christine Piatko. 2010. A Modality Lexicon and its Use in Automatic Tagging. In *Proceedings of the 7th International Conference on Language Resources and Evaluation (LREC'10)*, pages 1402-1405, May 19-21, 2010, Valetta, Malta.

Kathryn Baker, Michael Bloodgood, Bonnie J. Dorr, Chris Callison-Burch, Nathaniel W. Filardo, Christine Piatko, Lori Levin and Scott Miller. 2012. Modality and Negation in SIMT. *Computational Linguistics*. volume 38, issue 2, pages 411-438.

Samuel R. Bowman and Harshit Chopra. 2012. Automatic Animacy Classification. In *Proceedings of the NAACL HTL 2012 Student Research Workshop*, pages 7-10, June 3-8, 2012, Montreal, Canada.

Kristen E. Brustad. 2000. *The Syntax of Spoken Arabic: A Comparative Study of Moroccan, Egyptian, Syrian and Kuwaiti Dialects*. Georgetown University Press, Washington DC, USA.

Cohan Sujay Carlos and Madulika Yalamanchi. 2012. Intention Analysis for Sales, Marketing and Customer Service. In *Processing of COLING 2012: Demonstration Papers*, pages 33-40, December 2012, Mumbai, India.

Baptiste Chardon, Farah Benamara, Yannick Mathieu, Vladimir Popescu and Nicholas Asher. 2013. Sentiment Composition Using a Parabolic Model. In *Proceedings of the 10th International Conference on Computational Semantics (IWCS 2013)*, pages 47-58, March 20-22, 2013, Potsdam, Germany.

Yanyan Cui and Ting Chi. 2013. Annotating Modal Expressions in the Chinese Treebank. In *Proceedings of the IWC 2013Workshop on Annotation of Modal Meaning in Natural Language (WAMM)*, pages 24-32, March 2013, Potsdam, Germany.

Iris Hendrickx, Amàlia Mendes and Silvia Mencarelti. 2012. Modality in Text: A Proposal for Corpus Annotation. In *Proceedings of the 8th International Conference on Language Resources and Evaluation (LREC'12)*, pages 1805-1812, May 21-27, 2012, Istanbul, Turkey.

Klaus Krippendorff. 2011. Computing Krippendorff's Alpha-Reliability. Annenberg School of Communication, Departmental Papers: University of Pennsylvania.

Andrew Lampert, Robert Dale and Cecile Paris. 2010. Detecting Emails Containing Requests for Action. In *Proceedings of Human Language Technologies: the 2010 Annual Conference of the North American Chapter of the ACL*, pages 984-992, June 2010, Los Angles, California.

Ying-Shu Liao and Ting-Gen Liao. 2009. Modal Verbs for the Advice Move in Advice Columns. In *Proceedings of the 23rd Pacific Asia Conference on language, Information and Computation*, pages 307-316, December 3-5, 2009, Hong Kong, China.

Suguru Matsuyoshi, Megumi Eguchi, Chitose Sao, Koji Murakami, Kentaro Inui and Yuji Matsumoto. 2010. Annotating Event Mentions in Text with Modality, Focus and Source Information. In *Proceedings of LREC'10*, pages 1456-1463, May 19-21, 2010, Valletta, Malta.

T. F. Mitchell and S. A. Al-Hassan. 1994. *Modality, Mood and Aspect in Spoken Arabic with Special Reference to Egypt and the Levant*. London and NY: Kegan Paul International.

Ola Moshref. 2012. *Corpus Study of Tense, Aspect, and Modality in Diglossic Speech in Cairene Arabic*. PhD Thesis. University of Illinois at Urbana-Champaign.

Frank R. Palmer. 2001. *Mood and Modality*. 2nd Edition. Cambridge University Press, Cambridge, UK.

J. Ramanand, Krishna Bhavsar and Niranjan Pedanekar. 2010. Wishful Thinking: Finding Suggestions and "Buy" Wishes for Product Reviews. In *Proceedings of the NAACL HLT 2010 Workshop on Computational Approaches to the Analysis and Generation of Emotion in Text*, pages 54-61, June 2010, Los Angeles, California.

Aynat Rubinstein, Hillary Harner, Elizabeth Krawczyk, Daniel Simoson, Graham Katz and Paul Portner. 2013. Toward Fine-Grained Annotation of Modality in Text. In *Proceedings of the IWC 2013Workshop on Annotation of Modal Meaning in Natural Language (WAMM)*, pages 38-46, March 2013, Potsdam, Germany.

Roser Saurí and James Pustejovsky. 2009. FactBank: A Corpus Annotated with Event Factuality. *Language Resources and Evaluation*, 43:227-268

György Szarvas, Veronika Vincze, Richárd Farkas and János Csirik. 2008. The BioScope Corpus: Annotation for Negation, Uncertainty and their Scope in Biomedical Texts. In *Proceedings of BioNLP 2008: Current Trends in Biomedical Natural Language Processing*, pages 38-45, June 2008, Columbus, Ohio, USA.

Janyce Wiebe, Theresa Wilson and Claire Cardie. 2005. Annotating Expressions of Opinions and Emotions in Language. *Language Resources and Evaluation*, volume 39, issue 203, pages 1663-210.

Situation entity annotation

Annemarie Friedrich **Alexis Palmer**
Department of Computational Linguistics
Saarland University, Saarbrücken, Germany
{afried,apalmer}@coli.uni-saarland.de

Abstract

This paper presents an annotation scheme for a new semantic annotation task with relevance for analysis and computation at both the clause level and the discourse level. More specifically, we label the finite clauses of texts with the type of *situation entity* (e.g., eventualities, statements about kinds, or statements of belief) they introduce to the discourse, following and extending work by Smith (2003). We take a feature-driven approach to annotation, with the result that each clause is also annotated with fundamental aspectual class, whether the main NP referent is specific or generic, and whether the situation evoked is episodic or habitual. This annotation is performed (so far) on three sections of the MASC corpus, with each clause labeled by at least two annotators. In this paper we present the annotation scheme, statistics of the corpus in its current version, and analyses of both inter-annotator agreement and intra-annotator consistency.

1 Introduction

Linguistic expressions form patterns in discourse. Passages of text can be analyzed in terms of the individuals, concepts, times and *situations* that they introduce to the discourse. In this paper we introduce a new semantic annotation task which focuses on the latter and in particular their aspectual nature. Situations are expressed at the clause level; **situation entity (SE)** annotation is the task of associating individual clauses of text with the type of SE introduced to the discourse by the clause. Following Smith (2003), we distinguish the following *SE types* (see Sec. 3.1): EVENTS, STATES, GENERALIZING SENTENCES, GENERIC SENTENCES, FACTS, PROPOSITIONS, QUESTIONS and IMPERATIVES. Although these categories are clearly distinct from one another on theoretical grounds, in practice it can be difficult to cleanly draw boundaries between them. We improve annotation consistency by defining the SE types in terms of features whose values are easier for annotators to identify, and which provide guidance for distinguishing the more complex SE types.

As with most complex annotation tasks, multiple interpretations are often possible, and we cannot expect agreement on all instances. The feature-driven approach (see Sec. 3.2) is a valuable source of information for investigating annotator disagreements, as the features indicate precisely how annotators differ in their interpretation of the situation. Analysis of intra-annotator consistency shows that personal preferences of annotators play a role, and we conclude that disagreements often highlight cases where multiple interpretations are possible. We further argue that such cases should be handled carefully in supervised learning approaches targeting methods to automatically classify situation entity types.

As the first phase of the SE annotation project, we are in the process of annotating the written portion of MASC (Ide et al., 2010), the manually-annotated subcorpus of the Open American National Corpus. MASC provides texts from 20 different genres and has already been annotated with various linguistic and semantic phenomena.[1] MASC offers several benefits: it includes text from a wide variety of genres, it facilitates study of interactions between various levels of analysis, and the data is freely available with straightforward mechanisms for distribution. In this paper we report results for three of the MASC

[1] http://www.americannationalcorpus.org/MASC/Full_MASC.html

LAW VIII - The 8th Linguistic Annotation Workshop, pages 149–158,
Dublin, Ireland, August 23-24 2014.

genres: news, letters, and jokes. Once a larger portion of MASC has been labeled with SEs and their associated features, we will add our annotations to those currently available for MASC. We mark the SE types of clauses with the aim of providing a large corpus of annotated text for the following purposes:

(1) To assess the applicability of SE type classification as described by Smith (2003): to what extent can situations be classified easily, which borderline cases occur, and how do humans perform on this task? (see Sec. 4)

(2) Training, development and evaluation of automatic systems classifying situation entities, as well as sub-tasks which have (partially) been studied by the NLP community, but for which no large annotated corpora are available (for example, automatically predicting the fundamental aspectual class of verbs in context (Friedrich and Palmer, 2014) or the genericity of clauses and noun phrases).

(3) To provide a foundation for analysis of the theory of Discourse Modes (Smith, 2003), which we explain next (Sec. 2).

2 Background and related work

Within a text, one recognizes stretches that are intuitively of different types and can be clustered by their characteristic linguistic features and interpretations. Smith (2003) posits five *discourse modes*: Narrative, Report, Description, Informative and Argument/Commentary. Texts of almost all genre categories have passages of different modes. The discourse modes are characterized by (a) the type of situations (also called *situation entities*) introduced in a text passage, and (b) the principle of text progression in the mode (temporal or atemporal, and different manners of both temporal and atemporal progression). This annotation project directly addresses the first of these characteristics, the *situation entity types (SE types)*.

Some previous work has addressed the task of classifying SE types at the clause level. Palmer et al. (2004) enrich LFG parses with lexical information from both a database of lexical conceptual structures (Dorr, 2001) and hand-collected groups of predicates associated with particular SE types. The enriched parses are then fed to an ordered set of transfer rules which encode linguistic features indicative of SE types. The system is evaluated on roughly 200 manually-labeled clauses. Palmer et al. (2007) investigate various types of linguistic features in a maximum entropy model for SE type classification. The best results are still below 50% accuracy (with a most-frequent-class baseline of 38%), and incorporating features from neighboring clauses is shown to increase performance. Palmer et al. (2007) annotate data from one section of the Brown corpus and a small amount of newswire text, with two annotators and no clear set annotation guidelines. In addition, work by Cocco (2012) classifies clauses of French text according to a six-way scheme that falls somewhere between the SE level and the level of discourse modes. The types are: narrative, argumentative, descriptive, explicative, dialogal, and injunctive.

Other related works address tasks related to the features we annotate. One strand of work is in automatic classification of aspectual class (Siegel and McKeown, 2000; Siegel, 1999; Siegel, 1998; Klavans and Chodorow, 1992; Friedrich and Palmer, 2014) and its determination as part of temporal classification (UzZaman et al., 2013; Bethard, 2013; Costa and Branco, 2012). A second aims to distinguish generic vs. specific clauses (Louis and Nenkova, 2011) or to identify generic noun phrases (Reiter and Frank, 2010). The latter work leverages data with noun phrases annotated as either generic and specific from the ACE-2 corpus (Mitchell et al., 2003); their definitions of these two types match ours (see Sec. 3.2.1).

3 Annotation Scheme and Process

In this section, we first present the inventory of SE types (Sec. 3.1). We then describe our feature-driven approach to annotation (Sec. 3.2) and define the SE types with respect to three situation-related features: main referent type, fundamental aspectual class, and habituality. Some situation entity types are easier to recognize than others. While some can be identified on the basis of surface structure and clear linguistic indicators, others depend on internal temporal (and other) properties of the verb and its arguments. Annotators take the following approach: first, easily-identifiable *SE types* (Speech Acts and Abstract Entities) are marked. If the clause's SE type is not one of these, values for the three features are determined, and the final determination of SE type is based on the features.

3.1 Situation entity types

Following Smith (2003), we distinguish the following *SE types*:

Eventualities. These types describe particular situations such as STATES (1a) or EVENTS (2). The type REPORT, a subtype of EVENT, is used for situations introduced by verbs of speech (1b).

*(1) (a) "Carl is a tenacious fellow", (*STATE*)*
*(b) said a source close to USAir. (*EVENT – REPORT*)*

*(2) The lobster won the quadrille. (*EVENT*)*

General Statives. This class includes GENERALIZING SENTENCES (3), which report regularities related to specific main referents, and GENERIC SENTENCES (4), which make statements about kinds.

*(3) Mary often feeds my cats. (*GENERALIZING*)*

*(4) The lion has a bushy tail. (*GENERIC*)*

Abstract Entities are the third class of SE types, and comprise FACTS (5) and PROPOSITIONS (6). These situations differ from the other types in how they relate to the world: Eventualities and General Statives are located spatially and temporally in the world, but Abstract Entities are not. FACTS are objects of knowledge and PROPOSITIONS are objects of belief from the respective speaker's point of view.

*(5) I know that Mary refused the offer. (*FACT*)*

*(6) I believe that Mary refused the offer. (*PROPOSITION*)*

We limit the annotation of Abstract Entities to the clausal complements of certain licensing predicates, as well as clauses modified by a certain class of adverbs, as it is not always possible to identify sentences directly expressing Facts or Propositions on linguistic grounds (Smith, 2003). In (6), *believe* is the licensing predicate, and *Mary refused the offer* is a situation that is introduced as not being *in* the world, but *about* the world (Smith, 2003). Annotators are asked to additionally label the embedded SE type when possible. For example, *that Mary refused the offer* in (5) and (6) would be labeled as EVENT.

Speech Acts. This class comprises QUESTIONS and IMPERATIVE clauses (Searle, 1969).

Derived SE types. In some cases, the SE type of a clause changes based on the addition of some linguistic indication of uncertainty about the status of the situation described. We refer to these as derived SE types. More specifically, clauses that would otherwise be marked as EVENT may be coerced to the type STATE due to negation, modality, future tense, conditionality, and sometimes subjectivity: e.g. *John did not win the lottery*, a negated event, introduces a STATE to the discourse.

3.2 Features for distinguishing situation entity types

In this section, we describe three features that allow for the clear expression of differences between SE types. Fleshing out the descriptions of SE types with these underlying features is useful to convey the annotation scheme to new annotators, to get partial information when an annotator has trouble making a decision on SE type, and to analyze disagreements between annotators.

3.2.1 Main referent type: specific or generic

This feature indicates the type of the most central entity mentioned in the clause as a noun phrase. We refer to this entity as the clause's *main referent*. This referent can be found by asking the question: *What is this clause about?* Usually, but not always, the main referent of a clause is realized as its grammatical subject. We appeal to the annotator's intuitions in order to determine the main referent of a clause. In case the main referent does not coincide with the grammatical subject as in example (7), this is to be indicated during annotation.

*(7) There are two books on the table. (**specific** main referent, *STATE*)*

Some SE types (STATES, GENERALIZING SENTENCES and GENERIC SENTENCES, for details see Table 1) are distinguished by whether they make a statement about some *specific* main referent or about a *generic* main referent. Specific main referents are particular entities (8), particular groups of entities (9), organizations (10), particular situations (11) or particular instantiations of a concept (12).

*(8) Mary likes popcorn. (particular entity → **specific**,* STATE*)*

*(9) The students met at the cafeteria. (a particular group → **specific**,* STATE*)*

*(10) IBM was a very popular company in the 80s. (organization → **specific**,* STATE*)*

*(11) That she didn't answer her phone really upset me. (particular situation → **specific**,* EVENT*)*

*(12) Today's weather was really nice. (particular instantiation of a concept → **specific**,* STATE*)*

The majority of generic main referents are noun phrases referring to a *kind* rather than to a particular entity, and generic mentions of concepts or notions (14). Definite NPs and bare plural NPs (13) are the main kind-referring NP types (Smith, 2003).

*(13) The lion has a bushy tail. / Dinosaurs are extinct. (**generic**,* GENERIC SENTENCE*)*

*(14) Security is an important issue in US electoral campaigns. (**generic**,* GENERIC SENTENCE*)*

While some NPs clearly make reference to a well-established kind, other cases are not so clear cut, as humans tend to make up a context in which an NP describes some kind (Krifka et al., 1995). Sentence (15) gives an example for such a case: while *lions in captivity* are not a generally well-established kind, this term describes a class of entities rather than a specific group of lions in this context.

*(15) Lions in captivity have trouble producing offspring. (**generic**,* GENERIC SENTENCE*)*

Gerunds may occur as the subject in English sentences. When they describe a *specific* process as in (16a), we mark them as specific. If they instead describe a *kind* of process as in (16b), we mark them as generic.

*(16) (a) Knitting this scarf took me 3 days. (**specific**,* EVENT*)*
*(b) Knitting a scarf is generally fun. (**generic**,* GENERIC SENTENCE*)*

We also give annotators the option to explicitly mark the main referent as *expletive*, as in (17).

*(17) It seemed like (**expletive** = no main referent,* STATE*)*
*he would win. (**specific**,* STATE*)*

3.2.2 Fundamental aspectual class: stative or dynamic

Following Siegel and McKeown (2000), we determine the *fundamental aspectual class* of a clause. This notion is the extension of *lexical aspect* or *aktionsart*, which describe the "real life shape" of situations denoted by verbs, to the level of clauses. More specifically, aspectual class is a feature of the main verb and a select group of modifiers, which may differ per verb. The stative/dynamic distinction is the most fundamental distinction in taxonomies of aspectual class (Vendler, 1967; Bach, 1986; Mourelatos, 1978).

We allow three labels for this feature: **dynamic** for cases where the verb and its arguments describe some event (something happens), **stative** for cases where they introduce some properties of the main referent to the discourse, or **both** for cases where annotators see both interpretations.

It is important to note that the fundamental aspectual class of a verb can be different from the type of situation entity introduced by the clause as a whole. The basic situation type of *building a house* is **dynamic**, and in the examples below we see this fundamental aspectual class appearing in clauses with different situation entity types. Example (18) describes an EVENT. Clause (19), on the other hand, is a GENERALIZING SENTENCE, as it describes a pattern of events; this is a situation with a *derived* type. The same is true for example (20), which is a STATE because of its future tense.

*(18) John built a house. (*EVENT*, **dynamic** fundamental aspectual class)*

*(19) John builds houses. (*GENERALIZING SENTENCE*, **dynamic** fundamental aspectual class)*

*(20) John is going to build a house. (*STATE*, **dynamic** fundamental aspectual class)*

3.2.3 Habituality

Another dimension along which situations can be distinguished is whether they describe a **static** state, a one-time (**episodic**) event (21) or some regularity of an event (22) or a state (23), which is labeled **habitual**. The term *habitual* as used in this annotation project covers more than what is usually considered a matter of habit, extending to any clauses describing regularities (24). The discussion related to this linguistic feature in this section follows Carlson (2005). If one can add a frequency adverbial such as *typically/usually* to the clause and the meaning of the resulting sentence differs at most slightly from the meaning of the original sentence, or the sentence contains a frequency adverbial such as *never*, the sentence expresses a regularity, i.e., is habitual. Another property of habituals is that they are generalizations and hence have the property of tolerating exceptions. If we learn that Mary eats oatmeal for breakfast, it does not necessarily need to be true that she eats oatmeal at every breakfast. It is important to note that unlike fundamental aspectual class, *habituality* is an attribute of the <u>entire</u> situation.

*(21) Mary ate oatmeal for breakfast this morning. (**episodic**, EVENT)*

*(22) Mary eats oatmeal for breakfast. (**habitual**, GENERALIZING SENTENCE)*

*(23) I often feel as if I only get half the story. (**habitual**, **stative** fundamental aspectual class, GENERALIZING SENTENCE)*

*(24) Glass breaks easily. (**habitual**, GENERIC SENTENCE)*

3.3 SE types and their features

The feature-driven approach to annotation taken here is defined such that, ideally, each unique combination of values for the three features leads to one SE type. Table 1 shows the assignment of SE types to various combinations of feature values. This table covers all SE types except ABSTRACT ENTITIES and SPEECH ACTS, which are more easily identifiable based on lexical and/or syntactic grounds. Annotators are also provided with information about linguistic tests for some SE types and feature values, both for making feature value determinations and to support selection of clause-level SE type labels.

SE type	main referent	aspectual class	habituality
EVENT	specific	eventive	episodic
	generic		
STATE	specific	stative	static
GENERIC SENTENCE	generic	eventive	habitual
		stative	static, habitual
GENERALIZING SENTENCE	specific	eventive	habitual
		stative	
General Stative	specific	eventive	habitual
	generic		

Table 1: Situation entity types and their features.

4 Annotator agreement and consistency

This section presents analyses of inter-annotator agreement and intra-annotator consistency, looking at agreement for individual feature values as well as clause-level SE type.

4.1 Data and annotators

The current version of our corpus consists of three sections (news, letters and jokes) of MASC corpus (Ide et al., 2010). We hired three annotators, all either native or highly-skilled speakers of English, and had a training phase of 3 weeks using several Wikipedia documents. Afterwards, annotation of the texts began and annotators had no further communication with each other. Two annotators (A and B) each marked the complete data set, and one additional annotator (C) marked the news section only.

ANNOTATORS	NUMBER OF SEGMENTS	MAIN REFERENT	ASPECTUAL CLASS	HABITUALITY	SE TYPE	SE TYPE (REP=EVT)
A:B	2563	0.35	0.81	0.77	0.56	0.66
A:C	2524	0.29	0.77	0.76	0.55	0.65
B:C	2556	0.45	0.73	0.76	0.76	0.74
average	2545	0.36	0.77	0.76	0.62	0.68

Table 2: **Cohen's** κ, for pairs of annotators on the MASC `news` section.

GENRE	NUMBER OF SEGMENTS	MAIN REFERENT	ASPECTUAL CLASS	HABITUALITY	SE TYPE	SE TYPE (REP=EVT)
jokes	3455	0.57	0.85	0.81	0.74	0.73
news	2563	0.35	0.81	0.77	0.56	0.66
letters	1851	0.41	0.71	0.65	0.56	0.56
all	7869	0.47	0.80	0.77	0.64	0.68

Table 3: **Cohen's** κ, for two annotators on three different sections of MASC.

4.2 Segmentation into clauses

We segment the texts into finite clauses using the SPADE discourse parser (Soricut and Marcu, 2003), applying some heuristic post-processing and allowing annotators to mark segments that do not contain a situation (for instance, headlines or by-lines) or that should be merged with another segment in order to describe a complete situation. We filter out all segments marked by any annotator as having a *segmentation problem.* Of the 2823 segments automatically created for the news section, 4% were marked as containing no situation by at least one of the three annotators, and 7% were merged to a different segment by at least one annotator. All three annotators agree on the remaining 2515 segments (89%). Of the 9428 automatically-created segments in the full data set, 11.5% were marked as no-situation by at least one of two annotators, and a further 5% were merged to other segments by at least one annotator. 7869 segments remain for studying agreement between two annotators on the full data set.

The three genres vary as to the average segment length. Segments in the letters texts have the longest average length (11.1 tokens), segments in jokes are the shortest (6.9 tokens on average), and segments in news fall in the middle with an average length of 9.9 tokens.

4.3 Inter-annotator agreement

As we allow annotators to mark a segment as Speech Acts or Abstract Entities and in addition mark the SE type of the embedded situation with a non-surface type, we compute agreement for Eventualities and General Statives in the following, and present the results for Speech Acts and Abstract Entities separately.

news section, 3 annotators. We compute Cohen's unweighted κ between all three pairs of annotators for the news section, as shown in Table 2. We compute agreement for the segments where both respective annotators agree on the segmention, i.e., that the segment describes a situation. For aspectual class, we compute agreement over the three labels *stative*, *dynamic* and *both*; for main referents, we compute agreement over the three labels *specific*, *dynamic* and *expletive*; for habituality, we compute agreement over the three labels *episodic*, *habitual* and *static*. In each case, we omit segments for which one of the annotators did not give a label, which in each case are fewer than 26 segments.

We observe good agreement for the features aspectual class and habituality, and for SE type between annotators B and C. Pairs involving annotator A reach lower agreement; we identify two causes. Annotator A marks many segments marked as REPORT by the others as the corresponding supertype EVENT. This shows up in Table 2 as higher values of κ when considering REPORT to match its supertype EVENT. The second cause is A's different preference for marking main referents, causing lower κ scores for agreement on the main referent type and also influencing agreement for situation entity types. In more than 92% of the 183 clauses on which annotators B and C agree with each other, but disagree with A, B and C assigned the value specific while A marked the main referent as generic. Early in the annotation project, a revision was made to the scheme for labeling main referents – one hypothesis is that A might not have updated her way of labeling these. We estimate that roughly 40% of these cases were due to

A's misunderstanding of feature value definitions, but around 30% of these cases do allow for both interpretations. In the following sentence, the main referent of the second segment could either refer to the specific set of all kids in New York, or to the class of children in New York: *As governor, I'll make sure // that every kid in New York has the same opportunity.* Another frequent case is the main referent *you*, which can be interpreted in a generic way or as specifically addressing the reader (e.g. of a letter). Such disagreements at the level of feature annotations allow us to detect cases where several interpretations are possible. Having annotators with different preferences on difficult cases can actually be a valuable source of information for identifying such cases.

The distribution of labels for main referents is highly skewed towards specific main referents for the `news` section; when comparing B and C, they agree on 2358 segments to have a specific main referent. However, only 122 segments are labeled as having a generic main referent by at least one annotator, and they agree only on 43 of them. A further 49 are labeled generic by B but specific by C and a further 30 vice versa. In order to collect more reliable data and agreement numbers for the task of labeling main referent types, we plan to conduct a focused study with a carefully-balanced data set.

news, jokes, letters: 2 annotators. We report agreement for three sections, corresponding to three genres, for two annotators (A and B) in Table 3. We observe higher agreement for jokes than for news, and higher agreement for news than for letters. Figure 1 shows the distribution of situation entity types per genre. The numbers express averages of percentages of label types assigned to the clauses of one genre by the two annotators. The letters genre is different in that it has more STATES, far fewer EVENTS, which are usually easy to detect, and more General Statives. Most cases of confusion between annotators occur between General Statives and STATES, so the more EVENTS texts have, the higher the agreement.

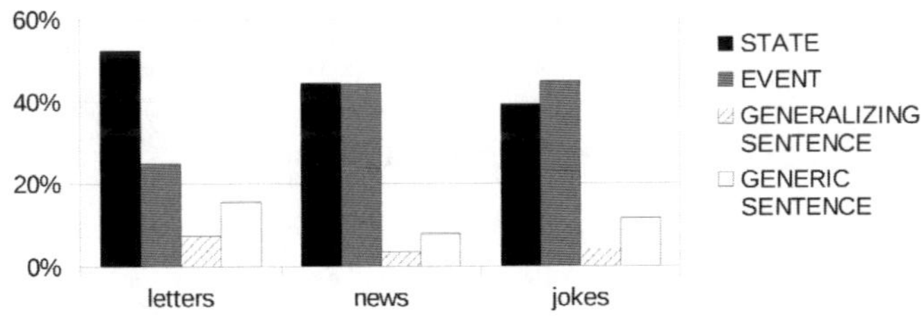

Figure 1: Distribution of situation entity types in three different genres.

Speech Acts and Abstract Entities. Figure 2 shows the percentage of segments of each genre that were marked as a Speech Act or an Abstract Entity by at least one annotator. QUESTIONS are most frequent in the jokes genre, but about half of them are just marked by one annotator, which has to do with how consistently indirect questions are marked. The two annotators agree on almost all segments labeled as imperatives; while there are only very few IMPERATIVES in the news section, there are more in the jokes and letters sections. The letters are mainly fund-raising letters, which explains the high percentage of IMPERATIVES (*Please help Goodwill. // Use the enclosed card // and give a generous gift today.*). FACTS and PROPOSITIONS, on the other hand, are rather infrequent in any genre, and annotators tend to mark them inconsistently. We take from this analysis that we need to offer some help to the annotators in detecting Abstract Entities. We plan to compile a list of verbs that may introduce Abstract Entities and specifically highlight potential licensing constructions in order to increase recall for these types.

4.4 Intra-annotator consistency

After the first round of annotation, we identified 11 documents with low inter-annotator agreement on SE type (5 news, 5 letters, 1 jokes) and presented them to two annotators for re-annotation. For each annotator, the elapsed time between the first and second rounds was at least 3 weeks. We observe that in general, the agreement of each annotator with herself is greater than agreement with the other annotator. This shows that the disagreements are not pure random noise, but that annotators have different preferences for certain difficult decisions. It is interesting to note that annotator B apparently changed how

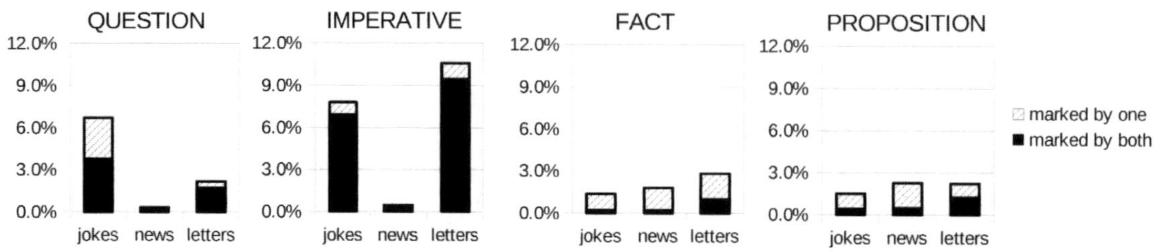

Figure 2: Percentage of segments marked as Speech Act or Abstract Entity by at least one annotator.

GENRE	NUMBER OF SEGMENTS	MAIN REFERENT	ASPECTUAL CLASS	HABITUALITY	SE TYPE	SE TYPE (REP=EVT)
A1:B1	636	0.15	0.79	0.64	0.40	0.45
A2:B2	599	0.12	0.78	0.70	0.42	0.48
A1:A2	596	0.79	0.88	0.78	0.75	0.75
B1:B2	620	0.55	0.84	0.78	0.75	0.75

Table 4: Consistency study: **Cohen's** κ, for two annotators, comparing against each other and against themselves (re-annotated data). A1 = annotator A in first pass, B2 = annotator B in second pass etc.

she annotates main referents; possibly this is also due to the above mentioned revision to the annotation scheme. On the other hand, B annotated very few segments as generic (only 61 segments were marked as having a generic main referent in either the first or second pass, 27 of them in both passes), which may also have led to the low κ value. The fact that annotators *do* disagree with themselves indicates that there are noisy cases in our data set, where multiple interpretations are possible. However, we want to point out that the level of noise estimated by this intra-annotator consistency study is an upper bound as we chose the most difficult documents for re-annotation; the overall level of noise in the data set can be assumed to be much lower.

5 Conclusion

We have presented an annotation scheme for labeling clauses with their situation entity type along with features indicating the type of main referent, fundamental aspectual class and habituality. The feature-driven approach allows for a detailed analysis of annotator disagreements, showing in which way the annotators' understandings of a clause differ. The analysis in the previous chapter showed that while good inter-annotator agreement can be reached for most decisions required by our annotation schema, there remain hard cases, on which annotators disagree with each other or with their own first round of annotations. We do not yet observe satisfying agreement for main referent types or for identifying abstract entities. In both cases, data sparseness is a problem; there are only very few generic main referents and abstract entities in our current corpus. We plan to conduct case studies on data that is specifically selected for these phenomena.

However, in many of the hard cases, several readings are possible. Rather than using an adjudicated data set for training and evaluation of supervised classifiers for labeling clauses with situation entities, we plan to leverage such disagreements for training, following proposals by Beigman Klebanov and Beigman (2009) and Plank et al. (2014).

The annotation reported here is ongoing; our next goal is to extend annotation to additional genres within MASC, starting with essays, journal, fiction, and travel guides. Following SE annotation, we will extend the project to annotation of discourse modes. Finally, we are very interested in exploring and annotating SEs in other languages, as we expect a similar inventory but different linguistic realizations.

Acknowledgments We thank the anonymous reviewers, Bonnie Webber and Andreas Peldszus for helpful comments, and our annotators Ambika Kirkland, Ruth Kühn and Fernando Ardente. This research was supported in part by the MMCI Cluster of Excellence, and the first author is supported by an IBM PhD Fellowship.

References

Emmon Bach. 1986. The algebra of events. *Linguistics and philosophy*, 9(1):5–16.

Beata Beigman Klebanov and Eyal Beigman. 2009. From annotator agreement to noise models. *Computational Linguistics*, 35(4):495–503.

Steven Bethard. 2013. ClearTK-TimeML: A minimalist approach to TempEval 2013. In *Second Joint Conference on Lexical and Computational Semantics (* SEM)*, volume 2, pages 10–14.

Greg Carlson. 2005. Generics, habituals and iteratives. *The Encyclopedia of Language and Linguistics*.

Christelle Cocco. 2012. Discourse type clustering using pos n-gram profiles and high-dimensional embeddings. In *Proceedings of the Student Research Workshop at the 13th Conference of the European Chapter of the Association for Computational Linguistics*, EACL 2012.

Francisco Costa and António Branco. 2012. Aspectual type and temporal relation classification. In *Proceedings of the 13th Conference of the European Chapter of the Association for Computational Linguistics (EACL)*, pages 266–275.

Bonnie J. Dorr. 2001. LCS verb database. Online software database of Lexical Conceptual Structures, University of Maryland, College Park, MD.

Annemarie Friedrich and Alexis Palmer. 2014. Automatic prediction of aspectual class of verbs in context. In *Proceedings of the 52nd Annual Meeting of the Association for Computational Linguistics (ACL). Baltimore, USA*.

Nancy Ide, Christiane Fellbaum, Collin Baker, and Rebecca Passonneau. 2010. The manually annotated sub-corpus: A community resource for and by the people. In *Proceedings of the ACL 2010 conference short papers*, pages 68–73.

Judith L. Klavans and Martin S. Chodorow. 1992. Degrees of stativity: The lexical representation of verb aspect. In *Proceedings of the 14th COLING*, Nantes, France.

Manfred Krifka, Francis Jeffry Pelletier, Gregory Carlson, Alice ter Meulen, Gennaro Chierchia, and Godehard Link. 1995. Genericity: an introduction. *The Generic Book*, pages 1–124.

Annie Louis and Ani Nenkova. 2011. Automatic identification of general and specific sentences by leveraging discourse annotations. In *Proceedings of IJCNLP 2011*.

Alexis Mitchell, Stephanie Strassel, Mark Przybocki, JK Davis, George Doddington, Ralph Grishman, Adam Meyers, Ada Brunstein, Lisa Ferro, and Beth Sundheim. 2003. ACE-2 Version 1.0. *Linguistic Data Consortium, Philadelphia*.

Alexander PD Mourelatos. 1978. Events, processes, and states. *Linguistics and philosophy*, 2(3):415–434.

Alexis Palmer, Jonas Kuhn, and Carlota Smith. 2004. Utilization of multiple language resources for robust grammar-based tense and aspect classification. In *Proceedings of LREC 2004*.

Alexis Palmer, Elias Ponvert, Jason Baldridge, and Carlota Smith. 2007. A sequencing model for situation entity classification. *Proceedings of ACL 2007*.

Barbara Plank, Dirk Hovy, and Anders Søgaard. 2014. Learning part-of-speech taggers with inter-annotator agreement loss. In *Proceedings of EACL 2014*.

Nils Reiter and Anette Frank. 2010. Identifying generic noun phrases. In *Proceedings of the 48th Annual Meeting of the Association for Computational Linguistics (ACL)*.

John Searle. 1969. *Speech Acts*. Cambridge University Press.

Eric V Siegel and Kathleen R McKeown. 2000. Learning methods to combine linguistic indicators: Improving aspectual classification and revealing linguistic insights. *Computational Linguistics*, 26(4):595–628.

Eric V. Siegel. 1998. Disambiguating verbs with the WordNet category of the direct object. In *Proceedings of Workshop on Usage of WordNet in Natural Language Processing Systems*, Universite de Montreal.

Eric V. Siegel. 1999. Corpus-based linguistic indicators for aspectual classification. In *Proceedings of ACL37*, University of Maryland, College Park.

Carlota S Smith. 2003. *Modes of discourse: The local structure of texts*. Cambridge University Press.

Radu Soricut and Daniel Marcu. 2003. Sentence level discourse parsing using syntactic and lexical information. In *Proceedings of the 2003 Conference of the North American Chapter of the Association for Computational Linguistics on Human Language Technology-Volume 1*, pages 149–156. Association for Computational Linguistics.

Naushad UzZaman, Hector Llorens, Leon Derczynski, Marc Verhagen, James Allen, and James Pustejovsky. 2013. Semeval-2013 task 1: Tempeval-3: Evaluating time expressions, events, and temporal relations. In *Second joint conference on lexical and computational semantics (* SEM)*, volume 2, pages 1–9.

Zeno Vendler, 1967. *Linguistics in Philosophy*, chapter Verbs and Times, pages 97–121. Cornell University Press, Ithaca, New York.

Focus Annotation in Reading Comprehension Data

Ramon Ziai **Detmar Meurers**
Sonderforschungsbereich 833
Eberhard Karls Universität Tübingen
{rziai,dm}@sfs.uni-tuebingen.de

Abstract

When characterizing the information structure of sentences, the so-called *focus* identifies the part of a sentence addressing the current question under discussion in the discourse. While this notion is precisely defined in formal semantics and potentially very useful in theoretical and practical terms, it has turned out to be difficult to reliably annotate focus in corpus data.

We present a new focus annotation effort designed to overcome this problem. On the one hand, it is based on a task-based corpus providing more explicit context. The annotation study is based on the CREG corpus (Ott et al., 2012), which consists of answers to explicitly given reading comprehension questions. On the other hand, we operationalize focus annotation as an incremental process including several substeps which provide guidance, such as explicit answer typing.

We evaluate the focus annotation both intrinsically by calculating agreement between annotators and extrinsically by showing that the focus information substantially improves the automatic meaning assessment of answers in the CoMiC system (Meurers et al., 2011).

1 Introduction

This paper discusses the interplay of linguistic and computational linguistic aspects in the analysis of focus as a core notion of information structure. Empirically, our work focuses on analyzing the responses to reading comprehension questions. In computational linguistics, automatic meaning assessment determining whether a response appropriately answers a given question about a given text has developed into an active field of research. Short Answer Assessment recently was also highlighted by the *Joint Student Response Analysis and Textual Entailment Challenge* (Dzikovska et al., 2013). Some research in this domain has pointed out the relevance of identifying which parts of a response are given by the question (Bailey and Meurers, 2008; Mohler et al., 2011), with recent work pointing out that the relevant notion here is that of *focus* as discussed in formal pragmatics (Meurers et al., 2011; Hahn and Meurers, 2012).

Figure 1 provides an example of answer comparison for meaning assessment, where the focus (marked by square brackets) can effectively be used to zoom in on the information that is relevant for comparing a target answer (TA) with a student answer (SA) given a question (Q).

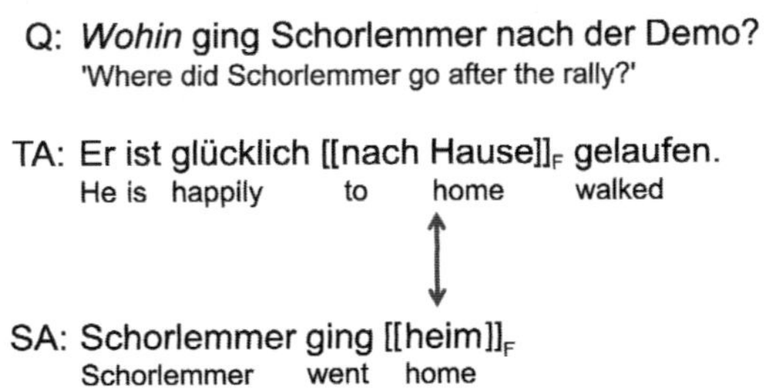

Figure 1: Answer comparison with the help of focus

LAW VIII - The 8th Linguistic Annotation Workshop, pages 159–168,
Dublin, Ireland, August 23-24 2014.

To support this line of research, one needs to be able to identify the focus in a response. As a first step, we have designed an annotation scheme and manual annotation process for identifying the focus in a corpus of reading comprehension responses. Focus here is understood in the sense of Krifka (2007) as indicating the presence of alternatives in the context and being a direct answer to the Question Under Discussion (QUD, Roberts 1996). This semantic view of focus is essentially language-independent.

Some attempts at systematically identifying focus in authentic data have been made in the past (Dipper et al., 2007; Calhoun et al., 2010). However, most approaches either capture a notion of focus more closely related to particular language features, such as the Topic-Focus Articulation and its relation to the word order in Czech (Buráňová et al., 2000), or the approaches were not rewarded with much success (Ritz et al., 2008). The latter have tried to identify focus in newspaper text or other data types where no explicit questions are available, making the task of determining the QUD, and thus reliably annotating focus, very hard. In contrast, in the research presented here, we work with responses to explicitly given questions that are asked about an explicitly given text. Thus, we can make use of the characteristics of the questions and text to obtain reliable focus annotation for the responses.

Theoretical linguists have discussed the notion of focus for decades, cf., e.g., Jackendoff (1972), Stechow (1981), Rooth (1992), Schwarzschild (1999) and Büring (2007). However, for insights and arguments from theoretical work to be applicable in computational linguistics, they need to be linked to thorough empirical work – an area where some work remains to be done (cf., e.g., De Kuthy and Meurers, 2012), with some recent research making significant headway (Riester and Baumann, 2013). As it stands, computational linguists have not yet been able to fully profit from the theoretical debate on focus. An important reason complementing the one just mentioned is the fact that the context in which the text to be analyzed is produced has rarely been explicitly taken into account and encoded. Yet, many of the natural tasks in which focus annotation would be relevant actually do contain explicit task and context information of relevance to determining focus. To move things forward, this paper builds on the availability and relevance of task-based language data and presents an annotation study of focus on authentic reading comprehension data. As a second component of our proposal, we operationalize the focus annotation in terms of several incremental steps, such as explicit answer typing, which provide relevant information guiding the focus annotation as such.

Overall, the paper tries to accomplish two goals, which are also reflected in the way the annotation is evaluated: i) to present an effective focus annotation scheme and to evaluate how consistently it can be applied, and ii) to explore the possible impact of focus annotation on Short Answer Assessment. Establishing a focus annotation scheme for question-response pairs from authentic reading comprehension data involves sharpening and linking the concepts and tests from theoretical linguistic with the wide range of properties realized in the authentic reading comprehension data. The work thus stands to contribute both to an empirical evaluation and enrichment of the linguistic concepts as well as to the development of automatic focus annotation approaches in computational linguistics.

The paper is organized as follows: Section 2 presents the corpus data on which we base the annotation effort and the annotation process. Section 3 introduces the scheme we developed for annotating the reading comprehension data. Section 4 then launches into both intrinsic and extrinsic evaluation of the manual annotation, before section 5 concludes the paper.

2 Data and Annotation Setup

We base our work on the CREG corpus (Ott et al., 2012), a task-based corpus consisting of answers to reading comprehension questions written by learners of German at the university level. The overall corpus includes 164 reading texts, 1,517 reading comprehension questions, 2,057 target answers provided by the teachers, and 36,335 learner answers. We use the CREG-1032 data subset (Meurers et al., 2011) for the present annotation work in order to enable comparison to previously published results on that data set (Meurers et al., 2011; Hahn and Meurers, 2012; Horbach et al., 2013). The CREG-1032 data set consists of two sub-corpora, which correspond to the sites they were collected at, Kansas University (KU) and Ohio State University (OSU). For the present work, we limited ourselves to the OSU portion of the data because it contains longer answers and more answers per question.

The OSU subset consists of 422 student answers to 60 questions, for which 87 target answers are available. The student answers were produced by 175 intermediate learners of German in the US, who on average wrote about 15 tokens per answer. All student answers were rated by two annotators with respect to whether they answer the question or not. The subset is balanced, i.e. it contains the same number of correct and incorrect answers, and both annotators agreed on the meaning assessment.

To obtain a gold-standard focus annotation for this data set, we set out to manually annotate both target answers and student answers with focus. We also annotated the question forms in the question. The annotation was performed by two graduate research assistants in linguistics using the *brat*[1] rapid annotation tool directly on the token level. Each annotator was given a separate directory containing identical source files to annotate. In order to sharpen distinctions and refine the annotation scheme to its current state, we drew a random sample of 100 questions, target answers and student answers from each sub-corpus of CREG and trained our two annotators on them. During this piloting process, the first author met with the annotators to discuss difficult cases and decide how the scheme would accommodate them.

Figure 2 shows a sample screenshot of the *brat* tool. The question asks for a person, namely the one 'wandering through the dark outskirts'. The target response provides an answer with an appropriate focus. The student response instead appears to answer a question about the reason for this person's action, such as 'Why did he wander through the dark outskirts?'.

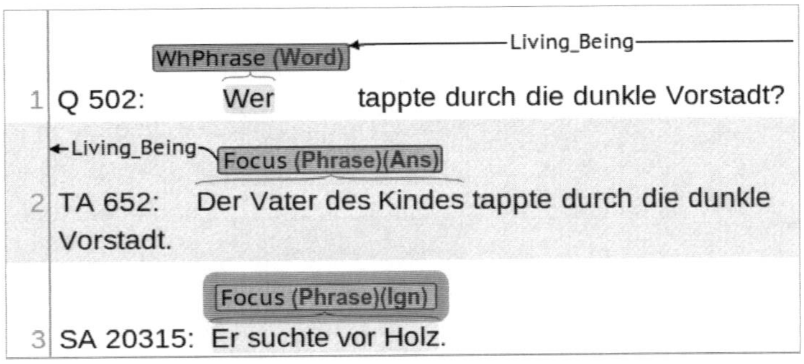

Q: 'Who wandered through the dark outskirts?'
TA: 'The child's father wandered through the dark outskirts.'
SA: 'He searched for wood.'

Figure 2: Example with a *who*-question and a different QUD for the student answer

3 Annotation Scheme

In this section, we introduce the annotation scheme we developed. An important characteristic of our annotation scheme is that it is applied incrementally: annotators first look at the surface question form, then determine the set of alternatives (Krifka, 2007, sec. 3), and finally they mark instances of the alternative set in answers. The rich task context of reading comprehension data with its explicit questions allows us to circumvent the problem of guessing an implicit QUD, except in the cases where students answer a different question (which we account for separately, see below). In the following, we present the three types of categories our scheme is built on.

Question Form is used to mark the surface form of a question, where we distinguish *wh*-questions, polarity questions, alternative questions, imperatives and noun phrase questions. In themselves, question forms do not encode any semantics, but merely act as an explicit marker of the surface question form. Table 1 gives an overview and examples of this dimension.

Focus is used to mark the focused words or phrases in an answer. We do not distinguish between contrastive and new information focus, as this is not relevant for assessing an answer. Multiple foci can be encoded and in fact do occur in the data.

[1] http://brat.nlplab.org

Category	Example	Translation
`WhPhrase`	'Warum hatte Schorlemmer zu Beginn Angst?'	'Why was Schorlemmer afraid in the beginning?'
`YesNo`	'Muss man deutscher Staatsbürger sein?'	'Does one have to be a German citizen?'
`Alternative`	'Ist er für oder gegen das EU-Gesetz?'	'Is he for or against the EU law?'
`Imperative`	'Begründen Sie diesen anderen Spitznamen.'	'Give reasons for this other nickname.'
`NounPhrase`	'Wohnort?'	'Place of residence?'

Table 1: Question Forms in the annotation scheme

The starting point of our focus annotation is Krifka (2007)'s understanding of focus as the part of an utterance that indicates the presence of alternatives relevant to the interpretation. We operationalize this by testing whether a given part of the utterance is needed to distinguish between alternatives in the QUD. Concretely, we train annotators to perform substitution tests in which they compare two potential extents of the focus to identify whether the difference in the extent of the focus also selects a different valid alternative in the sense of discriminating between alternatives in the QUD. For instance, consider the example in (1), where the focus is made explicit by the square brackets.

(1) Where does Heike live?
She lives ⟦in Berlin.⟧$_F$

Here "in" needs to be part of the focus because exchanging it for another word with the same POS changes the meaning of the phrase in a way picking another alternative, as in "She lives *near* Berlin". Consider the same answer to a slightly different question in (2). Here the set of alternatives is more constrained and hence "in" is not focused.

(2) In what city does Heike live?
She lives in ⟦Berlin⟧$_F$.

Other criteria we defined to guide focus annotation include the following:

- Coordination: If several foci are coordinated, each should be marked separately.
- Givenness: Avoid marking given material except where needed to distinguish between alternatives.
- Each sentence is assumed to include at least one focus. If it does not answer the explicit question, it must be annotated with a different QUD (discussed below).
- Focus never crosses sentence boundaries.
- Focus does not apply to sub-lexical units, such as syllables.
- Punctuation at focus boundaries is to be excluded.

In addition to marking focus, we annotate the relation between the explicitly given question and the Question Under Discussion actually answered by a given response. In the most straightforward case, the QUD is identical to the explicit question given, which in the annotation scheme is encoded as *question answered*. In cases where the QUD differs from the explicitly given question, we distinguish three cases: In the cases related to the implicit moves discussed in Büring (2003, p. 525) exemplified by (3), the QUD answered can be a subquestion of the explicit question, which we encode as *question narrowed down*. When it addresses a more general QUD, as in (4), the response is annotated as *question generalized*.

(3) What did the pop stars wear?
The female pop stars wore caftans.

(4) Would you like a Coke or a Sprite?
I'd like a beer.

Finally, we also mark complete failures of question answer congruence with *question ignored*. In all cases where the QUD being answered differs from the question explicitly given, the annotator is required to specify the QUD apparently being answered.

Answer Type expresses the semantic category of the focus in relation to the question form. It further describes the nature of the question-answer congruence by specifying the semantic class of the set of alternatives. The answer types discussed in the computational linguistic literature generally are specific to particular content domains, so that we developed our own taxonomy. Examples include `Time/Date`, `Location`, `Entity`, and `Reason`. In addition to semantically restricting the focus to a specific type, answer types can also provide syntactic cues restricting focus marking. For example, an `Entity` will typically be encoded as a nominal expression. For annotation, the advantage of answer types is that they force annotators to make an explicit commitment to the semantic nature of the focus they are annotating, leading to potentially higher consistency and reliability of annotation. On the conceptual side, the semantic restriction encoded in the answer type bears an interesting resemblance to what in a Structured Meaning approach to focus (Krifka, 1992) is referred to as *restriction of the question* (Krifka, 2001, p. 3).

Category	Description	Example (translated)
`Time_Date`	time/date expression, usually incl. preposition	The movie starts *at 5:50*
`Living_Being`	individual, animal or plant	*The father of the child* padded through the dark outskirts.
`Thing`	concrete object which is not alive	For the Spaniards *toilet and stove* are more important than the internet.
`Abstract_Entity`	entity that is not concrete	The applicant needs *a completed vocational training as a cook.*
`Report`	reported incident or statement	The speaker says *"We ask all youths to have their passports ready."*
`Reason`	reason or cause for a statement	The maintenance of a raised garden bed is easier *because one does not need to stoop.*
`Location`	place or relative location	She is from *Berlin.*
`Action`	activity or happening.	In the vegetable garden one needs to *hoe and water.*
`Property`	attribute of something	Reputation and money are *important* for Til.
`Yes_No`	polar answer, including whole statement if not elliptic	*The mermaid does not marry the prince.*
`Manner`	way in which something is done	The word is used *ironically* in this story.
`Quantity/Duration`	countable amount of something	The company seeks *75* employees.
`State`	state something is in, or result of some action	If he works hard now, *he won't have to work in the future.*

Table 2: Answer Types with examples

4 Evaluation

The approach is evaluated in two ways. First, the consistency with which the focus annotation scheme was applied is evaluated in section 4.1 by calculating inter-annotator agreement. In section 4.2 we then explore the effect of focus annotation on Short Answer Assessment. For both evaluations, we provide a qualitative discussion of characteristic examples.

4.1 Intrinsic Evaluation

4.1.1 Quantitative Results

Having carried out the manual annotation experiment, the question arises how to compare and calculate agreement of spans of tokens in focus annotation. While comparing individual spans and calculating some kind of overlap measure is certainly possible, it is hard to interpret the meaning of such numbers. We therefore decided to make as few assumptions as possible and treat each token as a markable for which the annotator needs to make a decision. On that basis, we then follow standard evaluation procedures in calculating percentage agreement and Cohen's Kappa (Artstein and Poesio, 2009).

Table 3 summarizes the agreement results. For both student and target answers, we report the granularity of the distinction being made (focus/background vs. all answer types), the number of tokens the distinction applies to, and finally percentage and Kappa agreement.

Type of distinction	Type of answers	# tokens	%	κ
Binary	Student	6329	82.8	.65
(focus/background)	Target	6983	84.9	**.69**
Detailed	Student	5198	72.6	.61
(13 Answer Types + background)	Target	6839	76.5	.67

Table 3: Inter-annotator agreement on student and target answers

The results show that all numbers are in the area of substantial agreement ($\kappa > .6$). This is a noticeably improvement over the results obtained by Ritz et al. (2008), who report $\kappa = .51$ on tokens in questionnaire data, and it is on a par with the results reported by Calhoun et al. (2010). Annotation was easier on the more well-formed target answers than on the often ungrammatical student answers. Moving from the binary focus/background distinction to the one involving all Answer Types, we still obtain relatively good agreement. This indicates that the semantic characterization of foci via Answer Types works quite well, with the gap between student and target answers being even more apparent here.

In order to assess the effect of answer length, we also computed macro-average versions of percentage agreement and κ for the binary focus distinction, following Ott et al. (2012, p. 55) but averaging over answers. We obtained 84.0% and $\kappa = .67$ for student answers, and 87.4% and $\kappa = .74$ for target answers. A few longer answers which are harder to annotate thus noticeably affected the agreement results of Table 3 negatively.

4.1.2 Examples

To explore the nature of the disagreements, we showcase two characteristic issues here based on examples from the corpus. Consider the following case where the annotators disagreed on the annotation of a student answer:

Q: Warum nennt der Autor Hamburg das "Tor zur Welt der Wissenschaft"?
'Why does the author call Hamburg the "gate to the world of science"?'

SA: ⟦Hamburg hat viel renommierte Universitäten⟧$_F$ (annotator 1)
Hamburg hat ⟦viel renommierte Universitäten⟧$_F$ (annotator 2)
'Hamburg has many renowned universities'

Figure 3: Disagreement involving given material

Whereas annotator 1 marks the whole answer on the grounds that the focus is of Answer Type `Reason` and needs to include the whole proposition, annotator 2 excludes material given in the question. Both can in theory be justified, but annotator 1 is closer to our guidelines here, taking into account that "Hamburg" indeed discriminates between alternatives (one could give reasons that do not include "Hamburg") and thus needs to be part of the focus.

The second example illustrates the issue of deciding where the boundary of a focus is:

Q: Wofür ist der Aufsichtsrat verantwortlich?
'What is the supervisory board responsible for?'

SA: Der Aufsichtsrat ist für ⟦die Bestellung⟧$_F$ verantwortlich. (annotator 1)
Der Aufsichtsrat ist ⟦für die Bestellung⟧$_F$ verantwortlich. (annotator 2)
'The supervisory board is responsible for the appointment.'

Figure 4: Disagreement on a preposition

Annotator 1 correctly excluded "für" ('for') from the focus, only marking "die Bestellung" ('the appointment') given that "für" is only needed for reasons of well-formedness. Annotator 2 apparently thought that "für" makes a semantic difference here, but it is hard to construct a grammatical example with a different preposition that changes the meaning of the focused expression.

4.2 Extrinsic Evaluation

It has been pointed out that evaluating an expert annotation of a theoretical linguistic notion only intrinsically is problematic because there is no non-theoretical grounding involved (Riezler, 2014). Therefore, besides calculating agreement measures, we also evaluated the resulting annotation in a larger computational task, the automatic meaning assessment of answers to reading comprehension questions.

We used the CoMiC system (Comparing Meaning in Context, Meurers et al., 2011) as a testbed for our experiment. CoMiC is an alignment-based system operating in three stages:

1. Annotating linguistic units (words, chunks and dependencies) in student and target answer on various levels of abstraction

2. Finding alignments of linguistic units between student and target answer based on annotation

3. Classifying the student answer based on number and type of alignments, using a supervised machine learning setup with 13 features in total

In stage 2, CoMiC integrates a simplistic approach to givenness, excluding all words from alignment that are mentioned in the question. We transferred the underlying method to the notion of focus and implemented a component that excludes all non-focused words from alignment, resulting in alignments between focused parts of answers only. We only used the foci where students did not ignore the question according to the annotators.

For the present evaluation, we experimented with three different settings involving the basic givenness filter and our focus annotations: i) using the givenness filter by itself as a baseline, ii) aligning only focused tokens as described above and iii) combining both by producing a givenness and a focus version of each classification feature. All three settings were tried out for annotator 1 and 2.

4.2.1 Quantitative Results

Table 4 summarizes the quantitative results. It shows that focus beats the basic givenness baseline of 84.6% on its own, pushing the classification accuracy to 86.7% for annotator 1 and 87.2% for annotator 2.

	Annotator 1	Annotator 2
Basic givenness only	84.6	
Focus only	86.7	87.2
Focus + givenness	**90.3**	89.3

Table 4: Answer classification accuracy with the CoMiC system

While this is an encouraging result already, the combination of basic givenness and focus performs substantially better, reaching 90.3% accuracy for annotator 1 and 89.3% for annotator 2.

In terms of the conceptual notions of formal pragmatics, this is an interesting result. While the notion of givenness implemented here is surface-based and mechanistic and thus could be improved, the results support the idea that both of the commonly discussed dimensions, focus/background and new/given, are useful and informative information-structural dimensions that complement each other in assessing the meaning of answers.

Interestingly, the focus annotation of annotator 2 on its own performed better than that of annotator 1, but worse when combined with basic givenness. We suspect that annotator 2's understanding of focus relied more on the concept of givenness than annotator 1's, causing the combination of the two to be less informative than for annotator 1.

4.2.2 Alignment Example

The possible benefits of using focus to constrain alignment can take different forms: focus can lead us to exclude extra, irrelevant material, but it can also uncover the fact that the relevant piece of information has in fact not been included, as in the following corpus example:

Q: Was machen sie, um die Brunnen im Winter zu schützen?
'What do they do to protect the wells in winter?'

TA: Zwölf der 47 Brunnen werden im Winter aus Schutz vor dem Frost und Witterungsschäden ⟦eingehaust⟧$_F$
'Twelve of the 47 wells are encased in winter for protection from freezing and damage from weather conditions'

SA: im Winter gibt es Frost und Witterungsschäden
'in winter there is freezing and damage from weather conditions'

Figure 5: No alignments because the student answer ignores the question

The question asks what is being done to protect the wells in winter, for which the text states that twelve of wells are encased for protection (technically, this is an answer to a sub-question since nothing is asserted about the other wells). Additional new information such as "vor dem Frost und Witterungsschäden" does not distinguish between alternatives to the question "Was machen sie...?", which clearly asks for an `Action`. The target and student answer have high token overlap due to the presence of such extra information, but only the target answer contains the relevant focus "eingehaust". Without the focus filter, CoMiC wrongly classifies this answer as correct, but with the added focus information, it has the means to judge this answer adequately.

5 Conclusion and Outlook

We presented a focus annotation study based on reading comprehension data, which we view as a contribution to the general goal of analyzing and annotating focus. Motivated by the limited success of approaches trying to tackle focus annotation from a general conceptual level, we aim to proceed from the concrete task to the more general setting. This allows us to separate a) identifying the QUD and b) determining the location and extent of the focus in the language material, where a) is informed and greatly simplified by the explicit question.

Using this approach in combination with semantically motivated annotation guidelines, we showed that focus annotation can be carried out systematically with Kappa values in the range of .61 to .69, depending on the well-formedness of the language and the number of classes distinguished.

With respect to the practical goal of improving automatic assessment of short student answers, we showed that information structural distinctions are relevant and able to quantitatively improve the results, as demonstrated by an increase from 84.6% to 90.3% accuracy in a binary classification task on a balanced data set.

While the manual annotation showcases the relevance and impact of focus annotation, we see the design of an automatic focus/background classification system on the basis of our annotated data as the logical next step. As such a system cannot perform the kind of introspective language analysis our human annotators employed, we will have to approximate focus through surface criteria such as word order, syntactic categories and focus sensitive particles. It remains to be seen how much of the potential benefit of focus annotation can be reached by automatic focus annotation using machine learning.

Finally, in order to obtain more human-annotated data, we are planning to turn focus annotation of answers to questions into a feasible crowd-sourcing task.

Acknowledgements

We are grateful to Heike Cardoso and Stefanie Wolf for carrying out the manual annotation and providing valuable feedback. We also would like to thank Kordula De Kuthy, Verena Henrich, Niels Ott and the three anonymous reviewers for their helpful comments.

References

Ron Artstein and Massimo Poesio. 2009. Survey article: Inter-coder agreement for computational linguistics. *Computational Linguistics*, 34(4):1–42.

Stacey Bailey and Detmar Meurers. 2008. Diagnosing meaning errors in short answers to reading comprehension questions. In Joel Tetreault, Jill Burstein, and Rachele De Felice, editors, *Proceedings of the 3rd Workshop on Innovative Use of NLP for Building Educational Applications (BEA-3) at ACL'08*, pages 107–115, Columbus, Ohio.

Eva Buráňová, Eva Hajičová, and Petr Sgall. 2000. Tagging of very large corpora: topic-focus articulation. In *Proceedings of the 18th conference on Computational linguistics - Volume 1*, COLING '00, pages 139–144, Stroudsburg, PA, USA. Association for Computational Linguistics.

Daniel Büring. 2003. On d-trees, beans, and b-accents. *Linguistics and Philosophy*, 26(5):511–545.

Daniel Büring. 2007. Intonation, semantics and information structure. In Gillian Ramchand and Charles Reiss, editors, *The Oxford Handbook of Linguistic Interfaces*. Oxford University Press.

Sasha Calhoun, Jean Carletta, Jason Brenier, Neil Mayo, Dan Jurafsky, Mark Steedman, and David Beaver. 2010. The NXT-format switchboard corpus: A rich resource for investigating the syntax, semantics, pragmatics and prosody of dialogue. *Language Resources and Evaluation*, 44:387–419.

Kordula De Kuthy and Detmar Meurers. 2012. Focus projection between theory and evidence. In Sam Featherston and Britta Stolterfoth, editors, *Empirical Approaches to Linguistic Theory – Studies in Meaning and Structure*, volume 111 of *Studies in Generative Grammar*, pages 207–240. De Gruyter.

Stefanie Dipper, Michael Götze, and Stavros Skopeteas, editors. 2007. *Information Structure in Cross-Linguistic Corpora: Annotation Guidelines for Phonology, Morphology, Syntax, Semantics and Information Structure*, volume 7 of *Interdisciplinary Studies on Information Structure*. Universitätsverlag Potsdam, Potsdam, Germany.

Myroslava Dzikovska, Rodney Nielsen, Chris Brew, Claudia Leacock, Danilo Giampiccolo, Luisa Bentivogli, Peter Clark, Ido Dagan, and Hoa Trang Dang. 2013. Semeval-2013 task 7: The joint student response analysis and 8th recognizing textual entailment challenge. In *Second Joint Conference on Lexical and Computational Semantics (*SEM), Volume 2: Proceedings of the Seventh International Workshop on Semantic Evaluation (SemEval 2013)*, pages 263–274, Atlanta, Georgia, USA, June. Association for Computational Linguistics.

Michael Hahn and Detmar Meurers. 2012. Evaluating the meaning of answers to reading comprehension questions: A semantics-based approach. In *Proceedings of the 7th Workshop on Innovative Use of NLP for Building Educational Applications (BEA-7) at NAACL-HLT 2012*, pages 94–103, Montreal.

Andrea Horbach, Alexis Palmer, and Manfred Pinkal. 2013. Using the text to evaluate short answers for reading comprehension exercises. In *Second Joint Conference on Lexical and Computational Semantics (*SEM), Volume 1: Proceedings of the Main Conference and the Shared Task: Semantic Textual Similarity*, pages 286–295, Atlanta, Georgia, USA, June. Association for Computational Linguistics.

Ray Jackendoff. 1972. *Semantic Interpretation in Generative Grammar*. MIT Press, Cambridge, MA.

Manfred Krifka. 1992. A compositional semantics for multiple focus constructions. In Joachim Jacobs, editor, *Informationsstruktur und Grammatik*, pages 17–54. Westdeutscher Verlag, Opladen.

Manfred Krifka. 2001. For a structured meaning account of questions and answers. In C. Fery and W. Sternefeld, editors, *Audiatur Vox Sapientia. A Festschrift for Arnim von Stechow*, volume 52 of *studia grammatica*, pages 287–319. Akademie Verlag, Berlin.

Manfred Krifka. 2007. Basic notions of information structure. In Caroline Fery, Gisbert Fanselow, and Manfred Krifka, editors, *The notions of information structure*, volume 6 of *Interdisciplinary Studies on Information Structure (ISIS)*, pages 13–55. Universitätsverlag Potsdam, Potsdam.

Detmar Meurers, Ramon Ziai, Niels Ott, and Janina Kopp. 2011. Evaluating answers to reading comprehension questions in context: Results for german and the role of information structure. In *Proceedings of the TextInfer 2011 Workshop on Textual Entailment*, pages 1–9, Edinburgh, Scotland, UK, July. Association for Computational Linguistics.

Michael Mohler, Razvan Bunescu, and Rada Mihalcea. 2011. Learning to grade short answer questions using semantic similarity measures and dependency graph alignments. In *Proceedings of the 49th Annual Meeting of the Association for Computational Linguistics: Human Language Technologies*, pages 752–762, Portland, Oregon, USA, June. Association for Computational Linguistics.

Niels Ott, Ramon Ziai, and Detmar Meurers. 2012. Creation and analysis of a reading comprehension exercise corpus: Towards evaluating meaning in context. In Thomas Schmidt and Kai Wörner, editors, *Multilingual Corpora and Multilingual Corpus Analysis*, Hamburg Studies in Multilingualism (HSM), pages 47–69. Benjamins, Amsterdam.

Arndt Riester and Stefan Baumann. 2013. Focus triggers and focus types from a corpus perspective. *Dialogue & Discourse*, 4(2):215–248.

Stefan Riezler. 2014. On the problem of theoretical terms in empirical computational linguistics. *Computational Linguistics*, 40(1):235–245.

Julia Ritz, Stefanie Dipper, and Michael Götze. 2008. Annotation of information structure: An evaluation across different types of texts. In *Proceedings of the 6th International Conference on Language Resources and Evaluation*, pages 2137–2142, Marrakech, Morocco.

Craige Roberts. 1996. Information structure in discourse: Towards an integrated formal theory of pragmatics. In Jae-Hak Yoon and Andreas Kathol, editors, *OSU Working Papers in Linguistics No. 49: Papers in Semantics*. The Ohio State University.

Mats Rooth. 1992. A theory of focus interpretation. *Natural Language Semantics*, 1(1):75–116.

Roger Schwarzschild. 1999. GIVENness, AvoidF and other constraints on the placement of accent. *Natural Language Semantics*, 7(2):141–177.

Arnim von Stechow. 1981. Topic, focus, and local relevance. In Wolfgang Klein and W. Levelt, editors, *Crossing the Boundaries in Linguistics*, pages 95–130. Reidel, Dordrecht.

Author Index

Association for Computational Linguistics
209 N. Eighth Street
Stroudsburg, Pennsylvania 18360

CURRAN ASSOCIATES INC
proceedings.com